ROYAL CENTRAL
SCHOOL OF SPEECH & DRAMA
UNIVERSITY OF LONDON

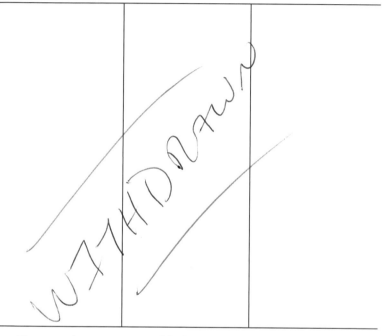

Please return or renew this item by the last date shown.

The Royal Central School of Speech and Drama
Eton Avenue, London, NW3 3HY
http://heritage.cssd.ac.uk
library@cssd.ac.uk
Direct line: 0207 559 3942

W

imprint-academic.com

Published in the UK by Imprint Academic
PO Box 200, Exeter EX5 5YX, UK

Published in the USA by Imprint Academic
Philosophy Documentation Center
PO Box 7147, Charlottesville, VA 22906-7147, USA

ISBN 9 781845 400873

A CIP catalogue record for this book is available from the
British Library and US Library of Congress

Contents

ABOUT AUTHORS

Julian Asher is a PhD student in the Department of Psychiatry in Cambridge University. He is also based in the Wellcome Trust Centre for Human Genetics in Oxford.

Chris Ashwin is a Senior Research Associate in the Autism Research Centre (ARC) at the University of Cambridge, and also works as a post-doctoral fellow in the University of Essex Affective Science Lab.

Grant C. Baldwin is a graduate student in Cognition/Perception at the University of Texas at Austin. In addition to his research on motivation and categorization, his interests include auditory perception and music cognition.

Simon Baron-Cohen is Professor of Developmental Psychopathology at the University of Cambridge, Departments of Psychiatry and Experimental Psychology. He is also Director of the Autism Research Centre (ARC) and a clinic for the diagnosis of Asperger Syndrome (AS) in Cambridge.

John Beeckmans graduated in chemical engineering from University College (London) in 1953 and obtained a PhD in physical chemistry from the University of Toronto in 1958. After a career as professor of chemical engineering at the University of Western Ontario he retired in 1995 and has since pursued his lifelong interest in consciousness.

José Luis Bermúdez is Professor of Philosophy and Director of the Philosophy-Neuroscience-Psychology program at Washington University in St. Louis. His books include *The Paradox of Self-Consciousness* (MIT, 1998), *Thinking without Words* (OUP, 2003) and *Philosophy of Psychology: A Contemporary Introduction* (Routledge, 2005).

Jaclyn Billington is is an affiliated researcher of the Autism Research Centre (ARC), University of Cambridge, and a Postdoctoral Research Associate at Royal Holloway, University of London.

Daniel Bor is a Career Development Fellow at the MRC Cognition and Brain Sciences Unit in Cambridge, and an investigator within the Wolfson Brain Imaging Centre (WBIC) at Addenbrooke's Hospital, Cambridge.

Peter Carruthers is Professor of Philosophy at the University of Maryland. His most recent books are *Consciousness: Essays from a*

Higher-Order Perspective (OUP, 2005), and *The Architecture of the Mind: Massive Modularity and the Flexibility of Thought* (OUP, 2006).

Philippe Chuard is Assistant Professor of Philosophy at Southern Methodist University. He works in the philosophy of perception and epistemology. His dissertation (Australian National University, 2006) was on Conceptualism and he has articles in *Philosophical Studies* and the *Australasian Journal of Philosophy*.

Rocco J. Gennaro is Professor of Philosophy at Indiana State University in Terre Haute. His books include *Consciousness and Self-Consciousness* (John Benjamins, 1996) and *Mind and Brain: A Dialogue on the Mind-Body Problem* (Hackett, 1996). He has also edited *Higher-Order Theories of Consciousness* (John Benjamins, 2004) and co-edited, with Charles Huenemann, *New Essays on the Rationalists* (OUP, 1999).

W. Todd Maddox is Professor of Psychology, a member Institute for Neuroscience, and a member of the Center for Perceptual Systems at the University of Texas, Austin. His research interests include the Cognitive Neuroscience of Classification and Decision Making and Motivational Influences on Cognition. He is currently associate editor of *Perception and Psychophysics*.

Arthur B. Markman is Annabel Irion Worsham Centennial Professor of Psychology and Marketing at the University of Texas at Austin. His research interests include similarity and analogy, categorization, decision making, and motivational processes. He is currently executive editor of *Cognitive Science*.

Jesse Prinz is Professor of Philosophy at the University of North Carolina at Chapel Hill. His published books are *Furnishing the Mind: Concepts and Their Perceptual Basis* (MIT, 2002) and *Gut Reactions: A Perceptual Theory of Emotion* (OUP, 2004). He has several forthcoming books, including *The Emotional Construction of Morals*.

David H. Rakison is an Associate Professor of Psychology at Carnegie Mellon University. For the last fifteen years he has conducted research on category and concept development in infants and young children with a focus on the animate-inanimate distinction and early mechanisms of learning. He has co-edited two volumes; one with Lisa M. Oakes called *Category and Concept Development: Making sense of the blooming, buzzing confusion*, and one with Lisa Gershkoff-Stowe called *Building Object Categories in Developmental Time*.

Georges Rey is Professor of philosophy at the University of Maryland at College Park. He is the author of *Contemporary Philosophy of Mind*, and of numerous articles on concepts, intentionality, qualia and consciousness. He is presently finishing a book on the role on intentional inexistents in cognitive theories of early vision, sensation and language processing.

Bénédicte Veillet is completing a PhD in philosophy at the University of Maryland at College Park, writing on representational theories of consciousness.

Daniel A. Weiskopf is Assistant Professor of Philosophy at the University of South Florida. He works on topics in the philosophy of mind and language, particularly on concepts and mental content.

Sally Wheelwright is a Senior Research Associate in the Autism Research Centre (ARC) at the University of Cambridge, and serves as the Deputy Director of the ARC.

Darrell A. Worthy is a graduate student in cognitive psychology at the University of Texas at Austin. His research interests include, but are not limited to, categorization, motivation, decision-making, mathematical modelling, consciousness, and social pressure.

Rocco J. Gennaro

Consciousness and Concepts

An Introductory Essay

1. The Central Problem

Much has been written over the past few decades on the nature of concepts in philosophy, psychology, and cognitive science. Questions such as 'What are concepts?' and 'What is it to possess a concept?' are central to these fields and notoriously difficult to answer. One major anthology (Margolis & Laurence, 1999) and a number of other important works (such as Prinz, 2002; Murphy, 2002) have contributed greatly to the debate. Some of the issues are familiar and longstanding. For example, are concepts abstract mind-independent objects in some Platonic or Fregean sense, or are they better understood as mental representations, such as constituents of thoughts? If the latter, it is sometimes said that concepts are to thoughts as words are to sentences. A common view in cognitive science is that thought is based on word-like mental representations, which is often referred to as the 'language of thought hypothesis' (Fodor, 1975). Others argue that possessing a concept C involves demonstrating some kind of ability with respect to C's. But which ability? The ability to form an image of C's? To display linguistic competence with C's? To behaviourally discriminate C's from non-C's? It seems that all of these options suffer from insuperable difficulties. Counter-examples abound for any proposed answer; for example, having the concept ELECTRON or JUSTICE cannot involve forming an image, and tying concept possession too closely to linguistic competence is highly problematic because some concepts are arguably possessed by non-linguistic creatures.

Similar longstanding issues arise for a proper theory of the *structure* of concepts. For example, the classical theory of concepts, according to which simpler concepts express necessary and sufficient conditions for falling under any concept C, has fallen out of favour due to the obvious difficulty of discovering just what those conditions are in many instances. There are also other well-known theories that attempt to articulate the structure of concepts, such as the prototype theory, theory theory, conceptual atomism, and Jesse Prinz's more recent 'proxytype' theory (Prinz, 2002).[1] My main point, however, is that despite the recent explosion in work on concepts, one finds very little explicitly connecting concepts to the philosophical problem of consciousness. There is often no attempt at all to shed light on the nature of conscious experience in these works (e.g. Fodor, 1998; Peacocke, 1992).

On the other hand, the literature on consciousness is enormous with many important books and anthologies published in just the last decade or so.[2] Once again, however, with very few exceptions, those who write on consciousness rarely draw *extensive* connections between their theories of consciousness and the literature on concepts. Part of the aim of this volume is to remedy this gap in the literature by bringing together a number of interdisciplinary articles explicitly involving the interplay between concepts and consciousness. My main goal in this essay is to set forth a framework for future research on this topic, as well as a context for the essays that follow. I will present a taste of various actual and potential areas of research and gesture toward some different areas of investigation.

First, however, a word about terminology. The concept 'consciousness' is notoriously ambiguous. The abstract noun 'consciousness' is not frequently used by itself in the contemporary literature, but it originally derives from the Latin *con* (with) and *scire* (to know). Perhaps the most commonly used contemporary notion of a 'conscious' mental state is captured by Thomas Nagel's famous 'what it is like' sense (Nagel, 1974). When I am in a conscious mental state, there is 'something it is like' for me to be in that state from the subjective or first-person point of view. When I am, for example, smelling a rose or having a conscious visual experience, there is something it 'seems' or 'feels' like from my perspective. An organism, such as a bat, is

---

[1] I will not review those here, but the interested reader should refer to the books cited above and the references therein.

[2] See e.g. Chalmers (1996), Lycan (1996), Block *et al.* (1997), Carruthers (2000), Tye (2000; 2005), Levine (2001), Papineau (2002), Smith & Jokic (2003), Baars *et al.* (2003), Koch (2004), Dennett (2005), Rosenthal (2005) and Revonsuo (2006).

conscious if it is able to experience the outer world through its (echo-locatory) senses. There is something it is like to be a conscious *crea-ture* whereas there is nothing it is like, for example, to be a table or tree. There are still, though, a cluster of expressions and terms related to Nagel's sense, and some authors simply stipulate the way that they use such terms. For example, philosophers sometimes refer to con-scious states as *phenomenal* or *qualitative* states. More technically, they often view such states as having qualitative properties called 'qualia' (singular, quale). There is significant disagreement over the nature, and even the existence, of qualia, but they are perhaps best understood as the felt properties or qualities of conscious states.

Ned Block (1995) makes an often cited distinction between *phe-nomenal* consciousness (or 'phenomenality') and *access* conscious-ness. The former is very much in line with the Nagelian notion described above. However, Block also defines the quite different notion of access consciousness in terms of a mental state's relation-ship with other mental states; for example, a mental state's 'availabil-ity for use in reasoning and rationality guiding speech and action' (Block, 1995, p. 227). This would, for example, count a visual percep-tion as (access) conscious not because it has the 'what it's likeness' of phenomenal states, but rather because it carries visual information which is generally available for use by the organism, regardless of whether or not it has any qualitative properties. Access consciousness is therefore more of a functional notion and more concerned with what such states *do*. Although this concept of consciousness is certainly very important in cognitive science and philosophy of mind generally, not everyone agrees that access consciousness deserves to be called 'consciousness' in any important sense of the term.[3]

In what follows, I will outline a number of areas of research which either are or should be at the intersection of work on concepts and consciousness.

2. Conceptualism

One area where there has been some overlap on consciousness and concepts is in the dispute over whether or not there is 'nonconceptual content' in experience (see e.g. Gunther, 2003). Thus, a central issue is

---

[3] For more on these definitional matters as well as an overview of contemporary work on consciousness, see Gennaro (2005a). Of course, explaining the nature of conscious expe-rience in some deep sense is certainly one of the most important and perplexing areas of philosophy. For example, the so-called 'hard problem' of consciousness has attracted much attention (Chalmers, 1995; Shear, 1997). The problem is basically explaining exactly how or why subjective experiences are produced at all from brain activity.

whether or not one can have conscious experience of certain objects
or properties without having the corresponding concepts. Conceptualism is basically the view that all conscious experience is structured by
concepts possessed by the subject (e.g. McDowell, 1994). In a somewhat Kantian spirit, we might say that all conscious experience presupposes the application of concepts, or the way one experiences the
world is determined by the concepts one possesses. One motivation
for this view stems from the observation that concept acquisition col-
ors the very experiences that we have. Another influential motivation
for the conceptualist is to explain how perceptual experience can provide reasons for empirical beliefs about objects in the world (Brewer
1999). However, there has been a growing chorus of philosophers
arguing that conceptualism is false; for example, that perceptual experience can outstrip the concepts that one possesses.[4]

Part of the issue centres on just how 'rich' the content of conscious
perceptual experience is. It seems, for example, that we can experience a complex visual scene, such as a landscape, without having all
of the concepts of the objects or properties experienced. Another
related issue has to do with the so-called 'fineness of grain' in our
experience. Thus, it is often said that conscious perceptual experience
is much more fine-grained than the concepts one possesses. In other
words, it seems that one can experience many objects or properties
without having the concept of that specific object or property. For
example, it seems that a subject could experience a novel shade of red
without having the corresponding concept and then without being
able to re-identify that shade on a future occasion. Conceptualists
have replies to these arguments but there is significant question as to
their success. The conceptualist might reply that we can form 'demonstrative concepts,' such as 'this shade of red,' for a specific new color
that is experienced (McDowell, 1994). However, some doubt that
such concepts really deserve the name 'concept' at all since the subject is unable to re-identify things which fall under it.

Concerning the richness of experience, a conceptualist might even
challenge the claim that conscious experience is very rich and that we
therefore do not consciously experience very much at any given time.
For example, some argue that the phenomena of inattentional blindness and change blindness might call the richness of experience into
doubt (Noë, 2004). Inattentional blindness occurs when normal subjects do not notice other objects in their visual field while the attention

---

[4]   See e.g. the essays by Michael Tye, Sean Kelly, and José Bermúdez in Gunther (2003).
      See also Tye (2006).

of subjects is occupied by a specific task (Mack and Rock, 1998). Change blindness occurs when normal subjects fail to notice a fairly obvious change in some object or scene (Simons, 2000). In any case, the fascinating dispute between conceptualists and non-conceptualists raises some of the most fundamental questions about conscious experience and the relationship between concepts and consciousness.

In this volume, **Philippe Chuard** clarifies the definition of Conceptualism and first argues that there is indeed reason to accept the idea that experience can be very rich in content. However, he then goes on to reject various attempts to show that the falsity of Conceptualism follows from this fact, while still maintaining that Conceptualists need to provide more details about what it means to deploy concepts in experience. Much of the theoretical work in this area has come from philosophers, but it would also be good for psychologists to get in on the act. Perhaps various experiments can be designed to address some of these issues.

3. Recognitional (or Phenomenal) Concepts

Another area where consciousness and concepts have been brought together to some extent has to do with so-called 'phenomenal' and 'recognitional' concepts (Loar, 1997; Papineau, 2002; Carruthers, 2005). Carruthers, for examples, describes purely recognitional concepts as those 'we either have, or can form…that lack any conceptual connections with other concepts of ours, whether physical, functional, or intentional. I can, as it were, just recognize a given type of experience as *this* each time it occurs, where my concept *this* lacks any conceptual connections with any other concepts of mine — even the concept *experience*' (2005, p. 67). Part of the rationale of recognitional concepts is to explain why there at least *seems* to be an 'explanatory gap' (Levine, 2001) between the mental and physical, and also to counter various well-known 'zombie' and 'conceivability' thought-experiments used against reductive materialism. The appeal to the possibility of zombies is often taken both as a problem for materialism and as a more positive argument for some form of dualism, such as property dualism (i.e. mental properties are distinct from physical or neural properties). The philosophical notion of a 'zombie' refers to conceivable creatures which are physically indistinguishable from us but lack consciousness entirely (Chalmers, 1996). It certainly seems logically *possible* for there to be such creatures: 'the conceivability of zombies seems … obvious to me. …While this possibility is probably empirically impossible, it certainly seems that a coherent situation is described; I can discern no contradiction in the description.' (Chalmers, 1996, p. 96)

Philosophers often contrast what is logically possible (in the sense of 'that which is not self-contradictory') from what is empirically possible given the actual laws of nature. Thus, it is logically possible for me to jump eighty feet in the air, but not empirically possible. Philosophers often use the notion of 'possible worlds,' or different ways that the world might have been, in describing such non-actual situations or possibilities. The objection, then, typically proceeds from the possibility of zombies to the conclusion that materialism is false because materialism would seem to rule out that possibility. It has been fairly widely accepted (since Kripke, 1972) that all identity statements are necessarily true (that is, 'true in all possible worlds'), and the same should therefore go for mind-brain identity claims. Since the possibility of zombies shows that it doesn't, then we should conclude that materialism is false.

However, given our possession of recognitional (or phenomenal) concepts, it is replied that any alleged explanatory gap or apparent lack of identity between the mental and physical can be explained away. If we possess purely recognitional concepts of the form '*This* type of experience,' we will still always be able to have that thought while, at the same time, conceiving of the absence of any corresponding physical or intentional property. On the one side, we are dealing with scientific third-person concepts and, on the other, we are employing phenomenal concepts. We are, perhaps, simply not in a position to understand completely the connection between the two, but the mere possibility of zombies is explained away in a manner that is harmless to materialism. It may be that there is a very good reason why such zombie scenarios seem possible; namely, that we do not (at least, not yet) see what the necessary connection is between neural events and conscious mental events.

The literature in response to zombie, and related 'conceivability,' arguments is enormous.[5] Perhaps most important for the materialist, however, is recognition of the fact that different *concepts* can pick out the same *property* or object in the world (Loar, 1997). Out in the world there is only the one 'stuff,' which we can conceptualize either as 'water' or as 'H_2O.' The traditional distinction, made most notably by Gottlob Frege in the late 19th century, between meaning (or 'sense') and reference is also relevant here. Two or more concepts, which can

---

[5] A sample includes Hill (1997), Hill and McLaughlin (1999), Papineau (1998; 2002), Balog (1999), Block and Stalnaker (1999), Loar (1999), Yablo (1999), Perry (2001), Botterell (2001), Kirk (2005).

have different meanings, can refer to the same property or object, much like 'Venus' and 'The Morning Star.' Materialists, then, explain that it is essential to distinguish between mental properties and our concepts of those properties. By analogy, then, there are recognitional concepts which use a phenomenal or 'first-person' property to refer to some conscious mental state, such as a sensation of red. In contrast, we can also use various concepts couched in physical or neurophysiological terms to refer to that same mental state from the third-person point of view. There is thus but one conscious mental state which can be conceptualized in two different ways: either by employing first-person experiential phenomenal concepts or by employing third-person neurophysiological concepts. It may just be a brute fact about the world that there are such identities and so the appearance of a contingent connection between brain properties and mental properties is just that — an *apparent* problem leading many to wonder about the alleged explanatory gap. Qualia would then still be identical to physical properties. Thus, this response provides a diagnosis for why there even *seems* to be such a gap; namely, that we use very different *concepts* to pick out the same *property*.

Most recently, David Chalmers (2007) has argued that the entire phenomenal concept strategy fails.[6] In this volume, **Peter Carruthers and Bénédicte Veillet** defend the strategy and offer what is largely a reply to Chalmers' (2007) argument. **Jesse Prinz** presents a theory about what it is to think about phenomenal states and phenomenal knowledge, and defends the claim that there are no phenomenal concepts (as this idea has been understood in recent philosophy). In doing so, Prinz draws on both philosophical and empirical work as well as his own theory of consciousness.

4. Representationalism

Representationalism is the thesis that phenomenal properties are identical to certain representational properties. There is a dizzying array of representational theories which I cannot summarize here (Chalmers 2004, Lycan 2005). But one question that should be answered by any theory of consciousness is: What makes a mental state a conscious mental state? There is a long tradition that has attempted to understand consciousness in terms of some kind of higher-order awareness. For example, John Locke (1689/1975) once said that 'consciousness is the perception of what passes in a man's own mind.' This intuition has

[6]   See Alter and Walter (2007) for many other important essays on this topic.

been revived by a number of philosophers over the past few decades (Armstrong, 1968; 1981; Rosenthal, 1986; 1997; 2005; Gennaro, 1996; 2005b; Lycan, 1996; 2001). In general, the idea is that what makes a mental state conscious is that it is the object of some kind of higher-order representation (HOR). A mental state M becomes conscious when there is a HOR of M. A HOR is a 'meta-psychological' state, i.e. a mental state directed at another mental state. So, for example, my desire to write a good introductory essay becomes conscious when I am (non-inferentially) 'aware' of the desire. Intuitively, it seems that conscious states, as opposed to unconscious ones, are mental states that I am 'aware of' in some sense. Any theory which attempts to explain consciousness in terms of higher-order states is known as a higher-order (HO) theory of consciousness. It is best initially to use the more neutral term 'representation' because there are a number of different kinds of higher-order theory, depending upon how one characterizes the HOR in question. HO theories, thus, attempt to explain consciousness in mentalistic and reductionist terms, that is, by reference to such notions as 'thoughts' and 'awareness.' Conscious mental states arise when two *unconscious* mental states are related in a certain specific way; namely, that one of them (the HOR) is directed at the other (M). HO theorists are united in the belief that their approach can better explain consciousness than any purely *first-order* representational (FOR) theory of consciousness, such as those offered by Tye (1995; 2000) and Dretske (1995).[7]

There are various flavors of HO theory with the most common division between higher-order *thought* (HOT) theories and higher-order *perception* (HOP) theories. HOT theorists, such as David Rosenthal, think it is better to understand the HOR as a thought of some kind. HOTs are treated as *cognitive* states involving some kind of conceptual component. HOP theorists urge that the HOR is a *perceptual* or *experiential* state of some kind (Lycan 1996) which does not require the kind of conceptual content invoked by HOT theorists. Partly due to Kant (1781/1965), HOP theory is sometimes referred to as 'inner sense theory' as a way of emphasizing its sensory or perceptual aspect. Although HOT and HOP theorists agree on the need for a HOR theory

---

[7]   It should also be noted that one of the authors in this volume (Georges Rey) has also defended a version of FOR theory (Rey, 1998). For much more on his theory, see his essay in this volume.

of consciousness, they do sometimes argue for the superiority of their respective positions (Rosenthal, 2004; Lycan, 2004).[8]

Peter Carruthers (2000) has proposed another possibility within HO theory; namely, that it is better to think of the HOTs as *dispositional* states instead of the standard view that the HOTs are *actual*, though he also understands his 'dispositional HOT theory' (or 'dual-content theory') to be a form of HOP theory (Carruthers, 2004; 2005). The basic idea is that the conscious status of an experience is due to its *availability* to higher-order thought. So 'conscious experience occurs when perceptual contents are fed into a special short-term buffer memory store, whose function is to make those contents available to cause HOTs about themselves.' (Carruthers, 2000, p. 228). Some first-order perceptual contents are available to a higher-order 'theory of mind mechanism,' which transforms those representational contents into conscious contents. Thus, no actual HOT occurs. Instead, according to Carruthers, some perceptual states acquire a dual intentional content; for example, a conscious experience of red not only has a first-order content of 'red,' but also has the higher-order content 'seems red' or 'experience of red.' Carruthers also makes interesting use of so-called 'consumer semantics' in order to fill out his theory of phenomenal consciousness. The content of a mental state depends, in part, on the powers of the organisms which 'consume' that state, e.g. the kinds of inferences which the organism can make when it is in that state.

However, there is again not very much explicitly written on concepts by either FO or HO theorists. To be sure, the topic does arise in some areas. For example, due to the fact that HOT theorists view HOTs as constituted by concepts, it is natural to ask just what the

---

[8] A common initial objection to HOR theories is that they are circular and lead to an infinite regress. It might seem that the HOT theory results in circularity by defining consciousness in terms of HOTs. It also might seem that an infinite regress results because a conscious mental state must be accompanied by a HOT, which, in turn, must be accompanied by another HOT *ad infinitum*. However, the standard reply is that when a conscious mental state is a first-order world-directed state the higher-order thought (HOT) is *not* itself conscious; otherwise, circularity and an infinite regress would follow. When the HOT is itself conscious, there is a yet higher-order (or third-order) thought directed at the second-order state. In this case, we have *introspection* which involves a conscious HOT directed at an inner mental state. When one introspects, one's attention is directed back into one's mind. For example, what makes my desire to write a good essay a conscious *first-order* desire is that there is a (nonconscious) HOT directed at the desire. In this case, my conscious focus is directed at the entry and my computer screen, so I am not consciously aware of having the HOT from the first-person point of view. When I introspect that desire, however, I then have a *conscious* HOT (accompanied by a yet higher, third-order, HOT) directed at the desire itself. See Gennaro 2004a for a much more detailed introduction on higher-order theories including several additional objections.

nature of those concepts might be. And how do those concepts relate to the content of the first-order states? How sophisticated are the self-concepts ('I') and the mental state concepts which constitute the HOT? How can animals and infants have such concepts?

In this volume, there are two papers which fall under this general heading. First, **John Beeckmans** takes up the key issue of whether or not various HOR theories can 'pass scientific muster.' He critically examines various central aspects of HOR theory with special attention to the role of conceptual short-term memory in consciousness, and argues that HOR theories seem sometimes to be at odds with the empirical evidence. Second, **Georges Rey** summarizes and then defends his well-known 'narrow' representationalist account of phenomenal experience and his eliminativism about 'qualia' largely against a criticism presented by Joseph Levine (2001). In doing so, Rey also focuses on the richness and determinacy of color experience and the nature of phenomenal concepts (see the previous section).

5. Concept Acquisition/Possession

There is a tremendous 'developmental' experimental literature mainly aimed at researching how infants and young children acquire concepts.[9] How do we learn concepts? What can empirical results from developmental psychology teach us about how we acquire concepts? Other related questions include: Are some concepts innate? (Cowie, 1999; Carruthers *et al.*, 2005.) What is the relationship between language use and concept formation? This is a fascinating area of ongoing research with psychologists often using the term 'categories' in addition to 'concepts.' To categorize is basically the 'ability to group discriminable properties, objects or events into classes...' whereas a concept is the 'mental representation that encapsulates the commonalities and structure that exist within categories.' (Rakison & Oakes, 2003, p. 1).

One contentious issue, for example, is the distinction between perceptual and conceptual categorization. Using this somewhat misleading terminology, the idea of 'perceptual categorization' refers to those objects and properties that are observable features (such as 'has four legs' or 'is red') whereas 'conceptual categorization' refers to more abstract and nonobservable properties of objects (such as 'continuing to exist when unperceived' or 'being a self-propelled agent that causally interacts with other things'). The latter includes background

---

[9] For just a recent sample of the literature, see Rakison & Oakes (2003), Gellman (2003) and Mandler (2004).

knowledge and information about, say, the ontology, causation and function of objects. Some argue that there is a clear distinction between these two types of categorization and thus that infants have two distinct systems which operate in parallel from very early in infancy (Mandler, 2004). Some argue that infants and children form categories based on perceptual or conceptual information at different points in development. This is a highly controversial distinction with many researches arguing, for example, that there isn't such a clear line between perceptual and conceptual categorization. For one thing, many of the same objects or entities that one might categorize as 'self-propelled' (e.g. dogs, cats) also have certain characteristic observable properties (e.g. 'has legs').

In any case, a number of familiar testing methods are employed to determine just what kinds of concepts are acquired in infancy and early childhood. To mention just one, the *familiarization-test procedure* examines infants' response to novel items after they are shown a number of objects (or pictures of objects) from the same category. The duration of their looking at the novel items is recorded with the idea being that the longer they look at the novel objects (or pictures) it is reasonable to infer that they think of the comparative objects as belonging to different categories. Although there is often agreement about such methods and their results, there remains significant disagreement about just how to interpret the results.[10]

Some of the discussion on infant (and even adult) concept acquisition and possession also revolves around testing for a so-called 'mindreading' ability; that is, the capacity to attribute mental states to others and even to oneself (and thus to have concepts of mental states). There is much discussion about such 'theories of mind' in the contemporary literature (Carruthers & Smith, 1996; Nichols & Stich, 2003; Goldman, 2006). One of the disputes centres on those who think that our concepts of the mental are acquired through a process of simulating another's mental activity with one's own, and those who argue that some kind of background theory of mind is presupposed in the ability to mindread. Hence, there is the much discussed choice between so-called 'simulation theory' and 'theory theory' of mind, though many authors really hold some form of hybrid view. A related controversy is what the relationship is between understanding one's own mental states and being able to attribute mental states to others. That is, does having concepts of mental states at all (even one's own) imply a third-person mindreading ability? Or can one be aware of

[10] Once again, see the many papers in Rakison & Oakes (2003).

one's own mental states without being able to mindread others at all? Infants and animals are often tested experimentally for their ability to understand whether or not another is having a perception or belief. Being able to deceive is often taken as evidence for such mindreading ability since the infant or animal is presumably trying to get another to (falsely) acquire a mental state.

The so-called 'false belief task' is also commonly used. An object might be moved to another location while subject A is in the room but subject B is out of the room. When B returns, A might be asked where B will look for the object, or other behavioural evidence (e.g. expressions of surprise) might be used to determine whether or not A can successfully contrast its own belief from B's belief about where the object will be. Infants do not perform well on these tasks until at least age three. Infants and animals are also sometimes tested as to their ability to follow the gaze of an experimenter with the logic being that doing so indicates an understanding of the concept of (another's) perception. Once again, however, even when there is agreement about the methods, there remains significant disagreement about how to interpret the results.

In any case, there is still very little explicit discussion of consciousness in the psychological literature. In my view, the problem of concept acquisition may in fact be the real 'hard problem' of consciousness (cf. Chalmers, 1995). For one thing, it is unclear just what the relationship is between consciousness and acquiring concepts. Does one have to be conscious first in order to acquire concepts (or at least most concepts)? If so, how does coherent conscious experience get started in the first place? Moreover, if one has conceptualist tendencies, the problem arises even more forcefully as to how we can acquire concepts if conscious experience presupposes having concepts. This is indeed an important and potentially rich area of future interdisciplinary research.

In this volume, **José Luis Bermúdez** argues, among other things, for a 'middle ground' position such that a human infant's perceptual development should be understood in terms of perceptual sensitivity to an increasing range of object properties. **David H. Rakison** examines the developmental literature in the areas of mathematics, categorization, and induction in order to determine whether infants possess concepts that allow them explicitly (i.e. consciously) to reason and make inferences about objects and events in the world. He argues against the idea that infants have conscious access to such background knowledge and then speculates about the relationship between language development and consciousness.

6. Animals

Much like some of the research described in the previous section, there is a natural similarity to work on animal minds. Many of the experiments done on (prelinguistic) infants are clearly also relevant to non-linguistic animals. How does one determine whether or not an animal possesses a concept? Also, like some research on infants, the idea of 'mindreading' often takes center stage in this area. There is an enormous and interesting literature on animal cognition.[11] However, once again, there is rarely an explicit connection drawn between concepts and consciousness.[12]

There are also other well-known empirical methods used to determine whether or not animals have *self*-concepts and self-awareness, such as various mirror recognition tasks (Gallup, 1970; Keenan, Gallup & Falk, 2003). To what extent can animals recognize themselves or something on their bodies in a mirror? This is perhaps not the best way to determine whether or not animals have some form of self-consciousness. However, it does still offer us one way to determine whether or not animals have 'I-thoughts,' that is, thoughts about oneself or one's own mental states.

Finally, there is some dispute as to whether or not HOT theory rules out animal and infant consciousness with a prominent HO theorist arguing that it does (Carruthers, 2000; 2005). It may seem that the HOTs (along with their constituent concepts) are too sophisticated for many animals to have. However, others argue that there are, for example, degrees of self-concepts and that the HOTs need not be so sophisticated (e.g. Gennaro, 1993; 1996; 2004).[13] Thus, HOT theory would be consistent with animal consciousness after all.

7. Psychopathologies

One might also examine how self-concepts and the ability to mindread play a role in consciousness on several other related fronts. In some abnormal cases, one's self-consciousness seems deficient and, in turn, one's self-concepts do not operate properly. Two psychopathologies frequently mentioned along these lines are autism and schizophrenia. For example, it has been argued that autistic people are 'mindblind' (Baron-Cohen 1995) in the sense that their 'mindreading' abilities are deficient, as was discussed in section five. Others have argued that

---

[11] See most recently, e.g., Bekoff *et al.* (2002), Bermúdez (2003) and Hurley & Nudds (2006).

[12] For some discussion, see Allen and Bekoff (1997).

[13] See Gennaro (2006) for some additional arguments against Carruthers' overall position.

schizophrenia results from a self-monitoring deficiency (Frith, 1992).[14] In this volume, **Simon Baron-Cohen** *et al.* present an interesting case of a patient who has a form of autism, but also has savant memory (where memory is seemingly limitless) and synaesthesia (a condition where stimulation of one sensory modality, such as hearing a sound, automatically triggers a perception in a second modality, such as having a colour experience). One issue is what the connection is, if any, between having these conditions. Other issues include the impaired mindreading abilities found in these patients, such as a lack of empathy or an inability to form concepts of others' mental states, as well as challenging the assumption that other conscious minds are similar to our own.

8. Other Themes and Future Directions

Finally, there are many other miscellaneous areas where concepts and consciousness can overlap and yield interesting results. For example, in this volume, **Art Markman** *et al.* argue that by manipulating people's motivational state and the nature of the task performed, the influence of conscious processing on cognitive performance (such as concept learning) can be varied. Using primarily neuroscientific evidence, **Daniel Weiskopf** argues against the recently revived notion of 'concept empiricism,' roughly the view that the vehicles of thoughts, and their constituent concepts, are made up of internally reactivated traces of perceptions. In doing so, Weiskopf raises once again the important problem of just what the relationship is between concepts and conscious perception. His results might also be relevant to the viability of HOR theories and Conceptualism.

So where do we go from here? Of course, much more needs to be done on all of the above topics. In addition, there are other equally important areas of inquiry. For example, just as there is significant research into the so-called 'neural correlates of consciousness' or NCC's (Metzinger, 2000), so there is increasing interest in what we might term the 'neural correlates of *concepts*.' Some efforts have been made in this direction (e.g. Miller *et al.*, 2003) and the papers in this volume by **Jesse Prinz**, **Daniel Weiskopf**, and **John Beeckmans** also touch on this topic. However, it would be useful if these lines of research came together at various points instead of progress being made by independent researchers only concerned with one or the other. To the extent that having concepts and conscious experience are

---

[14] Cf. Stephens & Graham (2000), Zahavi (2000), but also see Nichols and Stich (2003).

intimately linked, it is imperative that these two areas of research come together. In doing so, perhaps more progress will be made in solving the hard problem of consciousness, as well as the so-called 'binding problem' and issues related to the unity of consciousness.[15] These overlapping areas are already garnering much attention by both philosophers and scientists.

It is also important to keep in mind that concepts are often treated as constituents of intentional states, such as beliefs and desires. This, in turn, raises the crucial question of just how intentionality and consciousness are related.[16] Some hold that intentional states (and thus concepts) can be attributed to animals and even some insects without any commitment to consciousness (e.g. Carruthers 2005). On the other hand, some have argued that having genuine intentional states entails, or is inseparable from, consciousness in some sense (Searle, 1992; Siewert, 1998; Horgan & Tienson, 2002). Wherever one comes down on this issue, it is clear that one ought not to ignore it when developing an account of concept attribution (and intentionality), on the one hand, and a theory of consciousness, on the other. Also at stake is whether or not consciousness can be *reduced* to intentionality in some way, as many representationalists would have it. If genuine intentionality presupposes consciousness, it is difficult to see how the latter can be reduced to the former, that is, how conscious mentality can be reduced to non-conscious states.

As was noted in section five, the problem of concept acquisition may in fact be the real hard problem of consciousness. Significant research is on the horizon with respect to concept acquisition and the related topic of innateness. Once again, though, such work should not take place in a vacuum or without some attention to the nature of consciousness. For example, addressing the question of infant consciousness can only shed light on how some concepts are acquired, and vice versa.

It is my hope that this volume will spawn new research on concepts and consciousness and renew a spirit of interdisciplinary thinking and cooperation among philosophers, psychologists, and cognitive scientists on the variety of topics discussed in these pages. Needless to say, virtually every problem addressed in this volume will be solved only with significant interdisciplinary work. I thank the authors for all their hard work and for taking an important step in that direction. I also

---

[15] See e.g. Cleeremans (2003) where the binding problem is defined as 'the problem of integrating the information processed by different regions of the brain.' (p. 1)

[16] See, for example, Siewert (2003) for a survey article. See also Gennaro (1996) chapters one and five; Kriegel (2003); Wilson (2003).

thank Anthony Freeman for his help and editorial guidance throughout the entire process of putting this special issue together.

References

Allen, C. & Bekoff, M. (1997), *Species of Mind* (Cambridge, MA: MIT Press).
Alter, T. & Walter, S. (eds. 2007), *Phenomenal Concepts and Phenomenal Knowl-
edge: New Essays on Consciousness and Physicalism* (New York: Oxford Uni-
versity Press).
Armstrong, D. (1968), *A Materialist Theory of Mind* (London: Routledge and
Kegan Paul).
Armstrong, D. (1981), 'What is consciousness?' In *The Nature of Mind* (Ithaca,
NY: Cornell University Press).
Baars, B., Banks, W., & Newman, J. (eds. 2003), *Essential Sources in the Scientific
Study of Consciousness* (Cambridge, MA: MIT Press).
Balog, K. (1999), 'Conceivability, possibility, and the mind-body problem', *Philo-
sophical Review*, **108**, pp. 497–528.
Baron-Cohen, S. (1995), *Mindblindness* (Cambridge, MA: MIT Press).
Bekoff, M., Allen, C., & Burghardt, G. (eds. 2002), *The Cognitive Animal* (Cam-
bridge, MA: MIT Press).
Bermúdez, J. (2003), *Thinking Without Words* (New York: Oxford University Press).
Block, N. (1995), 'On a confusion about the function of consciousness', *Behav-
ioral and Brain Sciences*, **18**, pp. 227–47.
Block, N., Flanagan, O. & Güzeldere, G. (eds. 1997), *The Nature of Consciousness*
(Cambridge, MA: MIT Press).
Block, N. & Stalnaker, R. (1999), 'Conceptual analysis, dualism, and the explana-
tory gap', *Philosophical Review*, **108**, pp. 1–46.
Botterell, A. (2001), 'Conceiving what is not there', *Journal of Consciousness
Studies*, **8** (8), pp. 21–42.
Brewer, B. (1999), *Perception and Reason* (New York: Oxford University Press).
Carruthers, P. (2000), *Phenomenal Consciousness.* (Cambridge, MA: Cambridge
University Press).
Carruthers, P. (2004), 'HOP over FOR, HOT Theory', in Gennaro (2004a).
Carruthers, P. (2005), *Consciousness: Essays from a Higher-Order Perspective*
(New York: Oxford University Press).
Carruthers, P., Laurence, S. & Stich, S. (eds. 2005), *The Innate Mind: Structure
and Contents* (New York: Oxford University Press).
Carruthers, P. & Smith, P. (eds. 1996), *Theories of Theories of Mind* (New York:
Cambridge University Press).
Chalmers, D.J. (1995), 'Facing up to the problem of consciousness', *Journal of
Consciousness Studies*, **2** (3), pp. 200–19.
Chalmers, D.J. (1996), *The Conscious Mind* (New York: Oxford University Press).
Chalmers, D.J. (ed. 2002), *Philosophy of Mind: Classical and Contemporary
Readings* (New York: Oxford University Press).
Chalmers, D.J. (2004), 'The Representational Character of Experience', in *The
Future for Philosophy*, ed. B. Leiter (Oxford: Oxford University Press).
Chalmers, D. J. (2007), 'Phenomenal concepts and the explanatory gap', in Alter
& Walter (2007).
Cleeremans, A. (ed. 2003), *The Unity of Consciousness: Binding, Integration and
Dissociation* (Oxford: Oxford University Press).
Cowie, F. (1999), *What's Within? Nativism Reconsidered* (New York: Oxford Uni-
versity Press).

Dennett, D.C. (2005), *Sweet Dreams* (Cambridge, MA: MIT Press).

Dretske, F. (1995), *Naturalizing the Mind* (Cambridge, MA: MIT Press).

Fodor, J. (1975), *The Language of Thought* (Cambridge, MA: Harvard University Press).

Fodor, J. (1998), *Concepts: Where Cognitive Science Went Wrong* (New York: Oxford University Press).

Frith, C. (1992), *The Cognitive Neuropsychology of Schizophrenia* (East Sussex, UK: Psychology Press).

Gallup, G. (1970), 'Chimpanzees: self-recognition', *Science*, **167**, pp. 86–87.

Gellman, S. (2003), *The Essential Child* (New York: Oxford University Press).

Gendler, T. & Hawthorne, J. (eds. 2006), *Perceptual Experience* (New York: Oxford University Press).

Gennaro, R. (1993), 'Brute experience and the higher-order thought theory of consciousness', *Philosophical Papers*, **22**, pp. 51–69.

Gennaro, R. (1996), *Consciousness and Self-consciousness: A Defense of the Higher-Order Thought Theory of Consciousness* (Amsterdam & Philadelphia: John Benjamins).

Gennaro, R. (2004), 'Higher-order thoughts, animal consciousness, and misrepresentation: A reply to Carruthers and Levine', in Gennaro (2004a).

Gennaro, R. (ed. 2004a), *Higher-Order Theories of Consciousness: An Anthology* (Amsterdam and Philadelphia: John Benjamins).

Gennaro, R. (2005a), 'Consciousness', *Internet Encyclopedia of Philosophy*. Available at: http://www.iep.utm.edu/c/consciou.htm.

Gennaro, R. (2005b), 'The HOT theory of consciousness: between a rock and a hard place?' *Journal of Consciousness Studies*, **12** (2), pp. 3–21.

Gennaro, R. (2006), 'Review of Peter Carruthers' *Consciousness: Essays from a Higher-Order Perspective*', *Psyche*, **12**.

Goldman, A. (2006), *Simulating Minds* (New York: Oxford University Press).

Gunther, Y. (ed. 2003), *Essays on Nonconceptual Content* (Cambridge, MA: MIT Press).

Hill, C. S. (1997), 'Imaginability, conceivability, possibility, and the mind-body problem', *Philosophical Studies*, **87**, pp. 61–85.

Hill, C. & McLaughlin, B. (1998), 'There are fewer things in reality than are dreamt of in Chalmers' philosophy', *Philosophy and Phenomenological Research*, **59**, pp. 445–54.

Horgan, T. & Tienson, J. (2002), 'The intentionality of phenomenology and the phenomenology of intentionality', in Chalmers (2002).

Hurley, S. & Nudds, M. (eds. 2006), *Rational Animals?* (New York: Oxford University Press).

Kant, I. (1781/1965), *Critique of Pure Reason.* Translated by N. Kemp Smith. (New York: MacMillan).

Keenan, J., Gallup, G., & Falk, D. (2003), *The Face in the Mirror* (New York: HarperCollins).

Kirk, R. (2005), *Zombies and Consciousness* (New York: Oxford University Press).

Koch, C. (2004), *The Quest for Consciousness: A Neurobiological Approach* (Englewood, CO: Roberts and Company).

Kriegel, U. (2003), 'Is intentionality dependent upon consciousness?', *Philosophical Studies*, **116**, pp. 271–307.

Kripke, S. (1972), *Naming and Necessity* (Cambridge, MA: Harvard University Press).

Levine, J. (2001), *Purple Haze: The Puzzle of Conscious Experience* (Cambridge, MA: MIT Press).

Loar, B. (1997), 'Phenomenal states', In *The Nature of Consciousness*, ed. N. Block, O. Flanagan, & G. Güzeldere (Cambridge, MA: MIT Press).

Loar, B. (1999), 'David Chalmers's *The Conscious Mind*', *Philosophy and Phenomenological Research*, **59**, pp. 465–72.

Locke, J. (1689/1975), *An Essay Concerning Human Understanding*. P. Nidditch ed.. (Oxford: Clarendon).

Lycan, W.G. (1996), *Consciousness and Experience* (Cambridge, MA: MIT Press).

Lycan, W.G. (2001), 'A simple argument for a higher-order representation theory of consciousness', *Analysis*, 61, pp. 3-4.

Lycan, W.G. (2004), 'The superiority of HOP to HOT', In Gennaro 2004a.

Lycan, W.G. (2005), 'Representational Theories of Consciousness', *The Stanford Encyclopedia of Philosophy* (Spring 2005 Edition), Edward N. Zalta (ed.), URL: <http://plato.stanford.edu/archives/spr2005/entries/consciousness-representational/>.

Mack, A. & Rock, I. (1998), *Inattentional Blindness* (Cambridge, MA: MIT Press).

Mandler, J. (2004), *The Foundations of Mind* (New York: Oxford University Press).

Margolis, E. & Laurence, S. (1999), *Concepts: Core Readings* (Cambridge, MA: MIT Press).

McDowell, J. (1994), *Mind and World* (Cambridge, MA: Harvard University Press).

Metzinger, T. (ed. 2000), *Neural Correlates of Consciousness: Empirical and Conceptual Questions* (Cambridge, MA: MIT Press).

Miller, E., Nieder, A., Freedman, D., & Wallis, J. (2003), 'Neural correlates of categories and concepts', *Current Opinion in Neurobiology*, **13**, pp. 198–203.

Murphy, G. (2002), *The Big Book of Concepts* (Cambridge, MA: MIT Press).

Nagel, T. (1974), 'What is it like to be a bat?', *Philosophical Review*, **83**, pp. 435–56.

Nichols, S. & Stich, S. (2003), *Mindreading* (New York: Oxford University Press).

Noë, A. (2002), *Action in Perception* (Cambridge, MA: MIT Press).

Papineau, D. (1998), 'Mind the gap', In *Philosophical Perspectives* 12, ed. J. Tomberlin (Atascadero, CA: Ridgeview Publishing Company).

Papineau, D. (2002), *Thinking about Consciousness* (Oxford: Oxford University Press).

Peacocke, C. (1992), *A Study of Concepts* (Cambridge, MA: MIT Press).

Perry, J. (2001), *Knowledge, Possibility, and Consciousness.* (Cambridge, MA: MIT Press).

Prinz, J. (2002), *Furnishing the Mind: Concepts and Their Perceptual Basis* (Cambridge, MA: MIT Press).

Rakison, D. & Oakes, L. (eds. 2003), *Early Category and Concept Development* (New York: Oxford University Press).

Revonsuo, A. (2006), *Inner Presence* (Cambridge, MA: MIT Press).

Rey, G. (1998), 'A narrow representationalist account of qualitative experience', In *Philosophical Perspectives* 12, ed. J. Tomberlin (Atascadero, CA: Ridgeview Publishing Company).

Rosenthal, D. M. (1986), 'Two concepts of consciousness', *Philosophical Studies*, **49**, pp. 329–59.

Rosenthal, D. M. (1997), 'A theory of consciousness', in *The Nature of Consciousness*, eds. N. Block, O. Flanagan, & G. Güzeldere (Cambridge, MA: MIT Press).

Rosenthal, D.M. (2004), 'Varieties of higher-order theory', in Gennaro (2004a).

Rosenthal, D.M. (2005), *Consciousness and Mind* (New York: Oxford University Press).

Searle, J. (1992), *The Rediscovery of the Mind* (Cambridge. MA: MIT Press).

Shear, J. (ed. 1997), *Explaining Consciousness: The Hard Problem* (Cambridge, MA: MIT Press).

Siewert, C. (1998), *The Significance of Consciousness* (Princeton, NJ: Princeton University Press).

Siewert, C. (2003), 'Consciousness and intentionality', *The Stanford Encyclopedia of Philosophy (Fall 2003 Edition)*, Edward N. Zalta (ed.) URL: <http://plato.stanford.edu/archives/fall2003/entries/consciousness- intentionality/>.

Simons, D. (2000), 'Current approaches to change blindness', *Visual Cognition*, **7**, pp. 1–15.

Smith, Q. & Jokic, A. (eds. 2003), *Consciousness: New Philosophical Perspectives* (New York: Oxford University Press).

Stephens, G.L., & Graham, G. (2000), *When Self-Consciousness Breaks* (Cambridge, MA: MIT Press).

Tye, M. (1995), *Ten Problems of Consciousness* (Cambridge, MA: MIT Press).

Tye, M. (2000), *Consciousness, Color, and Content.* (Cambridge, MA: MIT Press).

Tye, M. (2006), 'Nonconceptual content, richness, and fineness of grain', In Gendler and Hawthorne, 2006.

Wilson, R. (2003), 'Intentionality and phenomenology', *Pacific Philosophical Quarterly*, **84**, pp. 413–31.

Yablo, S. (1999), 'Concepts and consciousness', *Philosophy and Phenomenological Research*, **59**, pp. 455–63.

Zahavi, D. (ed. 2000), *Exploring the Self* (Amsterdam & Philadelphia: John Benjamins).

Philippe Chuard

The Riches of Experience

Suppose you see a red ball. Unless you are in a psychologist's lab, it is unlikely that you see *just* the red ball against, say, a white background. Rather, a myriad of objects is visually presented to you *simultaneously*. For instance, you see the cricket bat beside the red ball, the table upon which they both lie, as well as what's in the background of the table. You also see the shapes of these objects, together with the manifold of spatial relations connecting them. For some of these objects at least, you see their particular colour(s), even the texture of their surface(s).

Most of our visual experiences seem to be like that. This owes partly to the fact that the visual scenes we encounter are complex and 'contain' many objects — in contrast to the psychologist's lab. More importantly, each single experience has the propensity to convey a *rich amount of information* about the objects, properties and relations which make up such scenes — together with information about the scenes themselves. Call this the 'Informational Richness of Experience' or (IRE):

> **The Informational Richness of Perceptual Experience**
> any single perceptual experience e of a subject S can *simultaneously* represent many objects $o_1 \ldots o_n$, properties $P_1 \ldots P_n$ and relations $R_1 \ldots R_n$.

The rich information characteristic of visual experience appears to raise a difficulty for Conceptualism — the view that perceptual experiences are *akin* to thoughts in the sense that they represent the subject's environment in a way that *necessarily* engages (and depends upon) her conceptual capacities. On this view, the content of experience is conceptual: *what* is represented in an experience — and *how* it is represented — is determined by the concepts the perceiver deploys in that experience.

(IRE) is supposed to raise a difficulty for Conceptualism because it suggests that there is much more to perceptual representation than the deployment of concepts allows for. In particular, it seems as though perceivers do not always conceptualize (that is, deploy concepts for) everything they see. For instance, you might let your eyes wander on the above scene (the cricket bat and the red ball on the table), while thinking about the latest test match between Australia and New Zealand. Whilst your thoughts are thus occupied, it's not as if you stop experiencing the many objects and properties in front of you. In such a case, though, it is far from obvious that, as you deploy concepts in thought, you simultaneously conceptualize what you see. Hence, the suggestion goes, there may be limitations on *how much* information you can conceptualize at any given time. If so, it seems possible that perceivers do not always conceptualize *every* object, property or relation, etc., represented in their experience at a time, given the rich information such experiences can convey. In which case, Conceptualism is false.

This general line of thought can be encapsulated in a two-premise argument, or argument-template — call it the 'Argument from the Informational Richness of Experience' (AIRE):

1. for any single visual experience e of a subject S, e can simultaneously represent many objects $o_1 \ldots o_n$, properties $P_1 \ldots P_n$ and relations $R_1 \ldots R_n$.
2. if S's visual experience e represents simultaneously many objects $o_1 \ldots o_n$, properties $P_1 \ldots P_n$ and relations $R_1 \ldots R_n$, it is *possible* that S does *not* deploy any concept for *some* of the many objects $o_1 \ldots o_n$, properties $P_1 \ldots P_n$ and relations $R_1 \ldots R_n$, represented in e.

Therefore:

3. It is not the case that, for any object, property, relation, etc., x, a subject S has an experience e representing x *only if* S deploys a concept C for x in e.

Premise (1) expresses (IRE) — the idea that experiences are informationally replete. Premise (2) is a conditional, the antecedent of which summarizes premise (1), while its consequent, equivalent to the conclusion (3), amounts to the negation of the conceptualist thesis — the claim that, necessarily, perceivers conceptualize *everything* they experience. Such a conditional can be regarded as enthymematic for whatever additional assumption — or combination thereof — is needed to secure the entailment from (1) to (3): call this conditional the 'Bridging Thesis'. The argument is valid, as it contains a single instance of *modus ponens*.

The question to be considered in this article is whether (AIRE) can successfully serve to refute the conceptualist view of experience. To answer this, two further questions must be addressed. First, whether perceptual experiences *really* are so rich in information as premise (1) claims. Second, whether the key premise — the Bridging Thesis — is true and what considerations can be brought to bear in its favour. In short, if perceptual experiences are indeed so rich in information, how exactly does this falsify Conceptualism?

The article has two parts, each concerned with one of these questions. After a brief outline of the conceptualist doctrine (Section 1), I consider motivations for the claim that experiences are rich in information (Section 2). I shall argue that, properly understood, there are good reasons to accept this first premise. Unsurprisingly, premise (2) is where the trouble begins. The rest of the paper sketches four different ways to motivate the Bridging Thesis and assesses their respective merits (Section 3).

1. Conceptualism

What is it, exactly, that Conceptualists claim about perceptual experience? John McDowell and Bill Brewer often express the view in terms of the following slogans: that the representational content of perceptual experience is 'conceptual through and through' (McDowell, 1994, p. 46); that '[e]xperiences have their content by virtue of the fact that conceptual capacities are operative in them' (*ibid.*, p. 66); that experiences are 'actualisations of conceptual capacities' (McDowell, 1998, p. 438); or that their content 'is the content of a possible *judgement by the subject*' (Brewer, 1999, p. 149). According to Strawson (1992, p. 62), experience is 'thoroughly permeated — saturated [. . .] with concepts'. Unfortunately, little has been done to flesh out such slogans in any detail. In what follows, I will only offer a very minimal sketch of what Conceptualism — as I understand the view — amounts to.[1]

But first, a *caveat*. Obviously, the crucial notion here is that of 'conceptual content'. It is common to assume that a characterization of 'conceptual content' must start with the specification of a theory of concepts, together with some commitment to one of the main

---

[1] I defend this construal of Conceptualism in much more detail in Chuard (2006a).

contending theories of mental content (Fregean senses, Russellian sets, or sets of possible worlds). Another common assumption: Conceptualists like McDowell and Brewer are Fregeans: for them, concepts are abstract Fregean senses which compose or constitute larger Fregean senses (propositions). One problem with these assumptions is that the issue between Conceptualists and their critics turns into a rather narrow dispute among Fregeans, in which other theorists cannot partake (see, e.g., Crane, 2001, pp. 151–2; Stalnaker, 1998, p. 340).[2]

Surely, though, the issue is broader than this: the question is whether perceptual experiences represent the environment in the same *kind* of way that thoughts and beliefs do, or altogether differently. It seems as though *that* question is more general (and important) about the nature of experience than which theory of content and of concepts applies to experience. More importantly, it should be possible for proponents of any theory of content or concepts (insofar as such theories capture what we traditionally and intuitively take contents and concepts to be, of course) to address such a question in a substantial way — rather than as a simple matter of definition, say.[3] Thus, a proper specification of the notion of 'conceptual content', at least at a general level of description, ought to be compatible with different theories of content and concepts. The minimal account of 'conceptual content' to be sketched here respects this desideratum.

1.1. Conceptualist supervenience

One way in which to understand the notion of 'conceptual content' is suggested by McDowell's claim that '[e]xperiences have their content by virtue of the fact that conceptual capacities are operative in them' (1994, p. 66). The claim sounds very much like some sort of determination thesis: namely, that *what* a given experience represents — and *how* it represents it — is determined by *which* conceptual capacities the perceiver exercises in her experience.

A determination thesis can be formulated in terms of *supervenience*. If *A* determines *B*, *B* supervenes upon *A*, so that any variation in *B* necessarily comes with a variation in *A* (but not *vice versa*). McDowell's claim could then be paraphrased thus: no difference in perceptual

---

[2] Note that textual evidence for the assumption that McDowell and Brewer — in the way they describe their Conceptualism — are committed Fregeans, is rather scant. If anything, both seem rather non-committal.

[3] It may be that Conceptualists and their critics have different presuppositions about content and concepts, and are simply talking past one another rather than having a substantive dispute. Thus, given a certain theory of concepts and content, Conceptualism may be trivially true; given another, trivially false — true or false by definition, as it were.

content without a difference in the conceptual capacities 'operative' in experience. Call it thesis (C):

(C) Necessarily, for any objects, properties, relations, states-of-affairs, etc., x_1 and x_2, represented in the experience(s) of some subject S, if x_1 is represented differently from x_2, then S exercises different conceptual capacities for x_1 and x_2 in the experience(s) representing them.

Some brief clarifications. By 'representational difference', I mean the following: if x_1 and x_2 are represented differently, there is a difference in content — a difference in *what* is represented and/or in *how* it is represented, in the sense that different objects (properties) might be represented, or that the same object (property) might be represented in different ways.[4]

By conceptual differences and the exercise (or deployment) of different conceptual capacities, I have in mind the exercise *in* experience of conceptual capacities associated with *distinct* concepts. But what are conceptual capacities? How to individuate them? What does it mean to say that such capacities are 'operative' (or 'exercised') in experience? And what does all this have to do with concepts? I'll take some of these points in turn.

1.2. Conceptual capacities

Conceptual capacities are psychological capacities of a sort that play a central role in thinking and reasoning. Assuming that psychological subjects make use of concepts to perform certain operations in thinking and reasoning, conceptual capacities are the sorts of capacities subjects typically exploit in using concepts. Admittedly, this is rather vague. Some examples might help. There are many things one can do with a concept C. One can (i) use C in an inference (if x is C, then x is F), one can (ii) identify an object as falling under C, one can (iii) discriminate C from some other concept F, etc. Call the capacities to perform such tasks 'conceptual capacities'. More capacities may count as conceptual, but the above examples are reasonably familiar.

There are two aspects to the individuation of conceptual capacities: (a) the particular capacity at issue, and (b) the concept with which it is

---

[4] For instance, x_1 and x_2 might be represented differently without being represented as *being different*. Thus, two identical shades of red, r_1 and r_2, can be represented differently in experience if one (r_1) is shaded while the other (r_2) appears in full sunlight, say. Though r_1 and r_2 look different and their colour is represented differently, it's not as if these shades are represented *as being* different.

associated. The capacity to apply a concept C to some object is distinct from the capacity to infer that some x is C from the thought that all xs are C. Both are capacities involving concept C, but they are different capacities: it is possible to have the former without the latter. Similarly, the capacity to apply a concept C to some object is distinct from the capacity to apply a concept F to the same object. They are the same *kind* of capacity, but are associated with different concepts (so that one could have one capacity without the other).[5] Here, by 'distinct conceptual capacities', I mean conceptual capacities (no matter of which kind) associated with different concepts.

What does it mean to say that capacities are 'exercised', 'deployed' or 'operative', in a given mental state? Nothing more than this: capacities are psychological dispositions (states) to perform certain tasks or operations, and such dispositions can be manifested (an event) by performing the task or operation in question. For instance, while drawing the inference that there are marsupials in Australia from the propositions that there are kangaroos in Australia, one exercises (among others) a capacity associated with the concept *KANGAROO*. I take it that this is what McDowell means by conceptual capacities that are 'operative' in experience.[6]

Finally, what does this have to do with concepts? Irrespective of what concepts are (metaphysically speaking), most theories of concepts allow that subjects who possess concepts can do certain things with them. Thus, conceptual capacities come with the possession of concepts — whether concepts *are* such conceptual capacities, whether these capacities are necessary for the possession of concepts, or whether the possession of concepts merely makes it possible for subjects to have such capacities.

According to thesis (C), then, the representational content of a perceptual experience is fully conceptual in the sense that what the experience represents (and how it represents it) is entirely determined by the conceptual capacities the perceiver brings to bear in her experience. This specifies the nature of the relation between content and

---

[5] Two concepts C_1 and C_2 will be distinct just in case, either (i) they have a different extension, and/or (ii), although they happen to apply to exactly the same things, C_1 and C_2 pick out different features (properties, relations, etc.) of such things.

[6] Why do Conceptualists like McDowell insist that conceptual capacities must be 'operative' in experience? Because possession of such capacities alone isn't sufficient to characterize the conceptualist view. The fact that you have conceptual capacities associated with distinct concepts applicable to the same perceived object underdetermines the content of your experience, since it leaves it open *how* you are in fact conceptualizing the object in front of you.

concepts (or conceptual capacities).[7] For Non-conceptualists who reject (C), the content of experience is not so determined.

The characterization of 'conceptual content' advanced here is neutral between different theories of concepts and of content. (C) is compatible with a Fregean account, but doesn't make such an account mandatory — it is compatible with other accounts too. In this respect, thesis (C) captures what is common between different theorists who think that what an experience represents is determined by the perceiver's concepts, no matter how they think of content and concepts (in the same way as physicalist supervenience captures what is common between different Physicalists who endorse different conceptions of physical properties, facts, processes, etc.).

2. Informational Richness

Why think that the following — (IRE) — is true?

> **The informational richness of perceptual experience**
> any single perceptual experience e of a subject S can *simultaneously* represent many objects $o_1 \ldots o_n$, properties $P_1 \ldots P_n$ and relations $R_1 \ldots R_n$.

Before we look at reasons for accepting (IRE), a word about its scope: this will help set aside a certain type of objection.

2.1. The scope of (IRE)

Two cautionary remarks. First, to say that visual experiences can be very rich in information is not to say that *all* visual experiences are. There are exceptions, of course. Think of the red ball against a white background in the psychologist's lab — or think of tunnel vision (Martin, 1992b, p. 207).

Nor is it to say, second, that *every* perceivable object or property in the perceiver's visual field is perceived, let alone perceived *in all detail*. For instance, it might be that only those objects at the centre of the perceiver's visual field are represented in any detail — whereas their surrounding isn't.[8] Still, a visual experience can present a very rich body of information — including information about hue, shape,

---

[7]   This is compatible with the fact that there may be other relations between concepts and content — relations which might serve to explain why (C) is true. For instance, Fregeans will hold that (C) is true because contents are constituted by concepts.

[8]   This has to do, in part, with the distribution of receptor cells on the retina. The centre of the retina (fovea) contains a high density of cones with very high acuity. In contrast, the periphery of the retina (parafovea) consists mainly of rods, which are more dispersed, and thus give rise to a much lower resolution. Hence, only 'foveated' stimuli are perceived in any great detail (see, e.g., Findlay and Gilchrist, 2003, pp. 11–18).

size, location, etc., about an object at the centre of the perceiver's visual field. What's more, as Dretske (1981, pp. 152, 157) pointed out, information about some objects in the periphery can be conveyed in the same experience. Even if such objects are not represented in *all* detail, information about their location, size, shape, as well as the spatial relations between such objects, is nevertheless available to the perceiver.

This second *caveat* is important. (IRE) must be distinguished from the so-called 'snapshot conception of experience' (Noë, 2002, p. 4). According to the latter, experiences are not just rich in information, but represent *every* object in the subject's visual field and represent them in *all detail*. Since (IRE) doesn't claim as much, it is left untouched by various considerations raised against the 'snapshot conception'.

For instance, it has been observed that, when their attention is occupied with some specific task, normal subjects are often unable to notice other objects in their visual field. A typical example of this so-called 'inattentional blindness' (Mack and Rock, 1998) involves a group of people playing with a ball, among whom figures a man wearing a gorilla suit. When asked to follow the game, normal subjects usually fail to notice the fake gorilla.

Similarly, cases of 'change blindness', where subjects fail to notice an obvious change in some object well in sight, suggest that they do not see everything in their visual field (see, e.g., Simons, 2000). For instance, two pictures of the same building might differ in that one represents the building with more windows. Yet, the difference often escapes notice when subjects are presented with one picture of the building after the other.

Whether or not such cases really cause trouble for the snapshot conception of experience, they are perfectly compatible with (IRE).[9] To see this, consider two pictures of my bookshelf:

Picture A   Picture B

---

[9]   It isn't clear that such cases really undermine the 'snapshot conception of experience' — *pace* Noë (2002, p. 7). For one thing, inattentional and change blindness might only reveal failures to *notice* certain features — which is consistent with the claim that such features are nonetheless represented in experience (see Cohen, 2002; and Moore, 2001).

Admittedly, you do not notice all the information in each photograph: there are many differences between the arrangement of books in pictures A and B you fail to notice. Nevertheless, there are many differences you *do* notice, and this suggests that you see the different properties constituting such differences. You notice the shape, size and colours (assuming these are coloured photographs) of many of the books, the titles on some of the books, as well as the location of particular books in the arrangement. You also notice, for instance, that there is no gap in the arrangement.

To repeat, then, (IRE) does not require that (a) one perceives *everything* in one's visual field, let alone that (b) one perceives everything *in the utmost detail*. Thus, the content of one's visual experience may still be very rich even though one fails to *notice* some of the elements of a visual scene represented in experience. Hence, once the scope of (IRE) is laid out, we see that considerations like the above leave (IRE) untouched.

2.2. (IRE) and fineness of grain

It is also important to distinguish (IRE) — the claim that visual experiences can convey a rich amount of information — from another claim about the *fineness of grain* of experience — the idea that the information conveyed in experience is very specific, so that experiences can represent particular objects and features in all detail and nuance (as when visual experiences, for instance, make it possible for subjects to discriminate the very subtle differences between, say, highly similar shades of colour). These two claims, however, are often conflated (see, e.g., Dretske, 1981, p. 147; Heck, 2000, p. 489; Martin, 1992a, p. 758; Peacocke, 1989, p. 315).

They are, however, logically distinct: it's possible to have experiences which instantiate one property but not the other. Thus, suppose you are in the psychologist's lab, facing a red dot against a uniform white background. Although your experience of the whole scene accurately represents the specific shade of red of the dot, it conveys very little information — in contrast to a visual experience of a street scene, say. Your experience is fine-grained, because it represents the specific shade of the red dot, but not very rich in information.

Alternatively, imagine walking on a city street through heavy fog. Though you see the whole street, everything looks fuzzy: no object appears to have any definite shape or contour and colours appear all a bit shaded. There could be an experience of this kind such that, although the experience conveys a lot of information about the whole scene and about individual objects in it, such information is rather coarse-grained. No specific details are seen in any specific manner.[10] In this article, I am concerned solely with the claim that experiences contain a wealth of information, and leave aside the fineness of grain of such information.

2.3. Why believe (IRE)?

What reason(s) is there to accept that *visual experiences* are so rich in information? At first sight the answer seems straightforward. By its very nature (IRE) must be based on one's familiarity with one's experiences and their phenomenology.

Think again of your experience of the red ball described at the beginning of the article. Introspecting the phenomenology of your experience of such a scene reveals that you are being presented with a multitude of objects, many (though perhaps not all) of their visible properties and relations (spatial and mereological relations, as well as relations of chromatic difference and similarity, for instance). This is so, even if you briefly glance at the scene and close your eyes afterwards. Thus, for instance, it seems that the overall spatial arrangement of the scene is represented in your visual experience. But this means that the shape of the various objects that make up the display, together with their location and the spatial relations that hold between such objects, must also be represented in your experience. If you can perceive the shape and location of these objects, this must owe partly to the fact that their colour — as well as the chromatic differences between such objects and their respective backgrounds — are represented in your experience too. Phenomenological reflection thus suggests that a very rich amount of information can be conveyed in a single experience.

It is also possible that your experiences carry more information than you are able to notice. After all, what information is conveyed in

---

[10] To some extent, the difference between (i) fineness of grain and (ii) informational richness is a matter of degree, since a fine-grained representation of *x* will typically contain more information about *x* than a non-specific one. Nevertheless, the additional information involved in (i) is *about* particular properties or objects (the ones presented in more detail). With (ii), the additional information is about different objects and properties, so that it *need* not contain specific information about anything in particular. For a more detailed discussion of this difference, see Chuard (2006a). For a discussion of the objection from the fineness of grain, see Chuard (2006a, 2006b).

your experience is one thing, what you *make* of such information another. Futhermore, what remains unnoticed in experience can nevertheless contribute to the phenomenology of experience in an important way. The point can be made more vivid with the help of an example from Barry Dainton (2000). Dainton imagines what the phenomenology of experience would be like if visual experiences were indeed exhausted by what a subject actually notices:

> You are sitting in an armchair, you have stopped daydreaming and have become engrossed in your book, which has taken an interesting turn, when suddenly the *entire* phenomenal background disappears, not just peripheral sound and vision, but mood and bodily experience too. The effect would be dramatic: it would seem as though the surrounding world had vanished, and your body with it. You would not feel the surrounding and supporting armchair; and since the surrounding room would no longer be present in your experience — save for the page of the book you were reading — you would be both surrounded and filled by void, physically and emotionally. [. . .]
>
> Since the phenomenal background is not usually the object of our attention, we are rarely attentively aware of it. But it would be odd to say we have no awareness of it whatsoever, of any kind; it is, after all, a constant presence in our experience. (Dainton, 2000, p. 32)

Clearly, our visual experiences aren't like the one described in Dainton's thought-experiment. Phenomenologically, visual experiences seem to have a background: they represent more than just what is attended or noticed.[11] So information about some of the objects and properties in the background of visual experience makes a proper part of the content of such experiences.

To recapitulate: considerations in favour of (IRE) are based on the phenomenology of experience. Thus, if Conceptualists wish to resist (IRE), they must show either (i) that (IRE) mis-characterizes the phenomenology of experience, or (ii) that phenomenology is a poor guide to the nature of the representational content of experience.[12] But Conceptualists like McDowell and Brewer do not deny that perceptual

---

[11] The notion of 'background' at play in this context is contrastive: what is not attended figures in the background. In this respect, the background of experience need not coincide with the periphery of the subject's visual field: see Pashler (1998, p. 38), and Findlay and Gilchrist (2003) for a detailed and critical discussion of this distinction. Thus, items located at the periphery of the subject's visual field might nevertheless attract the perceiver's attention. For instance, while your gaze is directed at the car in front of you, your attention may be attracted by the flashing light — in the corner of your eye, as it were — of the police car about to overtake.

[12] For instance, Conceptualists could resort to a so-called 'Dual-Component' theory of perception, according to which the phenomenology of experience is independent from its representational content (for a critical discussion see Smith, 2002, ch. 3). Note that both

experiences can be very rich in information. For instance, remarking on the 'characteristic richness of experience', McDowell writes that experience is just 'a rich supply of already conceptualised content' (1994, p. 49, n.6; compare Brewer, 1999, pp. 240–1).

This means that the success of (AIRE) depends principally on the Bridging Thesis in premise (2). The disagreement has to do with the consequences allegedly following from the fact that perceptual experiences are rich in information. In the remainder of this article, I consider various attempts to motivate this second premise.

3. How to Exploit (IRE) against Conceptualism?

The crucial question about (AIRE) now is: what motivates premise (2)?

The Bridging Thesis:
if S's visual experience e simultaneously represents many objects $o_1 \ldots o_n$, properties $P_1 \ldots P_n$ and relations $R_1 \ldots R_n$, it is possible that S does *not* deploy a concept for at least one of the many objects $o_1 \ldots o_n$, properties $P_1 \ldots P_n$ and relations $R_1 \ldots R_n$, represented in e.

In this section I review three possible strategies to support such a claim. The first (Section 3.1) relies on a comparison between perception and belief. The second explores the possibility that premise (2) is grounded in some kind of general limitation(s) about concepts (Section 3.2). The third strategy focuses on a much narrower constraint upon the exercise of concepts in experience (Section 3.3). None of these strategies is of any help, I argue. The main point, here, is to illustrate how difficult it is to properly defend premise (2). In the final section (Section 3.4), I sketch a more promising — *albeit weaker* — approach.

3.1. Analog and digital representations

Consider the contrast between visual experiences and beliefs: think of the experience of the red ball described at the beginning, and compare it with your belief that, say, there is a red ball on the table. The information making up the content of your belief might be limited to the proposition that there is a red ball on some table. Your experience, in contrast, contains much more information about the red ball, the table and the surrounding environment. Hence, whereas your experience presents a *particular* visual scene, your belief is compatible with a whole range of such distinct scenes (Crane, 2001, p. 151). Thus,

Comparison between Experiences and Beliefs (CEB)
the content of experiences is richer in information than the content of beliefs and judgments.

McDowell and Brewer seem to deny such independence (Brewer, 1999, p. 156; McDowell, 1998, p. 441).

It often seems as though such a contrast is the driving intuition behind
(AIRE). Assuming that beliefs and judgments have conceptual content,
the suggestion is that there must be some correlation between the fact
that judgments and beliefs have such content and the (comparatively)
limited amount of information these states usually convey. One might
then hope to make use of this correlation to warrant the Bridging
Thesis.

Indeed, this seems to be what Fred Dretske (1981) had in mind
when he first drew attention to the fact that perceptual experiences are
very rich in information.[13] Dretske begins by distinguishing two ways
of encoding information:

> Suppose a cup has coffee in it, and we want to communicate this piece of
> information. If I simply *tell* you, 'The cup has coffee in it', this (acous-
> tic) signal carries the information that the cup has coffee in it in digital
> form. No more specific information is supplied about the cup (or the
> coffee) than that there is some coffee in the cup. You are not told *how*
> *much* coffee there is in the cup, how large the cup is, *how dark* the coffee
> is, what the shape and orientation of the cup are, and so on. If, on the
> other hand, I photograph the scene and show you the picture, the infor-
> mation that the cup has coffee in it is conveyed in analog form. The pic-
> ture tells you that there is some coffee in the cup by telling you, roughly,
> how much coffee is in the cup, the shape, size, and color of the cup, and
> so on. (Dretske, 1981, pp. 147–8)

With such a distinction in hand, he argues:

> The contrast between an analog and a digital encoding of information
> (as just defined) is useful for distinguishing between sensory and cogni-
> tive processes. Perception is a process by means of which information is
> delivered within a richer matrix of information (hence in *analog* form)
> *to* the cognitive centres for their selective use. Seeing, hearing, and
> smelling are different ways we have of getting information about *s* to a
> digital-conversion unit whose function it is to extract pertinent informa-
> tion from the sensory representation for purposes of modifying output.
> [. . .] The traditional idea that knowledge, belief, and thought involve
> *concepts* while sensation (or sensory experience) does not is reflected
> in this coding difference. (Dretske, 1981, p. 151)

The central point in this passage speaks directly to (CEB), the comparative claim about the information conveyed in perception and
judgment. According to Dretske, *only some* information carried by
perceptual states in analog form is *selected* — or 'extracted' — to

---

[13] To be fair, Dretske's primary target was not Conceptualism *per se*, but the view that sensory and cognitive phenomena are indistinguishable stages in our cognitive architecture.
Nevertheless, some of his remarks can be used against Conceptualism and have often been
interpreted in such a way.

be encoded *digitally* by thought-processes. In other words, *a loss of information* characterizes the transition from perception to belief (or judgment). Such a loss is explained by the fact that information conveyed in experiences and thoughts is encoded in different formats.

But how does this relate to the Bridging Thesis exactly? Perhaps the connection can be spelt out as follows:

i)   *first step*: the loss of information characteristic of the transition from experience to judgment suggests that judgments and experiences have different kinds of content: while the content of experiences — being informationally rich — is analog, the content of judgments — poorer in information — is digital.

ii)   *second step:* the content of beliefs and judgments is conceptual, and since conceptual content is a kind of digital content, the fact that beliefs and judgments have such content can explain why their content is poorer in information: digital contents carry less information.

iii)   *third step:* if so, the connection between conceptual content and digital content offers support for the idea that analog content, being richer in information, is not conceptual.

This would then explain why the Bridging Thesis is true and why normal subjects can fail to conceptualize everything they perceive.

Unfortunately, this attempt to motivate premise (2) leads nowhere. The main problem resides in the transition from step 2 to step 3. Suppose that the first step successfully establishes that the contents of experiences and judgments encode information differently; and suppose, more controversially, that this supports the claim that experiences and judgments have different *kinds* of contents.[14] The second step fails to show that such a *difference in kind* pertains to the allegedly *conceptual* (or non-conceptual) nature of the contents of experiences and judgments. Granting that the digital content of judgments and thoughts is conceptual, it doesn't follow that the analog content of experience isn't conceptual.

---

[14] Dretske (1981) distinguishes between analog and digital representations in terms of co-variance: analog representations co-vary in a continuous manner with what they represent, whilst digital representations are discrete and do not co-vary in the same way. So there are two differences between these kinds of representations: (i) the way in which they co-vary with what they represent (continuously or discretely), (ii) the fact that analog representations carry relatively more information than digital ones. The difficulty is that neither condition suffices to draw a clear contrast between the content of experience and that of judgements and beliefs. First, as Dretske himself points out that 'a signal carrying information in analog form will always carry some information in digital form' (1981, p. 147). Further, Dretske seems aware that it is possible to construct complex linguistic descriptions (made up, perhaps, of very long conjunctions of simpler sentences), which capture in exact detail the information contained in corresponding analog representations (p. 148).

Here is why. The argument exploits three distinctions: namely, between (i) *analog* and *digital* ways of encoding information, between (ii) content that is *informationally rich* and content that is less so; and finally, between (iii) *non-conceptual* and *conceptual* content. The argument would prove problematic for Conceptualists if it established that, whereas *conceptual* content is necessarily *digital* and *poorer in information*, analog and informationally rich content is *non-conceptual*. But nothing in the argument supports the assumption that these three distinctions actually map onto one another in such a way.[15]

In this respect, Conceptualists need not think of conceptual content as an entirely homogeneous kind. They could grant that, while perceptual experiences are analog and rich in information, judgments and beliefs are digital and poorer in information. But, they will insist, such differences capture a contrast between two different *types* of *conceptual* content, or between different *vehicles* of such content — not between conceptual and non-conceptual types of content. In which case we still have no reason to accept the Bridging Thesis: even if thoughts based on experience convey less information, it doesn't follow that the information carried in experience isn't conceptualized.

3.2. Limited concept deployment

Perhaps a more promising approach might exploit the existence of general limitations on our conceptual capacities — and limitations on our ability to *exercise* (or deploy) such capacities. If it could be shown that normal subjects are generally incapable of *simultaneously* exercising conceptual capacities for the many objects, properties, relations, etc., represented in a single visual experience, then we might have a reason to accept the Bridging Thesis. Perhaps, then, we can appeal to something like the following:

(L)   normal subjects can only *deploy* a certain number n of concepts in *any* psychological state ϕ at *any* given time.

Thus, if n were to fall well short of the amount of information contained in a single visual experience, it would follow that perceivers are incapable of exercising enough conceptual capacities at a given time to capture the information in their experience.[16] The main questions

---

[15] For instance, it could be that some conceptual thoughts are analog — mental images and perceptual beliefs, for instance.

[16] (L) presupposes a correlation between the amount of information conveyed in a given mental state and n, the number of concepts (or conceptual capacities associated with such

about (L), of course, are: (i) what n amounts to, (ii) whether (L) is true, and (iii) how we can find out.

It is hard to imagine what considerations could serve to answer questions (i) and (ii). For instance, it seems as though no phenomenological consideration — based, presumably, upon our familiarity with the way we *normally* deploy concepts in thought — will do. Insofar as it embodies a general limitation upon our ability to exercise concepts, (L) must entail that it is *not possible* to deploy so many concepts at the same time; and grounding this modal claim upon descriptions of the way thoughts, beliefs and other mental states *actually* engage our conceptual capacities, seems inappropriate. For the same reason, no empirical consideration seems apposite either. It may be that normal subjects never exercise their conceptual capacities to their limit. In which case an empirical investigation of the way we *usually* exercise such capacities may not reveal anything like (L). Finally, there is the difficulty that neither phenomenological, nor empirical, considerations can rest too heavily upon the way we exercise concepts in *beliefs* and other thoughts — on pain of raising the worry that such considerations are irrelevant to the way we exercise conceptual capacities *in experience*.

Similar difficulties plague one central empirical consideration proponents of (AIRE) have been keen to exploit (see Dretske, 1981; and Tye, 2006). In order to show that normal perceivers are unable to 'conceptualize' everything they see, Dretske (1981) resorts to Sperling's (1960) famous work on iconic memory:

> Subjects [in Sperling's experiment] are exposed to an array of nine or more letters for a brief period (50 milliseconds). It is found that after removal of the stimulus there is a persistence of the 'visual image'. Subjects report that the letters appear to be visually present and legible at the time of a tone occurring 150 milliseconds *after* removal of the stimulus. Neisser has dubbed this iconic memory — [. . .] it turns out that although subjects can identify only three or four under brief exposure, *which* letters they succeed in identifying depends on the nature of a later stimulus, a stimulus that appears only 150 milliseconds after removal of the original array of letters. [. . .]
>
> What [Sperling's] experiments show is that although there is a limit to the rate at which subjects can *cognitively* process information (*identify* or *recognize* letters in the stimulus array), the same limitation does

---

concepts) a subject can deploy in such a state. Thus, compare the content expressed by 'there is a red ball, a bat and a cap on the middle of the table in the living room' with that expressed by 'there is a red ball'. The former is both (a) richer in information and (b) seems to require the deployment of more concepts if one is to entertain that content. In this respect, it seems, the more information the content of a judgment conveys, the more conceptual capacities it mobilizes.

not seem to apply to sensory processes by means of which this information is made available to the cognitive centres. Although the subjects could identify only three or four letters, information about *all* the letters (or at least *more* of the letters) was embodied in the persisting 'icon'. (Dretske, 1981, p. 159)

The natural assumption, I take it, is that what subjects 'identify' and 'recognize' in experience strictly coincides with what they conceptualize. The thought, then, is that Sperling's research establishes that (1) normal perceivers are unable to report — and thus conceptually identify — more than four or five items in a display at the time, although (2) they can perceive more items, since they can retrieve information about the overall display on the basis of their iconic memory.

Note that different experiments support claims (1) and (2). The first set of experiments is supposed to establish that, in a variety of situations, subjects can typically report no more than four or five items, irrespective of the numbers of items in the display and the time during which the display is presented — claim (1). Sperling's proposed explanation for this fact is that short-term memory (STM) can only store information about four or five items, and that such stored information is lost rather slowly (see Pashler, 1998, p. 103).

Another set of experiments — where a probe cues the subject's attention towards a part of the display very shortly after the display's offset — suggests that (a) subjects are able to retrieve information about more items of the display when so cued, though (b) they are able to do so only for a very short amount of time. Sperling's explanation is that, since short-term memory can only store information about four or five items, there must be another kind of memory at play (dubbed 'iconic memory'), which (i) holds more information about the display and (ii) is subject to rapid decay (Pashler, 1998, pp. 103–4, 321). This is claim (2).

But how does this relate to the Bridging Thesis? While the first point (1) seems to support the existence of some limitation like (L) on the deployment of concepts, the second point (2) is meant to provide support for a version of (CEB), according to which experiences contain more information than a subject is able to conceptually identify. Put together, (1) and (2) suggest that subjects usually fail to conceptualize all the information conveyed in their experience: information which figures in their iconic memory but not in their short-term memory (STM), and which represents more than the four or five items subjects usually identify. (Note that this motivation for (L) even offers a precise number for *n*!)

There is one problem, though. The results of Sterling's first set of experiments show that normal perceivers can report only four or five items in a display of nine letters. The problem is that it is unclear whether such limitations indicate (i) a failure to *conceptually identify* all the letters in the display, rather than (ii) a mere failure to *report* what the subject has conceptually identified. The argument assumes that what is conceptually identified exactly corresponds with what is stored in short-term memory, and then reported by the subject. But why assume that? After all, the items that are reported could have been conceptually identified prior to being stored in the subjects' short-term memory. This means that more items might have been conceptualized, but weren't stored in STM.[17] Without a better understanding of how short-term memory relates to conceptual identification, Sperling's experiment fails to show that any limitation like (L) constrains our conceptual capacities. The Bridging Thesis is still ungrounded.

3.3. Noticing and conceptualizing

The previous approach failed to reveal any limitation on the deployment of concepts in experience. At this point, one might try to exploit a constraint *Conceptualists themselves* impose on conceptual capacities exercised in experience. But what might such a constraint be?

For Conceptualists, perceptual experience is essentially a *cognitive* state. What a perceptual experience represents is intrinsically connected, on their view, with what the perceiver *cognitively accesses* in experience — that is, with what the perceiver thinks and *would* form beliefs about, absent considerations that the world is not really as it seems to her. Hence, the Conceptualists' insistence on the role of concepts in experience. Besides conceptualization, it is natural to think that what perceivers *cognitively access* in experience — and what is represented in their experience — is constrained by what they *notice*.[18] In general, if a perceiver fails to notice some object x, it is likely her experience will not give rise to a belief about x (unless, of course, it concerns the absence of x).

---

[17] Indeed, Sperling's results are consistent with the possibility that information stored in iconic memory does involve information/categorization about the items (which letters they are): for a survey, see Pashler (1998), pp. 55, 132.

[18] Martin (1992a, p. 758) emphasizes this conceptualist commitment. Admittedly, it is difficult to specify exactly what *noticing* amounts to. According to Alan White (1964, pp. 22–31), noticing x requires at least (i) a focus of perceptual attention on x, (ii) where x is discriminated against a background, and (iii) the subject 'realizes' the presence of x; it is also (iv) involuntary and (v) effortless.

But if the content of experience is constrained by what the perceiver notices, and if such content is conceptual as Conceptualists claim, it seems to follow that, typically, a perceiver will exercise conceptual capacities only for what she notices in her experience. Hence, the deployment of concepts in experience is, too, constrained by what a subject notices:

> **The Noticing Constraint on Conceptual Deployment in Experience**
> a subject S deploys a concept for an object o (or property f) in an experience e *only if* S *notices* o (or f) in having e.

Call this (N). Now that we have (N), the strategy consists in finding cases where a subject's experience seems to represent more than she actually notices. Given (N), such an example might provide a reason to accept the Bridging Thesis.

Fred Dretske (1993) and M.G.F. Martin (1992a) have argued that a perceiver might remember an object she had previously experienced, even if she didn't notice that object at the time. This suggests that what she remembers was, although unnoticed at the time, nevertheless represented in her experience. Here is an example:

> THE GENERAL'S MOUSTACHE. You spent the evening talking to the General at the Regiment's party. You failed to notice the General's thin moustache, despite the fact that you were facing him for most of the evening. Perhaps, you were simply too absorbed in the General's conversation to notice his moustache.
>
> Later, you come to realise that he had a moustache, by recalling the way his face *looked like*. That is, you retrieve such information after having had the experience, on the basis of your *perceptual* memory. But if you can remember such information, this must mean that you *did* experience the General's moustache in the first place.

One natural assumption here is that perceptual memory is representational: the subject remembers the way something (e.g. the General's moustache) perceptually appeared to her. If the memory in question is faithful, it must contain information about the way the General's moustache *actually* appeared to her in her experience of the General (see Martin, 1992a, pp. 750–2).

This example suggests that there may be information in the representational content of experience which goes unnoticed. In other words, what is cognitively access*ible* is not necessarily access*ed* at the time of experience, although it might be accessed later. In turn, such a possibility, together with (N), shows that a subject might fail to conceptualize some of the things represented in her experience, provided she fails to notice them. This is all we need to motivate the

Bridging Thesis: the possibility that the subject does not deploy concepts for everything represented in her experience.

Unfortunately, Conceptualists could reject the example just described. They might insist that the example simply begs the question against their claim that only what the perceiver notices is represented in experience. Conceptualists will probably question the assumption that you could fail to notice the General's moustache — 'fail to notice' in what sense, they might ask? Perhaps, while listening carefully to what the General was saying, you did not consciously think about his moustache, Conceptualists will admit. But this doesn't show that you failed to *perceptually* notice it at the time.[19] After all, how could you fail to notice the General's moustache? Wasn't it right in front of you? If so, the example is inconclusive. Hence, the Bridging Thesis remains unmotivated.

3.4. An explanatory challenge

All three attempts to defend the Bridging Thesis considered so far have been unsuccessful. One key problem owes to a reliance on constraints about the deployment of concepts, which Conceptualists need not accept. First, there is no reason to think that how normal subjects exercise conceptual capacities in judgments and beliefs is entirely relevant for the way they deploy concepts in experience. Second, there doesn't seem to be any reason to think that our capacity for deploying concepts in general is limited. Finally, putative examples of unnoticed objects that are nevertheless represented in experience are just *that*: putative examples.[20] Thus, we have found no conclusive support for The Bridging Thesis. Without it, it's hard to see how one could derive a counterexample against the conceptualist supervenience thesis (C) based on the fact that experiences are informationally replete (IRE).

---

[19] At first sight, such a response seems less readily available with Martin's (1992a, p. 750) scenario, where a subject is looking for cufflinks in her cupboard, fails to find them, but later remembers that she had seen them in one of the drawers she searched. Here, had the subject noticed the cufflinks the first time around, she would presumably have found them. However, Conceptualists can reject the intuition that the subject could later remember having seen the cufflinks. Alternatively, they might argue that she might have noticed them in some way or other, without *realising* that they were the cufflinks she was looking for.

[20] Admittedly, many of the above arguments fail, partly because Conceptualists are elusive about the details of their own view. It is difficult to find any explicit constraint Conceptualists impose on the exercise of conceptual capacities in experience. Without such a constraint, one cannot even start to construct counter-examples which might cause trouble for Conceptualism. In this respect, Hume's dictum seems fitting: ' 'Tis impossible to refute a system, which has never yet been explain'd. In such a manner of fighting in the dark, a man loses his blows in the air, and often places them where the enemy is not present' (Hume, 1978, p. 464).

Does this mean that (IRE) is completely unproblematic for proponents of Conceptualism? Perhaps not. For it seems to raise an explanatory challenge for advocates of Conceptualism.[21] In particular, it is unclear at best how Conceptualists can plausibly and coherently accommodate in their account of the representational content of experience cases of visual experiences with an informationally rich content.

Consider for instance the spatial structure of a visual scene containing a variety of objects (a busy street scene, say), and the very rich spatial information conveyed in an experience of such a scene. Not only does your experience represent the shape of most — though perhaps not all — objects, their location and various spatial relations between such objects, as well as the spatial layout of the background, but it also represents the colour of some of these objects, their texture, differences in illumination, etc. If some of these objects happen to be moving (cars, pedestrians), your experience might represent the change in their location as well as the different spatial relations that get instantiated over time between the different objects as some of them move through your visual field. Admittedly, it's unclear exactly how much of such a scene gets to be represented in a single experience of the scene. But, as we have seen, there are good reasons to think that a fair amount of information can be represented.

So is it really plausible to suggest that, at the time of such an experience, you deploy enough distinct spatial concepts in a way that captures such information in its entirety? For one thing, it's unclear how the concepts you deploy for such spatial relations could match exactly the complex way in which these various relations make up the spatial structure of your visual field. For another, is it really the case that, for any difference in the content of your experience (such as a change in the location or orientation of a car to your left), you deploy different corresponding concepts? Here, it seems, there is some pressure on Conceptualists to ensure that their view can be developed in a way that escapes the appearance of implausibility generated by these sorts of examples.

The problem for Conceptualists is not just that, if Conceptualism is true, you should be exercising conceptual capacities associated with different concepts for every bit of information conveyed in your experience. The problem is that, according to thesis (C), your experience represents the objects in such a scene and their various properties and relations *in virtue of the fact* that you apply concepts to such

---

[21] Thanks here to Kim Sterelny.

objects, properties and relations. This also requires that any representational difference in your experience owes to the fact that you are deploying distinct concepts for the things thus represented.

Here, in particular, Conceptualists owe us some positive account of the exercise of conceptual capacities in experience since, according to thesis (C), experiences represent what they do in virtue of such deployment. The difficulty is to develop such an account in a way that it can plausibly make sense of the rich information conveyed in the content of many visual experiences.

4. Conclusion

The aim of this article was to assess what sort of argument could be constructed on the basis of the informational richness of experience (IRE), and how such an argument might fare against Conceptualism. Conceptualists, we have seen, appear to grant that the representational content of experiences can indeed be quite rich in information. On the other hand, the fact that experiences instantiate (IRE) does not seem to offer a conclusive argument against Conceptualism.

Nevertheless, we just saw how (IRE) might present an important challenge to the way Conceptualists develop their account of experience. It is difficult to imagine how perceivers might plausibly deploy concepts for everything they see at any one time, given the rich information carried in experience. So discussion of (IRE) ought to play a major part in the case against Conceptualism, at least insofar as it forces Conceptualists to substantiate their account of the representational content of experience.

Acknowledgments

A first shot at this material was presented at the ANU Philosophy Society in Canberra in September 2002 — thanks in particular to Laura Schroeter and Kim Sterelny for their questions. For helpful comments on various ancestors to this paper, many thanks to Alex Byrne, David Chalmers, Nic Damnjanovic, Martin Davies, Janice Dowell, Daniel Friedrich, Frank Jackson, John O'Dea, Sally Parker-Ryan, Adina Roskies, Daniel Stoljar and Susanna Siegel. Thanks also to the editor, Rocco Gennaro, and to an anonymous referee, for their suggestions to improve this version of the paper.

References

Brewer, Bill (1999), *Perception and Reason* (Oxford: Oxford University Press).

Byrne, Alex (2005). 'Perception and conceptual content', in *Contemporary Debates in Epistemology*, ed. M. Steup and E. Sosa (Oxford: Blackwell).

Chuard, Philippe (2006a), *Appearances without Concepts: A Critical Evaluation of Conceptualism* (PhD Dissertation, Australian National University).

Chuard, Philippe (2006b), 'Demonstrative concepts without re-identification', *Philosophical Studies*, **130**, pp. 153–201.

Cohen, Jonathan (2002), 'The Grand Illusion Illusion', in *Journal of Consciousness Studies: Is the Visual World a Grand Illusion (Special Issue)*, **9** (5/6), ed. Alva Noë.

Crane, Tim (2001), *The Elements of Mind* (Oxford: Oxford University Press).

Dainton, Barry (2000), *The Stream of Consciousness: Unity and Continuity in Conscious Experience* (London: Routledge).

Dretske, Fred (1981), 'Sensation and perception', in *Perceptual Knowledge*, ed. J. Dancy, 1988 (Oxford: Oxford University Press).

Dretske, Fred (1993), 'Conscious experience', *Mind*, **102**, pp. 263–83.

Findlay, John M. and Gilchrist, Iain D. (2003), *Active Vision: The Psychology of Looking and Seeing* (Oxford: Oxford University Press).

Heck, Richard (2000), 'Non-conceptual content and the "space of reasons" ', *The Philosophical Review*, **109** (4), pp. 483–523.

Hume, David (1978), *A Treatise of Human Nature*, ed. L.A. Selby-Bigge and P. Nidditch, 2nd edn. (Oxford: Oxford University Press).

McDowell, John (1994), *Mind and World* (Cambridge, MA: Harvard University Press).

McDowell, John (1998), 'Having the world in view: Sellars, Kant, and intentionality (The Woolbridge Lectures 1997)', *Journal of Philosophy*, **95** (9), pp. 431–91.

Mack, Arien and Rock, Irvin (1998), *Inattentional Blindness* (Cambridge, MA: MIT Press).

Martin, M.G.F. (1992a), 'Perception, concepts and memory', *Philosophical Review*, **101**, pp. 745–63.

Martin, M.G.F. (1992b), 'Sight and touch', in *The Contents of Experience*, ed. Tim Crane (Cambridge: Cambridge University Press).

Moore, Cathleen M. (2001), 'Inattentional blindness: perception or memory and what does it matter?', *Psyche*, **7** (2).
(http://psyche.cs.monash.edu.au/v7/psyche-7-02-moore.html)

Noë, Alva (2002), 'Is the visual world a grand illusion?', in *Journal of Consciousness Studies: Is the Visual World a Grand Illusion (Special Issue)*, **9** (5/6), ed. Alva Noë.

Pashler, Harold (1998), *The Psychology of Attention* (Cambridge, MA: MIT Press).

Peacocke, Christopher (1989), 'Perceptual content', in *Themes from Kaplan*, ed. J. Almog, J. Perry and H. Wettstein (Oxford: Oxford University Press).

Simons, Daniel J. (2000), 'Current approaches to change blindness', *Visual Cognition*, **7** (1/2/3), pp. 1–15.

Smith, A.D. (2002), The Problem of Perception (Cambridge, MA: Harvard University Press).

Sperling, G. (1960), 'The information available in brief visual presentations', *Psychological Monographs*, **74**, pp. 129.

Stalnaker, Robert (1998), 'What might non-conceptual content be?', in *Philosophical Issues: Concepts*, **9**, ed. E. Villanueva.

Strawson, P.F. (1992), *Analysis and Metaphysics* (Oxford: Oxford University Press).

Tye, Michael (2006), 'Nonconceptual content, richness, and fineness of grain', in *Perceptual Experience*, ed. Tamar Gendler and John Hawthorne (Oxford: Oxford University Press).

White, Alan R. (1964), *Attention* (Oxford: Blackwell).

José Luis Bermúdez

The Object Properties Model of Object Perception

Between the Binding Model and the Theoretical Model[1]

Abstract: *This article proposes an object properties approach to object perception. By thinking about objects as clusters of co-instantiated features that possess certain canonical higher-order object properties we can steer a middle way between two extreme views that are dominant in different areas of empirical research into object perception and the development of the object concept. Object perception should be understood in terms of perceptual sensitivity to those object properties, where that perceptual sensitivity can be explained in a manner consistent with the graded representation approach adopted by some connectionist modellers. The object properties approach does justice to the differences between a perceptual system solving the binding problem, on the one hand, and genuinely perceiving objects, on the other, without running into the theoretical problems associated with treating young infants as 'little scientists'.*

What are objects, and what is it to perceive them? These deceptively simple questions raise fundamental theoretical issues framing research into visual perception and the development of the object concept. This article discusses some of the implicit philosophical background that drives current research into object perception. In it I stake out a middle

---

[1] I am grateful to Rocco Gennaro and two referees for the *Journal of Consciousness Studies* for their comments on an earlier draft

ground between two extreme positions, each of which can fairly be described as the orthodox view in *one* aspect of research into object perception.

Researchers motivated by the *binding problem* tackle the problem of explaining how the various different features of an object, many of them processed separately in different areas of the brain, come to be bound to each other so that they are experienced as co-instantiated in a particular place. The default assumption behind much of this research is that objects are bundles or clusters of features and hence that perceiving an object is essentially a matter of perceiving a bundle of features co-instantiated in a particular place. I suggest that this *binding model* is not the best way to understand objects and what it is to perceive them. Perceiving a bundle of co-instantiated features is necessary but not sufficient for perceiving objects. I sketch out and defend an alternative account (the *object properties model*) of the metaphysics of object perception on which objects are bundles of features that obey certain high-level physical principles. On this account, perceiving objects is a much richer and more complex achievement than solving the binding problem.

Researchers into the development of the object concept in infancy, in contrast, are generally motivated by a model of what objects are and what it is to perceive them much richer than the binding model. It is standard among developmental psychologists to think of prelinguistic infants as possessing a highly developed theoretical understanding of what objects are and how they behave — an implicit naïve physics, an organized body of knowledge that defines a primitive object concept. This theoretical understanding is thought to explain the expectations manifested in the *dishabituation paradigm*. The object properties model is an alternative to this *theoretical model* of infant object perception. It understands object perception in terms of perceptual sensitivity to certain canonical high-level physical principles that define what it is for a bundle of features to count as an object. Recent work on modelling object permanence in connectionist networks shows how we might give a substantive explanation of infants' perceptual sensitivity to higher-order principles (such as the principle of object permanence) without assuming that they are exploiting theoretical principles.

Perceiving Objects vs Solving the Binding Problem

Let me begin with the first conception of what objects are and what it is to perceive them. This is the *binding model*. We can approach it through

Anne Treisman's experiments on illusory conjunctions (Treisman, 1988; Treisman and Schmidt, 1982). In certain experimental situations subjects can be induced to make errors in conjoining different features in a presented array. That is, when presented with an array of figures each of which has a distinctive colour and shape, subjects make mistakes putting colours and shapes together. In one experiment (Treisman and Schmidt, 1982) subjects were briefly presented with an array of coloured letters bounded on each side by a digit and told in advance that the task would be to identify the flanking digits. The array was displayed for 300ms — just long enough for the subjects to attend to the digits and succeed in identifying them. When the subjects were asked to report on the letters between the flanking digits it turns out that they regularly mixed up shapes and colours, so that the letters were correctly identified but with the wrong colours. The subjects correctly pick out all the relevant features in the perceptual array — the full range of shapes and visually presented colours. But they put them together (*bind* them) in the wrong way.

The binding problem, as generally understood, is the problem of explaining why our perceptual systems do not normally generate illusory conjunctions of this type. Our representations of objects tend to bind together different features in a way that more or less reflects the way in which those properties are bound together in the distal environment. How does this come about? What mechanisms are responsible?

Of course, there is no dispute about whether solving the binding problem is a *necessary* step in giving an adequate account of object perception. The real question is whether solving the binding problem as we find it characterized by Treisman and others is all that a theory of object perception has to do in order to explain what it is to perceive an object as an object — that is, whether solving the binding problem is not just necessary but also *sufficient*. Let me call the claim that it is both necessary and sufficient the *binding model* of object perception.[2]

---

[2] This is somewhat simplified. For one thing, Treisman herself thinks that we need to distinguish the property binding problem (which is the problem that we have just been discussing) from the location binding problem (Treisman, 1996). This problem, which arises on various versions of the two visual systems hypothesis (Goodale and Milner, 1996), is the problem of binding together separately processed 'what' and 'where' information. Moreover, Treisman's model of the relation between feature-coding, spatial attention and binding (as depicted in Figure 2 below) suggests that she may not subscribe to the binding model. Even if we take objection perception to be the process that yields what Treisman labels temporary object representations in her model, representations of objects that can serve as inputs to the recognition system, the fact remains that Figure 2 contains arrows in both directions between the temporary object representation and the recognition network. Nonetheless, the binding model is implicit in many psychological discussions of object

However, it seems to me that there are good reasons for thinking that the binding model cannot be right. The problem is that the model obscures a very important distinction between two different levels at which the world can be experienced — between two different ways of apprehending the world (Bermúdez, 1995a; 2003; Strawson, 1959). The key distinction here is between the recognition of bodies and the recognition of recurrent circumstances. It is possible for a perceiver to recognize certain, previously encountered features (such as food or water or danger or shelter) without experiencing the environment as containing objects. It might encounter a tree and perceive it as affording shelter without perceiving it as a tree. To perceive a tree as affording shelter one need only recognize its similarity to other things that have afforded shelter and to act accordingly. In contrast, to perceive a tree as a tree is to perceive it as an individual thing, as something that persists over time and can be encountered at different times and in different sensory modalities. It is to be able to reidentify the tree; to be able to pose the question, for example, whether the tree in front of one is the same tree one perceived earlier; or to be able to select one tree out from a group of perceptually similar trees; or to be able to count the number of trees in one's immediate vicinity.

We can follow Strawson in terming this the distinction between the feature-placing level of experience and the particular-involving level of experience (Strawson, 1959). At the feature-placing level of experience there is no continuity between one instantiation of treeness and another — much as we, at our vastly more sophisticated level of thought, find no continuity between two episodes of warmth. A creature at this level inhabits a world composed of different kinds of stuff. These different kinds of stuff can be encountered at different places, at different times and in different combinations. Some of these encounters and combinations are predictable, and the creature best able to make these predictions will flourish. But the regularities on which these predictions are based are simply conjunctions of features — associations of food with a particular perceptual *Gestalt* associated with a certain combination of leaves and branches, for example.

The fact that a creature's perceptual systems have solved the binding problem is perfectly compatible with its operating at the feature-placing level of experience. We can suppose that a creature is

---

perception. To take an example chosen more or less at random, Scholl *et al.* (2001) define an object as an 'independently attendable feature cluster' (p. 160). One might expect the binding model to be adopted by any account that identifies object perception with the results of what is often called mid-level vision and that holds, unlike Treisman, that mid-level vision is insulated from the high-level vision and object recognition systems.

perceptually sensitive to a range of different properties and that its perceptual system binds the representations of these properties in a way that more or less matches the way that those properties are co-instantiated in the world. Such a creature will experience the world as composed of bounded segments whose boundaries map onto the boundaries of the objects in the perceived environment. But that, I claim, is not enough for it to be perceiving objects.

Clearly, it is necessary for perceiving the world as divided up into objects that a perceiver be capable of recognizing that features are juxtaposed in a single place — that the perceiver be capable of responding to the presence of combinations of features as well as to individual features. To perceive a body is to perceive a compact clustering of visually detectable features and to recognize that that cluster is associated with further features detectable in different sensory modalities. But perceiving objects is not just a matter of how one parses the perceptual array. It is also a matter of the expectations one has about how those compact clusters of visually detectable features will behave, both when one is perceiving them and when one is not perceiving them.

Genuine objects obey certain principles and behave in certain regular ways. A world articulated in terms of genuine objects is a world that obeys certain basic physical regularities. Consequently, any creature that perceives such a world must be sensitive to these physical regularities that circumscribe what it is for something to count as a particular or a body at all. Bodies have certain higher-order physical properties in common. They tend, for example, to have sharply defined edges relative to their environment. They usually do not vary enormously in size and shape over short periods of time and consequently maintain certain forms of perceptual constancy relative to the perceiver when the perceiver moves or when they move themselves. Their properties can be detected in different perceptual modalities. They do not pop in and out of existence, but move through space-time on a single connected path. They are resistant to pressure and have a certain mass that governs their interactions with other individuals. No more than one individual can be in a place at a time. They are susceptible to gravity and interact with each other through transmitting energy. And so forth. These are higher-order similarities that are not immediately perceptually salient but to which a creature must be sensitive if it is properly to be described as perceiving and acting within a suitably objective and structured world.[3]

---

[3] The emphasis on acting is important here. It may well be that an agent's perceptual sensitivity to these basic physical regularities is inextricably linked to their abilities to act in

Suppose we have a creature perceiving a world of bounded segments with boundaries that map onto the boundaries of the objects in the perceived environment, and suppose moreover that it clusters perceptible properties in more or less the right way. That is to say, to put it in Triesman's terms, the representation of redness gets bound to the representations of size and shape in a way that matches the distribution of the relevant features in the environment. This does not imply any perceptual sensitivity to the higher-order physical regularities that govern the behaviour of objects. The binding can take place without there being any such sensitivity.

Here is a simple illustration. One of the characteristic regularities governing the behaviour of objects is that they tend to maintain their shape and size over relatively short periods of time. The perceptual systems of normal perceivers automatically compensate for variations in the size and shape of the image on the retina produced by a particular distal object. After a very early age normal humans, for example, do not see a person diminishing in size as it moves away from them — what they see is a person who retains a constant size relative to them moving into the distance. Similarly we are all capable of extracting a single perceptual form as an object's shape despite variations in its orientation. But it does not seem to be part of solving the binding problem that the perceptual system should be sensitive to this type of shape constancy and size constancy. We can appreciate this by thinking about how we would expect a perceptual system that is *not* sensitive to shape constancy and size constancy to operate. We would not expect such a system to produce the totally chaotic representations that would result if it had completely failed to solve the binding problem. Nor would we expect it to come up with the sort of illusory conjunctions that we considered earlier — illusory conjunctions in which, say, colour features and size features are mismatched. All that we would expect is that the system would not make the sort of compensations that we make. An organism with such a perceptual system would not see a retreating object as retaining its size — nor would it perceive a rotating object as retaining its shape. Nonetheless, it would still see a persisting cluster of co-instantiated features.

---

virtue of those physical regularities. The approach I am proposing is consistent with some aspects of the theory of sensorimotor contingencies proposed by O'Regan and Noë (2001) and, more broadly, with the stress on the 'active observer' to be found within the Piagetian and Gibsonian approaches to vision (although for Gibson the emphasis is often more on perceivers' movements through the environment than on their actions). We will return to this in the final section of the paper.

An example will help make the point. There is strong experimental evidence that size constancy is an acquired feature of infant perceptual systems. The experimental paradigm was originally developed by Thomas Bower, although it turned out that it proved impossible to replicate his early findings of size constancy as early as eight weeks of age (Bower, 1966). The paradigm involved operant conditioning (see Fig. 1). Infants were conditioned to respond to visually presented cubes of a particular size. The reinforced behaviour was head movement and the reinforcing was the appearance of the infant's mother. The infants were conditioned to respond when a cube of 30cm in diameter was presented one metre in front of them. The question that the experimenters posed was how this response would be generalized — on the standard assumption that a generalized response reflects a perceived similarity. Would the response generalize across similarities in retinal image size? Or would it generalize across similarities in real size, thus showing that the infants were compensating for differences in size of the retinal image and deploying a form of size constancy? It turns out (McKenzie *et al.*, 1980) that size constancy is present at six months although not much before.

Let us consider what happens in experiments that *fail* to detect size constancy in young infants (McKenzie and Day, 1972). Using an experimental set-up similar to Bower's, but using the dishabituation paradigm rather than operant conditioning, McKenzie and Day habituated infants between six and twenty weeks to one object at a set distance. They found that the infants' looking times increased when an object was presented at a different distance, irrespective of whether that object was the same size or projected the same retinal image. Infants seem to respond to actual distance, rather than constancy in either actual size or retinal size.

The point to extract from this is that the original processes of conditioning (Bower) and habituation (McKenzie and Day) would only work if the infant perceptual system had solved the binding problem — that is to say, if the features of the cube were all represented in a suitably integrated cluster. The very possibility of showing that infants fail to detect shape constancy requires assuming that the infant perceptual systems have solved the binding problem. Yet, since perceptual sensitivity to shape constancy seems to be integral to the perception of an object it seems clear that solving the binding problem does not guarantee object perception. Further operations are required.

There is an important distinction, therefore, between perceiving objects and solving the binding problem. The purely perceptual processing involved in solving the binding problem is not enough to

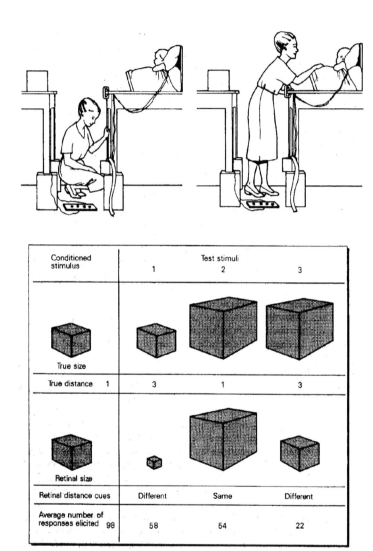

Figure 1

(a) Apparatus used by Bower (1966) to test for depth perception and size constancy.
(b) Test stimuli showing true sizes, distances and corresponding retinal image size. *Reproduced with permission from Bremner (1988), p. 78.*

give us perception of objects. It is possible for there to be perceptual sensitivity to the sort of compact clusters of features yielded by the binding mechanisms without this generating object perception. This has implications for theories of object perception. In particular, it suggests that there is something missing from many influential accounts of object perception which go directly from perceptual processing to object identification. Consider Anne Treisman's feature integration theory, for example (Treisman, 1988; Treisman and Gelade, 1980). The essence of the theory, as portrayed in Figure 2, is that the binding problem is solved by attending to the location of the object.

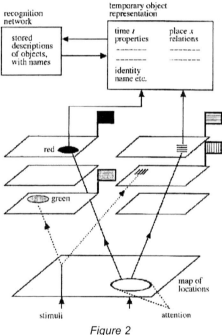

Figure 2

Treisman's model of the relation between feature coding, spatial attention, and binding in object perception.

Attention to location generates a temporary object representation that then feeds into the object recognition system where it is matched against various stored representations. What is missing here is any reference to the processing associated with sensitivity to the higher-order physical principles that define the nature of objects. The tacit assumption, I take it, is that this sort of processing takes place at a much higher level, after the processes of object-recognition have done their work. It seems to me that this tacit assumption is mistaken. Physical objects are not simply perceived as agglomerations of directly perceptible properties such as shape, size, texture and so forth, and there is more to perceiving objects than solving the binding problem for these perceptible properties. The processing that secures size constancy, for example, is reflected in the content of perception. That this is so is shown, I think, by the example we have considered. We can develop the idea further, and explore some of its implications, by thinking more about two important contemporary debates in developmental psychology. That is the topic of the next section.

Infant Naïve Physics: Against the Theoretical Model

As is well known, it has emerged from research on infant perception using the so-called *dishabituation paradigm* by Elizabeth Spelke, Rene Baillargeon and others that even very young infants inhabit a highly structured and orderly perceptual universe, composed of bounded individuals that they expect to obey certain very general physical principles (Baillargeon, 1987; Spelke, 1988).[4] That much at least is more or less beyond dispute. The disputes arise when we ask two further questions. First, how does infant perception relate to adult perception? Second, how should we understand the 'implicit knowledge' that infants seem to display about their physical environment? Or, to put it another way: how should we understand the infant's 'naïve physics'?

With regard to the first of these questions one influential answer has been given by Elizabeth Spelke, who suggests that infants possess a rudimentary form of the adult object concept from a very early age. She writes:

> The earliest developing conceptions of physical objects are the most central conceptions guiding mature object perception and physical reasoning. For adults, such conceptions are overlaid by a wealth of knowledge about the appearances and behaviour of particular kinds of objects. Even this more specific and limited knowledge, however, reflects the core knowledge from which it grew. (Spelke, 1993, p. 157)

---

[4] The basic principle behind the dishabituation paradigm is that suitably habituated infants look longer at surprising than at familiar stimuli (Bornstein, 1985), and hence that, by measuring looking time it is possible to work backwards to what infants find novel and what they find familiar — and hence to their perceptual expectations about the distal environment. See Cohen and Cashon (2003) for an overview of research into infant perception and cognition.

This passage from Spelke presents the strongest form of what I am calling the theoretical model of object perception. On the theoretical model, young infants' perceptual discriminations reflect their abilities to make inferences about the likely behaviour of physical objects; inferences that in turn are grounded in a stored and quasi-theoretical body of knowledge about the physical world. The theoretical model often goes hand in hand with a general form of *modularism* about the human mind (Carruthers *et al.*, 2005).[5] On Spelke's version of the conceptual model, the infant's naïve physics is essentially continuous with the body of knowledge that structures adult object perception. A weaker version of the conceptual model denies that the infant's naïve physics is simply an impoverished version of our own. This is proposed in recent work by Alison Gopnik and Andrew Meltzoff on the development of physical knowledge during infancy and early childhood (Gopnik and Meltzoff, 1997). Gopnik and Meltzoff identify a crucial difference between the criteria that young infants (before the age of about nine months) and adults deploy to determine object continuity. For infants movement information dominates information about features and properties, so that their principal criterion for whether or not something is the same object is simply that it should maintain a single observable trajectory, irrespective of any alterations that there might be in its general appearance. As a consequence infants will not show surprise when one object disappears behind a screen and a completely different object emerges on the other side. For adults, on the other hand, as Gopnik and Meltzoff elegantly point out, featural constancy frequently trumps continuity of trajectory in determining whether or not two perceptions are taken to be perceptions of a single object:

> As adults we individuate and reidentify objects by using both place and trajectory information and static-property information. We also use property information to predict and explain appearances and disappearances. If the same large, distinctive white rabbit appears in the box and later in the hat, I assume it's the same rabbit, even if I don't immediately see a path of movement for it. In fact, I infer an often quite complex invisible path for the object. If I see the green scarf turn into a bunch of flowers as it passes through the conjuror's hand while maintaining its trajectory, I assume it is a different object. On the other hand, if an object changes its trajectory, even in a very complex way, while maintaining its properties, I will assume it is still the same object. (Gopnik and Meltzoff, 1997, p. 86)

---

[5] For more on modularism see Bermúdez (2005) and the readings in section 3(c) of Bermúdez (2006).

If this is right then the process of moving from an infant 'naïve physics' to an adult naïve physics is not simply a matter of gradually becoming more and more sensitive to an increasing range of higher-order physical principles governing the behaviour and interaction of physical objects. The development will involve a certain amount of 'unlearning'.

This brings us neatly to the second question. What are we talking about when we talk about the infant's naïve physics? How should we understand the various transitions that occur from the initial naïve physics that emerges in early infancy to the naïve physics that we find in older children and adults. Do infant expectations about how bodies will behave reflect some sort of knowledge of objects? If so, what type of knowledge is this?

Both Gopnik and Meltzoff on the one hand, and Spelke on the other, answer this question in similar ways — reflecting their commitment to the theoretical model. According to Gopnik and Meltzoff, young infants do in fact possess a theory about the physical world, and they develop the suggestive proposal that even the youngest children are little scientists. Spelke herself shares this view, as we see in the following passage;

> I suggest that the infant's mechanism for apprehending objects is a mechanism of thought: an initial *theory* of the physical world whose four principles jointly define an initial *object concept*. (Spelke, 1988, p. 181)

There is a certain amount of haziness about what a theory actually is, but Gopnik and Meltzoff offer the following as characteristic features of theories, whether espoused by laboratory scientists or by 'little scientists':

- They postulate the existence of abstract entities.
- Those abstract entities are coherently organized with causal relations between them.
- Their causal generalizations support counterfactuals.
- Their generalizations support prediction and explanation.
- They change in response to counter-evidence in distinctive ways.

The theoretical model of object perception faces familiar problems. The most significant of these problems is that we have no clear account of what it is to have 'implicit' or 'tacit' knowledge of a naïve physics that (1) gives clear criteria for when to attribute such implicit knowledge and (2) is sufficiently independent of the explanandum to provide genuine explanatory leverage. The two desiderata pull in different directions. The closer our characterization of what is tacitly known stands to the phenomena it is trying to explain, the less it looks as if we have genuine explanation. But the more distance there is between explanans and explanandum the harder it is to give clear conditions on how and when such knowledge is to be attributed. Theorists have made some progress on resolving this tension in the relatively circumscribed sphere of tacit knowledge of semantics and grammar (Evans, 1981; Peacocke, 1989), but there has been no serious work on how such accounts might be carried over to tacitly known naïve physics.

The potential problems for developing the theoretical model are sufficiently serious for it to be worth considering an alternative way of conceptualizing the infant's understanding of certain basic physical principles — one that does justice to the same phenomena as the theoretical conception, but that inverts the standard order of explanation. Instead of understanding object perception in terms of tacit mastery of a theory of physical objects, we can understand tacit mastery of a theory of physical objects in terms of perceptual sensitivity to certain higher-order physical regularities.

The basic idea here, as I have discussed in more detail elsewhere (Bermúdez, 1998; 2003) is to start with the properties constitutive of something qualifying as an object (properties corresponding to the higher-order physical principles and regularities discussed in the previous section). I term these *canonical object-properties*. Examples include:

- the property of following a single continuous trajectory through space-time;
- the property of continuing to exist when unperceived;
- the property of being homogenous and internally unified;
- the property of only being able to undergo a fixed set of changes;
- the property of being impenetrable;
- the property of being subject to gravity;
- the property of being internally causally connected;
- the property of having a certain mass;
- the property of posing resistance to the touch;
- the property of having its state of motion or rest explicable in terms of mechanical forces acting upon it;
- the property of causally influencing other objects.

This is not a fixed and rigid list. Some objects lack one or more object properties, and certain object-properties may be reducible to others (as the property of presenting resistance to the touch might be reducible to the property of impenetrability). Objects that are lighter than air, for example, will not be subject to gravity in any interesting sense. Even more borderline are those objects like birds that are capable of overcoming the effects of gravity. Yet part of what it is to be perceptually sensitive to an object property is to be perceptually sensitive to the exceptional cases in which certain object properties cease to hold.

How might perceptual sensitivity to object properties be manifested? Some will be directly manifested in the manner revealed by the dishabituation experiments. So, for example, perceptual sensitivity to the object-property of gravity might be manifested in surprise if an object resting on a supporting surface stays where it is when the supporting surface is removed. Sensitivity to other object properties will be manifested indirectly. Consider the object-property of having a determinate shape. One would not expect infants sensitive to this object-property to be surprised by a thing that lacks it. After all, they might regularly be expected to encounter smoke rings, shadows, clouds of smoke and the like. But they might manifest their sensitivity to the object-property by showing surprise when an object that lacks it nonetheless appears to obey other object-properties, such as for example the object-property of impenetrability.

My proposal, therefore, is that human infant's perceptual development should be understood in terms of perceptual sensitivity to an increasing range of object properties. That sensitivity to certain object properties emerges at more or less constant stages in human ontogeny seems indubitable. It would appear, for example, that sensitivity to the object-property of causally influencing other bodies emerges in some form at around the age of seven months (Leslie, 1984). However, this account cannot be a complete account, even in the case of infants. Not all the 'properties' to which infants are perceptually sensitive are canonical object properties, as we have just seen in Gopnik and Meltzoff's account of the development of physical knowledge during infancy and early childhood. Young infants do not track the object-property of following a single, continuous trajectory through space-time. Rather, they track a *deviant object-property* of spatio-temporal continuity that can be best identified through its associated higher-order physical principle, namely, that everything that follows a single trajectory through space-time is a continuously existing body. This is in contrast to the higher-order physical principle associated with the canonical object-property of spatio-temporal continuity, which is that all continuously existing bodies follow a single trajectory through space-time.

There is a close connection between the two parts of this article. In the first part I argued that object perception requires more than simply solving the binding problem in a way that will give a suitably unified cluster of features. It requires perceptual sensitivity to the higher-level physical principles that govern the behaviour of objects. In the second part I suggested that we view what is sometimes called naïve physics or intuitive physics in terms of perceptual sensitivity to object properties and the higher-level physical principles associated with them. These are really two different sides of a single basic idea. This basic idea is that we cannot divorce our theories of objects and object perception, whether philosophical theories or psychological theories, from our implicit understanding of the higher-order physical principles to which they are subject. This implicit understanding of higher-order physical principles is part of the content of perception. Part of what we perceive when we perceive an object is that we are in front of something that is internally causally connected, that follows a single continuous path through space-time, that is impenetrable, that interacts causally with other objects and so forth. These object-properties are not directly perceptible. That is, one cannot just *see* the internal causal connectedness of an object in the way that one can just see its colour or its shape. But nor, on the other hand, are they inferred from what we do see directly. It is not the case that we see that something is an object and then infer on that basis that it must have the relevant object-properties. We couldn't see that something is an object unless we could also see that it has those properties.

A natural question at this point is how exactly this implicit understanding of higher-order principles is to be understood. After all, one of the principal motivations for the theoretical model is precisely to *explain* how infants can be perceptually sensitive to higher-order properties that are not directly perceptible. It is, so proponents of the theoretical model argue, because infants have a theoretical understanding (albeit a primitive one) of, say, the principle of object permanence that they can be perceptually sensitive to the higher-order object property of continuing to exist when unperceived. If we abandon the theoretical model, then what account can we give of perceptual sensitivity to properties that are not directly perceptible? This concern is a very real one, given my proposal to invert the standard order of explanation. If proponents of the theoretical model are correct to argue (in effect) that the infant's perceptual sensitivity to higher-order physical principles is only explicable as a theoretical achievement, then we plainly cannot take this type of perceptual sensitivity to be primary in the order of explanation.

What we need is an illustration of how organisms can be perceptually sensitive to the relevant object properties without having the sort of theoretical understanding required by the theoretical model. There are, I think, two complementary ways of proceeding. The first is to stress the relation between perceptual sensitivity to object properties and the perceiver's ability to act upon the world. Perceptual sensitivity to object properties is at the very least manifest in, and required by, the agent's capacity to interact with and manipulate objects. Some theorists have suggested that the motor dimension is constitutive of visual perception. This, if I understand them correctly, is the position proposed by O'Regan and Noe (2001). Weaker versions of this view were proposed by Piaget and Gibson and still have contemporary advocates (see Russell, 1996, for example). It might be argued that what it is to be perceptually sensitive to object properties is to act in ways that exploit the relevant physical properties.

Many theorists are likely to think, however, that the direction of explanation goes the other way. It is because agents are perceptually sensitive to object properties that they are capable of exploiting higher-order physical regularities. If this is right then even those sympathetic to active observer and sensorimotor contingency theories are still going to have to say something about the mechanisms underlying perceptual sensitivity to object properties.

This brings us to the second possible strategy, which is to appeal to recent work in the modelling of infant development (Mareschal and Johnson, 2002; Munakata and McClelland, 2003; Munakata *et al.*, 1997) to show how organisms can be perceptually sensitive to the relevant object properties without having the sort of theoretical understanding required by the theoretical model. These models are particularly relevant here, since they are explicitly proposed as alternatives to the theoretical model of infant perception. To see how they can help solve our problem we can look at the general approach to object permanence developed by Munakata *et al.* (since what developmental psychologists term object permanence is essentially the object-property of continuing to exist when unperceived). Connectionist models are, of course, only models. But the existence of models consistent with the known facts and lacking the types of stored knowledge required by the theoretical model shows at the very least that the object properties model is a genuine alternative to the theoretical model.[6]

---

[6] I am taking these connectionist models primarily as illustrations of the mechanisms that might underlie object perception, rather than as models of how the abilities associated with object perception might emerge in the course of development. The theoretical model is often developed in a nativist manner, but for present purposes my target is the thesis that perceptual sensitivity to object properties requires propositionally encoded theoretical knowledge. I am assuming that if a cognitive ability can be accurately modelled by a

Here is how Munakata *et al.* describe how their approach differs from the theoretical model.

> Because infants seem to behave in accordance with principles at times, there might be some use to describing their behavior in these terms. The danger, we believe, comes in the tendency to accept these descriptions of behavior as mental entities that are explicitly accessed and used in the production of behavior. That is, one could say that infants' behavior in a looking-time task accords with a principle of object permanence, in the same way one could say that the motions of the planets accord with Kepler's laws. However, it is a further — and we argue unfounded — step to then conclude that infants actually access and reason with an explicit representation of the principle itself. We present an alternative approach that focuses on the adaptive mechanisms that may give rise to behavior and on the processes that may underlie change in these mechanisms. We show that one might characterize these mechanisms as behaving in accordance with particular principles (under certain conditions); however, such characterizations would serve more as a shorthand description of the mechanism's behavior, not as a claim that the mechanisms explicitly consult and reason with these principles. (Munakata *et al.*, 1997, p. 687)

What they propose, in effect, is that the 'knowledge' reflected in an infant's successful performance on object permanence tasks (tasks that, when performed successfully, reveal the infant's understanding that objects continue to exist when unperceived) is not explicitly stored in the form of theoretical principles, but rather is implicitly stored in graded patterns of neural connections that evolve as a function of experience. Infants' understanding of object permanence is essentially practical. It is exhausted in the expectations that they have about how objects will behave. These expectations themselves reflect the persistence of patterns of neural activation — patterns that vary in strength as a function of the number of neurons firing, the strength and number of the connections between them, and the relations between their individual firing rates. The mechanisms that explain the type of perceptual sensitivity manifested in dishabituation paradigms are essentially associative mechanisms of pattern recognition of precisely the type well modelled by connectionist networks. As infants observe the 'reappearance' of occluded objects the connections between relevant neurons are strengthened. As a result, the representations of perceived objects (i.e. the patterns of neural activation that accompany

---

connectionist network then its exercise does not *require* propositionally encoded theoretical knowledge. In taking this approach I am following the spirit but not the terminology of Paul Churchland's deployment of connectionist models in, for example, Churchland (1989) (since Churchland thinks that there can be theoretical knowledge that is not propositional in form).

the visual perception of an object) persist longer when the object is
occluded.

So, according to Munakata *et al.* the infant's 'knowledge' of object
permanence should be understood in terms of the persistence of object
representations. This 'implicit' understanding of object permanence is
the foundation for the theoretical understanding that emerges at a
much later stage in development. One advantage of their approach is
the explanation it gives of well-documented behavioural dissociations
in infant development (Munakata, 2001). There is good evidence that
infants' abilities to act on occluded objects lags a long way behind
their perceptual sensitivity to object permanence, as measured in
preferential looking tasks. Although perceptual sensitivity to object
permanence emerges at around three and a half months (Baillargeon,
1987), infants succeed in searching for hidden objects only at around
eight months — and even then they make mistakes in Piaget's A not-B
task (Piaget, 1954) by searching in the original location even when
they see the object moved to a new location. Munakata *et al.* argue
(and their simulations illustrate) that it is possible for a visual object
representation to be sufficiently strong to generate expectations about
the reappearance of an occluded object, while still being too weak to
drive reaching behaviour.

One of the networks studied by Munakata *et al.* is designed to simu-
late a simple object permanence task involving a barrier moving in
front of a ball and occluding the ball for a number of time steps. Figure 3 shows the inputs to the network as the barrier moves in front of
the ball and then back to its original location.

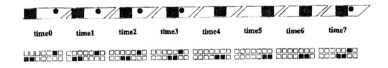

Figure 3

A series of inputs to the network as a barrier moves in front of a ball and
then back to its original location. The top row shows a schematic drawing of
an event in the network's visual field; the bottom row indicates the corresponding pattern of activation presented to the network's input units, with
each square representing one unit. Learning in the network is driven by
discrepancies between the predictions that the network makes at each time
step and the input it receives at the next time step. The correct prediction at
one time step corresponds to the input that arrives at the next time step.
Reproduced with permission from Munakata et al. (1997).

The network is a recurrent network, with a feedback loop that effectively serves as a memory of the hidden layer at the previous time step and makes it possible for the network to make predictions about the next state of the input.

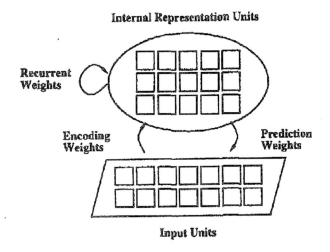

Figure 4

Recurrent network for learning to anticipate the future position of objects. The pattern of activation on the internal representation units is determined by the current input and by the previous state of the representation units by means of the encoding weights and the recurrent weights respectively. The network sends a prediction back to the input units to predict the next state of the input. The stimulus input determines the pattern of activation on the input units, but the difference between the pattern predicted and the stimulus input is the signal that drives learning. *Reproduced with permission from Munkata et al. (1997).*

The network's 'understanding' of object permanence is a function of its sensitivity to the ball's reappearance from behind the occluder. This sensitivity can in turn be measured in terms of the accuracy of the network's 'prediction' when the ball does eventually reappear. As training progresses the network becomes increasingly proficient at predicting the reappearance of occluded objects over longer and longer periods of occlusion.

So much for the fact of object permanence. What is the mechanism underlying it? Here Munakata *et al.* analyse the patterns of hidden unit activation in order to measure how the network represents the occluded ball. Their strategy is to identify which of the fifteen hidden units are sensitive to the ball (by identifying which hidden units showed the greatest difference in activation between stimuli with and without balls) and then to examine the activation of those hidden units during the occlusion period. They found that improved sensitivity to object permanence was directly correlated with the hidden units representing the ball showing similar patterns of activation when the ball is visible and when it is occluded. In effect, they claim, the network is learning to maintain a representation of an occluded object. The network's 'understanding' of object permanence is to be analysed in terms of its ability to maintain such representations; and this comes in degrees. As further simulations reported in the same paper show, a network can maintain representations sufficiently strong to drive perceptual 'expectations' but too weak to drive motor behaviour. Sensitivity to object permanence is, they suggest, a graded phenomenon — a function of strengthened connections allowing maintained activation patterns — rather than a theoretical achievement.

Of course, there is much more work to be done in this area. Quite apart from worries about particular connectionist models of infant development (see the commentaries in *Developmental Science* on Mareschal and Johnson, 2002, for example), and general concerns about the neural applicability of the connectionist approach, we know relatively little about how something like the mechanism that Munakata *et al.* propose might be neurally implemented.[7] Moreover, it remains to be seen whether this type of model can be extended to other types of object property. Questions also remain about how precisely such networks represent the world. In particular, what is the relation between the ability to represent object permanence and mastery of the concept of an object?[8] Nonetheless, the models and simulations that have been developed in this area do at least point towards how we might develop a substantive account of object perception that is both explanatory and a genuine alternative to the theoretical model.

Conclusion

The object properties approach has a number of implications for empirical study. In the first place, it predicts that the phenomenon identified in the earlier discussion of size constancy will be found more generally. That is, that young infants will be capable of solving

---

[7]   For discussion of the relation between computational models and neural mechanisms see O'Reilly and Munakata (2000).

[8]   Some of the theoretical issues here are discussed in Bermúdez (1995b and 1999).

the binding problem in a way that allows them to perceive bounded segments that map more or less onto the boundaries of physical objects without being perceptually sensitive to object properties. Second, it suggests a view of infant development on which infant development is at least in part a matter of their becoming perceptually sensitive to novel object properties (and losing sensitivity to deviant object properties). We would expect perceptual sensitivity to particular object properties to come onstream at different ages. Correlations between the child's sensitivity to particular object properties and their motor skills can profitably be studied. Third, the approach provides a framework for studying the similarities and dissimilarities between the 'perceptual universes' of different species in terms of the different sets of object properties to which members of those species are perceptually sensitive.

The principal challenge confronting the object properties approach is explaining the key notion of perceptual sensitivity. I have suggested that we can understand perceptual sensitivity partly in terms of motor behaviour and partly in terms of the type of processing that supports it. Neural network models of the type discussed in the final section go some way towards explaining what it is for an organism to be perceptually sensitive to the object property of object permanence, but it is still an open question whether these models can be extended to other object properties that are not directly perceptible — and we certainly need more information about the neural plausibility of these neural networks.

Nonetheless, the object properties approach has significant potential theoretical rewards. By thinking about objects as clusters of co-instantiated features that possess certain canonical higher-order object properties we can steer a middle way between two extreme views that are dominant in different areas of empirical research into object perception and the development of the object concept. In particular, we can do justice to the differences between a perceptual system solving the binding problem on the one hand, and genuinely perceiving objects on the other, without running into the theoretical problems associated with treating young infants as 'little scientists'. The prospect of these potential rewards should motivate further study.

References

Baillargeon, R. (1987), 'Object permanence in 3.5 and 4.5 month old infants', *Developmental Psychology*, **23**, pp. 655–64.

Bermúdez, J.L. (1995a), 'Ecological perception and the notion of a nonconceptual point of view', in *The Body and the Self*, ed. J.L. Bermúdez, A.J. Marcel and N. Eilan (Cambridge MA: MIT Press).

Bermúdez, J.L. (1995b), 'Non-conceptual content: From perceptual experience to sub-personal computational states', *Mind & Language*, **10** (4), pp. 333–69.

Bermúdez, J.L. (1998), *The Paradox of Self-Consciousness* (Cambridge MA: MIT Press).

Bermúdez, J.L. (1999), 'Cognitive impenetrability, phenomenology, and non-conceptual content', *Behavioral and Brain Sciences*, **22** (3), pp. 367–.

Bermúdez, J.L. (2003), *Thinking Without Words* (New York: Oxford University Press).

Bermúdez, J.L. (2005), *Philosophy of Psychology: A Contemporary Introduction* (London: Routledge).

Bermúdez, J.L. (2006), *Philosophy of Psychology: Contemporary Readings* (London: Routledge).

Bornstein, M.H. (1985), 'Habituation of attention as a measure of visual information processing in human infants: Summary, systematization, and synthesis', in *Measurement of Audition and Vision in the First Year of Postnatal Life*, ed. G. Gottleib and N.A. Krasnegor (Norwood, NJ: Ablex), pp. 253–300.

Bower, T.G.R. (1966), 'The visual world of infants', *Scientific American*, **215**, pp. 80–92.

Carruthers, P., Laurence, S. and Stich, S. (ed. 2005), *The Innate Mind: Structure and Content* (Oxford: Oxford University Press).

Cohen, L.B. and Cashon, C.H. (2003), 'Infant perception and cognition', in *Comprehensive Handbook of Psychology. Volume 6, Developmental Psychology*, ed. R. Lerner, A. Easterbooks and J. Mistry (New York: Wiley and Sons), pp. 65–89.

Evans, G. (1981), 'Semantic theory and tacit knowledge', in *Wittgenstein: To Follow a Rule*, ed. S.H. Holzman and C.M. Leich (London: Routledge and Kegan Paul).

Goodale, A.D. and Milner, M.A. (1996), *The Visual Brain in Action* (Oxford: Oxford University Press).

Gopnik, A. and Meltzoff, A. (1997), *Words, Thoughts, and Theories* (Cambridge, MA: MIT Press).

Leslie, A.M. (1984), 'Infant perception of a manual pick-up event', *British Journal of Developmental Psychology*, **2**, pp. 19–32.

Mareschal, D. and Johnson, S.P. (2002), 'Learning to perceive object unity: A connectionist account', *Developmental Science*, **5** (2), pp. 151–85.

McKenzie, B.E. and Day, R.H. (1972), 'Object distance as a determinant of visual fixation in early infancy', *Science*, **178**, pp. 1108–10.

McKenzie, B.E., Tootell, H.E. and Day, R.H. (1980), 'Development of visual size constancy during the first year of human infancy', *Developmental Psychology*, **16**, pp. 163–74.

Munakata, Y. (2001), 'Graded representations in behavioral dissociations', *Trends in Cognitive Science*, **5** (7), pp. 309–15.

Munakata, Y. and McClelland, J.L. (2003), 'Connectionist models of development', *Developmental Science*, **6** (4), pp. 413–29.

Munakata, Y., McClelland, J.L., Johnson, M.H. and Siegler, R.S. (1997), 'Rethinking infant knowledge: Toward an adaptive process account of successes and failures in object permanence tasks', *Psychological Review*, **104** (4), pp. 686–713.

O'Regan, K. and Noë, A. (2001), 'A sensorimotor account of vision and visual consciousness', *Behavioral and Brain Sciences*, **24**, pp. 883–917.

O'Reilly, R.C. and Munakata, Y. (2000), *Computational Explorations in Cognitive Neuroscience* (Cambridge MA: MIT Press).

Peacocke, C. (1989), 'When is a grammar psychologically real?', in *Reflections on Chomsky*, ed. A. George (Oxford: Basil Blackwell).

Piaget, J. (1954), *The Construction of Reality in the Child* (New York: Basic Books).

Russell, J. (1996), *Agency* (Brighton: Lawrence Erlbaum).

Spelke, E.S. (1988), 'The origins of physical knowledge', in *Thought without Language*, ed. L. Weiskrantz (Oxford: Oxford University Press).

Strawson, P.F. (1959), *Individuals: An Essay in Descriptive Metaphysics* (London: Methuen).

Treisman, A. (1988), 'Features and objects: The fourteenth Bartlett memorial lecture', *Quarterly Journal of Experimental Psychology*, **40A**, pp. 201–37.

Treisman, A. (1996), 'The binding problem', *Current Opinion in Neurobiology*, **6**, pp. 171–8.

Treisman, A. and Gelade, G. (1980), 'A feature integration theory of attention', *Cognitive Psychology*, **12**, pp. 97–136.

Treisman, A. and Schmidt, H. (1982), 'Illusory conjunctions in the perception of objects', *Cognitive Psychology*, **14**, pp. 107–41.

David H. Rakison

Is Consciousness in its Infancy in Infancy?

Abstract: *In this article, I examine the literature from three domains of cognitive development in the first years of life — mathematics, categorization and induction — to determine whether infants possess concepts that allow them explicitly to reason and make inferences about the objects and events in the world. To achieve this aim, I use the distinction between procedural and declarative knowledge as a marker for the presence of access consciousness. According to J.M. Mandler, infants' early concepts are represented as accessible declarative knowledge. However, the evidence discussed in this article indicates that infants' early concepts are best depicted as procedural, perceptually-based knowledge that are inaccessible to consciousness. I conclude by speculating about the role of language development on the emergence of consciousness towards the end of the second year of life.*

An underlying assumption in developmental science is that the foundations for consciousness are laid in the first years of life. Nonetheless, a scan of the subject indexes of five infancy textbooks and five developmental textbooks on my shelf, as well as Dennett's (1991) excellent book *Consciousness Explained*, revealed that not one included any mention of consciousness in the first two years of life. Similarly, a more detailed keyword search on PsychINFO — one of the most extensive databases available to psychologists — generated only a handful of articles that directly examined consciousness in infants. This scarcity of research on infant consciousness is somewhat at odds with a recent trend in developmental science whereby researchers have attempted to push back ever farther the onset of various conceptual abilities. It has been argued, for example, that infants within the first year of life are sensitive to the laws of physics such as solidity and gravity (Baillargeon, 1998; Baillargeon *et al.*, 1992; Spelke *et al.*, 1992), can perform simple addition and subtraction (Wynn, 1992) and understand that animals and vehicles engage in different action (e.g. animals drink and cars start with keys) (Mandler & McDonough, 1996, 1998). Surprisingly, however, no researchers have made the same attempts to show that consciousness is present in infants at such an early point in their development.

What is to account for this lack of attention on the part of developmental psychologists in studying consciousness in infants? One reason may be that it is unclear how researchers who believe that there is something of substance to the notion of consciousness in infants might go about studying it. Attempts have been made to examine when infants develop what is labelled *reflective-* or *self-consciousness*, or when they possess a representation of the self. One classic study that attempted to address this issue was the 'mark' or 'rouge' test in which infants around 18 months of age putatively show recognition of the self because they touch a dot of coloured rouge on their forehead rather than an image of themselves in a mirror (Gallup, 1970; Lewis & Brooks-Gunn, 1979). However, recognizing one's reflected image does not necessarily mean that one is self aware; that is, self-perception should be distinguished from self-conception. To succeed in the 'mark' test, infants must match their concept of what they think they look like to the image they observe in the mirror; but they need not possess consciousness, in the form of a cognitive representation of self founded on reflective self-awareness, to do so (Butterworth, 1992).

A second reason for the dearth of empirical evidence on infant consciousness is the longstanding assumption that infants do not possess the requisite representational capacities to be self-aware or to be able to access stored knowledge for cognitive tasks such as reasoning, induction and categorization (e.g. 'These things belong together because they are animals'). In particular, it has been argued that a crucial prerequisite of consciousness is language, and because infants by definition are non-linguistic — the etymology of the term 'infant' comes from the Latin 'unable to speak' — they cannot be conscious (e.g. Edelman & Tononi, 2000; Dennett, 1991; Zelazo, 2004). The crux of this argument is that language is necessary for a more sophisticated self-reflective form of what Block (1995) calls 'access consciousness', which he defines as the ability to use previously stored representations to direct thoughts and actions. (I will use the term 'access consciousness' to designate the more sophisticated notion of 'having conscious access to one's own concepts and thoughts' throughout this paper.)

Implicit in this view is the notion that infants' representations are impoverished versions of those possessed by adults and older children in that they are inaccessible to conscious awareness. As was briefly outlined above, however, research with infants over the past twenty years has putatively revealed surprisingly advanced perceptual and cognitive competencies in the first years of life. If infants' early concepts are relatively sophisticated and can support advanced interpretations of the world around them, one might ask whether these concepts are directly employed during this process. In other words, if infants are capable of induction, categorization, addition and subtraction, and are sensitive to the laws of physics, perhaps they are to perform these advanced cognitive tasks only with conscious application of their existing knowledge.

The aim of this article is to examine these issues. That is, I will address the nature of infants' early concepts of the world, discuss whether infants reveal evidence that they possess concepts that require conscious access to be employed, and speculate on how these concepts may act as the foundation for consciousness in later life. In so doing, I will focus mainly on evidence that speaks to whether access consciousness (in the sense described earlier) can be attributed to infants. I will also not discuss *phenomenal consciousness* (Block, 1995) which is the state of having experience — a pain-state, for example — because it is generally assumed that infants from birth (if not before) can be attributed with this form of consciousness. Thus, if infants' early concepts of the world have any relation to the development of consciousness they will most likely shed light on access consciousness.

Concepts in Infancy

I define a *concept* as a mental representation of the properties and structure among items within groups or *categories* of things in the world (Margolis, 1994; Smith, 1995). A common concept of 'cat' includes information about surface appearance (e.g. cats are fluffy and cat shaped), biological properties (e.g. cats have hearts, brains and cat DNA), motion capabilities (e.g. cats are self-propelled) and psychological states (e.g. cats have goals such as drinking milk and chasing mice). Over the last twenty years, researchers have built a large database on the development of early concepts for a wide range of objects and events in the world, which include, but are not limited to, concepts for objects and entities, physics, mathematics, causality, space and time.

In many of these domains, researchers have found evidence that suggests, at least on the surface, that infants are precocious concept formers. For example, Baillargeon has conducted a number of ingenious experiments to examine young infants' expectations about gravity, or whether an object should fall when it is only partly or not at all supported (Baillargeon, 1998; Baillargeon *et al.*, 1992; Needham & Baillargeon, 1993). In these experiments infants are presented repeatedly with the same events during a training or *habituation* phase, after which they are presented with a number of test events that differ in some way from those observed earlier. In experiments by Baillargeon *et al.* (1992), for instance, infants were habituated with events in which a human hand pushed a box horizontally on top of another box. In the test events, part of the lower box was removed and the hand pushed the upper box until it stopped completely supported by the lower box (possible event) or until only a small part of it or no part of it was supported by the lower box (impossible event). The reasoning behind this design is that if infants expect unsupported objects to fall, they will look longer at the event that violates this expectation — the impossible event in this case — than one that does not. Using this general procedure, Baillargeon and colleagues found that 3-month-olds looked longer at a box that is suspended in midair than one that falls to the ground, but not until three months later do they look longer at a box that is only supported slightly by another box.

The main question of interest here is as follows: Does infants' looking behaviour in this task, and their behaviour in similar experiments, imply that they possess concepts that allow the kind of cognitive reasoning that is accessible to consciousness? In other words, do infants use their representational knowledge of, in this case, support to make a 'decision' during the test trials about whether the box should fall or not? Before this judgment can be made, however, it must be determined whether such findings can be construed to mean that infants have concepts for support at all. Although the results described above seem clear cut, alternative interpretations have been presented by a number of researchers for these and similar results that purport to show conceptually rich representation in young infants (e.g. Bogartz *et al.*, 2000; Cashon & Cohen, 2000; Rakison, 2005). These alternative views suggest that infants come to the laboratory with either no knowledge about the domain under scrutiny or with impoverished and perceptually-bound concepts for them.[1] Thus, in some sense the issue of interest is the content and structure of information about the world that is encapsulated within infants' concepts.

Procedural and declarative knowledge

A potentially fruitful way to approach this issue is to consider whether infants' concepts scaffold behaviour because the information they represent is *procedural* or *declarative* (Mandler, 2004; Schacter, 1987). Representationally speaking, the difference between these two types of knowledge is that the former describes information that is often inaccessible to consciousness whereas the latter is accessible to consciousness. In other words, this distinction 'has to do with fundamentally different kinds of information that are represented in different ways' (Mandler, 2004, p. 53). A fine example of procedural knowledge concerns a myriad of motor behaviours in which we engage: we cannot verbalize how we catch a ball or tie our shoelaces. Such motor actions are fast, unselective, and occur automatically without attention. Declarative knowledge, in contrast, is slow and selective, and requires conscious attention; factual knowledge such as 'women generally have longer hair than men' is declarative in that it is accessible to us as adults.

According to one view, it is not just knowledge of motor actions in infancy that are procedural but also perceptual knowledge (Mandler, 2004). The claim, which is consistent with Piaget's view of the difference between perceptual/motor knowledge and conceptual knowledge, is that perceptual information is stored in procedural form because it is automatically processed without attention. Mandler (2004) cites evidence of face processing to support this view. Infants as young as 6 months of age can categorize male from female faces (Fagan & Singer, 1979), but adults are unable to describe how they

---

[1] These positions are often characterized in the literature as the *associationist* view versus the *theory theory* or *core knowledge* view. The crux of the distinction between them is that according to the first view infants rely on domain-general mechanisms (e.g. associative learning, habituation, condition) to learn about the world, whereas according to the second view infants are born with specialized mechanisms or innate knowledge to accomplish this task. Consequently, the associationist view implies that infants' early representations are grounded in the perceptual characteristics of objects and events, whereas the theory theory and core knowledge view implies that they are richer theory-based concepts that incorporate deeper properties of the input. I choose here not to use these labels in discussing infants' representations because the actual views of the theorists within each camp differ considerably in their approach and because terms such as 'theory-based concepts' are laden with a number of implications that are beyond the scope of this article. Instead I will apply the more general terms perceptually-based representations and conceptually rich representations and variants of these phrases.

accomplish this task. This view, then, suggests that such *perceptual categorization* tasks are performed quickly without conscious attention by the visual input system (Mandler, 2004; Moscovitch *et al.*, 1994). In contrast, *conceptual categorization* is, according to Mandler, a process whereby infants form an idea of the *meaning* of objects as they consciously analyse what they are doing. According to this view 5-month-old infants' behaviour in the support experiments by Baillargeon and colleagues are based on a cognitive interpretation of the events that are observed with reference to declarative, accessible concepts. Indeed, Baillargeon in an interview for *Scientific American Frontiers* described infants' mental behaviour in the support experiments in terms of 'actively thinking about what we show them, and actively searching for and finding explanations for what they see'.

Implicit in this perspective is the idea that conceptual knowledge and consciousness are inseparably intertwined and even that 'consciousness is required for concept formation to happen in the first place' (Mandler, 2004, p. 299). Consistent with this view is recent research on the development of memory in infancy. It has been suggested, for example, that deferred imitation is a measure of nonverbal declarative memory (see e.g. Bauer, 2005; Collie & Hayne, 1999), and that any memory recall implies declarative knowledge.[2] According to this perspective access consciousness is a precursor of concept formation and occurs prior to the onset of language. In other words, infants should be attributed with access consciousness within the first year of life and without such consciousness they would not be able to form concepts at all.

Clearly, the distinction between procedural and declarative knowledge is useful in examining the nature of infants' concepts of the world as they relate to consciousness. If infants' knowledge is purely procedural, as many would argue it is for motor skills and perceptual knowledge, then they cannot be attributed with access consciousness. On the other hand if infants possess conceptual knowledge and apply

---

[2] The veridicality of this claim — that deferred imitation, or memory recall, unavoidably implies consciousness — remains to be seen. For one thing, researchers who study infants' deferred imitation can only infer, not directly test, whether they tap declarative memory. Rovee-Collier (1997), for example, noted that it is not necessarily the case that one task maps onto a specific memory system, and Tulving (1990) suggested that little can be drawn from such studies because conscious recollection and declarative memory are not inevitably related. Researchers who study deferred imitation also cite evidence relating to adults who suffer damage to specific areas of the brain and the resulting effect on memory and consciousness. However, as Rovee-Collier (1997) pointed out, it is unclear whether conclusions can be drawn about the abilities of non-verbal infants from studies with normal or brain-damaged adults.

it in a task then they must, according to this view, have done so via declarative knowledge. There are, however, in my view two main problems with this approach. First, it should not be assumed that knowledge that is initially stored as procedural remains cognitively impenetrable for adults, because although it is in many cases (I am not very good at explaining how I ride a bike), it need not be (I can explain how I solve long-division problems). I agree, then, that some perceptual knowledge is acquired in the way that Mandler describes — automatically and quickly — and remains inaccessible to consciousness (face perception is an excellent example of this, probably because humans have an evolved adaptation for faces). I do take issue with the idea that all such information remains impenetrable to consciousness throughout the lifespan. The claim that I wish to put forward here is that infants' earliest representations are initially stored as clusters of perceptual features and are therefore best described as procedural knowledge. Later, after the onset of language, a number of these concepts become accessible to consciousness because labels are a mechanism by which information initially stored as procedural knowledge becomes stored as declarative knowledge (see also Nelson, 1996).

A second problem that is more within the scope of this article is that one must be careful in assuming that infants' behaviour in a particular task means that they have conceptual knowledge rather than more perceptually-bound concepts. There has been a recent research trend to ascribe infants with rich conceptual knowledge about the meaning of an object or an interpretation of an event that may simply not be warranted; in many cases, a more parsimonious explanation involves infants' responding to the perceptual cues in the events. Before jumping to the conclusion that infants are conscious because they have conceptual knowledge (Mandler, 2004), we must ascertain whether such conceptual knowledge is indeed present. The following section addresses this issue by focusing briefly on research with infants in a number of domains; namely, mathematics, object categorization, and induction of properties for objects.

Mathematical reasoning in infancy

To readers who are unacquainted with the developmental literature, it may seem preposterous to even ask whether young infants understand or are capable of simple mathematics such as addition and subtraction. Since the ground-breaking work of Piaget (1952) on children's inability to conserve solids, liquids, length and number, developmentalists have generally assumed that young infants do not possess the requisite concepts to make such calculations. It may come as something of a surprise, then, that 'more and more it appears that infants are capable of reasoning about the effects of the arithmetic operations of addition and subtraction' (Gelman & Williams, 1998, p. 588).

The conclusion that infants are able to 'reason' in this way is based on the findings of seminal work by Wynn (1992; see also Wynn, 1995). In one experiment, 5-month-olds were habituated to a single toy animal on a stage that was then occluded by a screen. A human hand was then observed putting a second, identical toy behind the screen. In the test phase of the experiment, the occluding screen was removed and infants saw either one or two toys on the stage. The rationale for this design was as follows. If infants represented separately each of the two objects behind the occluder — one object plus one object equals two objects — they would be expected to fixate visually longer at the display that violates this expectation than at the one that does not; that is, the event with one object on the stage. In contrast, if infants did not represent the two objects as separate — only one object at a time is visible during habituation — then they would be expected to look longer at the display that violates this expectation; namely, the test trial with the two toys. In fact, infants' looking behaviour was consistent with the idea that they represented the objects as separate and added them together; they looked longer at the test trial with one object than at the test trial with two objects. In a different experiment with the same basic procedure, Wynn (1992) habituated infants to events in which two objects were shown on the stage and then occluded by a screen, after which one was removed from behind the screen by a human hand. Consistent with the notion that infants can compute the subtraction of two minus one, 5-month-olds in this experiment visually fixated longer at the test event with two toys than the one with one toy.

According to Wynn (1998), these findings suggest that infants 'engage in numerical computation' (p. 296) and possess an evolved and innate system of simple mathematics. Wynn does not claim, to my knowledge, that this computation occurs with conscious awareness or that infants have access to the knowledge that $1+1=2$. Yet by the standards set by Mandler and others (e.g. Mandler, 2004; Baillargeon, 1998; Spelke et $al.$, 1992) this kind of finding is evidence of conceptual declarative knowledge rather than perceptual procedural knowledge. In other words, although Wynn does not argue that addition and subtraction in infants indicates conscious thought, the kinds of reasoning involved in this task and others on physics requires cognitive computation that should be available to consciousness.

The problem with such a conclusion in the domain of mathematics as well as in others, such as physics, is that in many cases there is a simpler perceptual explanation for infants' behaviour that eliminates the need to invoke conceptual knowledge. Cohen and Marks (2002), for example, suggested that infants looked longer at specific test events in the Wynn (1992) procedure not because they were reasoning about addition and subtraction but because of a preference for familiarity in conjunction with a tendency to look longer when more items were presented. To test this idea empirically, Cohen and Marks (2002) replicated the basic findings in the Wynn (1992) experiments. In subsequent experiments, they presented one group of 5-month-olds with the test events in Wynn (1992) without first habituating them to the addition or subtraction habituation events, and another group of 5-month-olds was presented with either one or two items before each test trial, again without showing any addition or subtraction events. Infants' visual fixations in this last experiment supported Cohen and Marks' idea that infants' behaviour in Wynn's studies were not based on numerical competence. Infants looked longer at familiar events — having seen one object prior to the test phase infants preferred to look at one object during the test phase — and they looked longer at more items than fewer items (e.g. two rather than one).

In light of the controversial nature of the notion of numerical competence in infants, Cohen and Marks' experiments have been on the receiving end of criticism from researchers on both sides of the theoretical fence (Mix, 2002; Wynn, 2002). For example, Wynn (2002) argued that Cohen and Marks failed to replicate the particulars of the experimental conditions in her studies and thus that comparisons between infants' behaviour in their and her experiment were not valid. Regardless of concerns over the robustness of Wynn's findings (if the parameters of the experiment change only slightly the effect should hold), more recent work by Clearfield and Westfahl (2006) has confirmed that infants in the original addition and subtraction experiments were responding to perceptual aspects of the display. First, Clearfield and Westfahl replicated Wynn's original experiment with great attention to the details of the procedure. Then, they showed that infants' looking behaviour is governed by what they observe in the familiarization phase of the experiment. That is, 5-month-old infants who were familiarized with eight possible mathematical events looked longer at the correct outcome, but 5-month-olds who were familiarized with eight impossible events showed no preference for either test.

My intention here is not to debunk the findings of Wynn (1992) *per se*. The key issue is whether there is reasonable doubt about whether infants in these kinds of studies are responding on the basis of declarative knowledge — which is assumed to be available for free use in reasoning and for the rational control of action (e.g. Mandler, 2004) — or on the basis of simple perceptual aspects of the display or procedural knowledge. Indeed, similar reinterpretations have been suggested for a number of findings that purport to reveal early conceptual competencies in infants. For example, a number of researchers (Bogartz *et al.*, 2000; Cashon & Cohen, 2000; Rivera *et al.*, 1999) have collected data that suggest that young infants do not have a conceptual understanding of object solidity and object permanence as was suggested in work by Baillargeon and colleagues (Baillargeon, 1987; Baillargeon *et al.*, 1985). The point, then, is that great care must be taken, and parsimony applied, before assuming that infants are consciously 'reasoning', 'computing' or 'thinking' about mathematics, physics or other domains in which conceptually rich and accessible representations are assumed to exist.

Categorization in infancy

Until thirty years ago it was widely believed that infants were unable to form categories of objects and events in the world. However, methodological advances in infant-related testing procedures — including the development of the habitation procedure as well as others outlined here — have allowed researchers to make significant insights into how infants representationally group things in the world. There is little debate that, whether one is discussing faces, animals or vehicles, the earliest categories are formed on the basis of perceptual, surface features (Mandler, 2003; Rakison, 2003). For example, infants within the first months of life are capable of forming categories by extracting correlations among surface features (Younger & Cohen, 1986) and perceptual prototypes for a wide range of stimuli including faces, animals and geometric shapes (Bomba & Siqueland, 1983; Langlois *et al.*, 1987; Quinn *et al.*, 1993). As I discussed earlier, these perceptual categories are assumed by many, if not all, researchers to be inaccessible to conscious awareness because they are procedural.

The ability to form what have been labelled *conceptual* categories is far more contentious however, both in their basis and at what age they are formed. According to Mandler (1992; 2003; 2004; see also Pauen, 2002), infants are able to form such conceptual categories towards the end of the first year of life through an innate, specialized process called *perceptual analysis*. This process, which abstracts what infants see into a more conceptual accessible form, means that infants are able to categorize objects and events on the basis of what things are rather than how they look. That is, Mandler (2003; 2004) argued that young infants initially categorize objects such as animals on the basis of their appearance (e.g. things that are animal shaped), but soon thereafter they categorize them because they understand that they are animals, move in certain ways (e.g. they are self-propelled) and are capable of certain actions (e.g. animals drink). Thus 'through perceptual meaning analysis they consciously analyse what objects are doing. The results of this process — interpretations of the world that suffuse the mind with meaning — are also accessible to consciousness' (Mandler, 2004, p. 292).

In support of this view, Mandler and colleagues have conducted a number of experiments on infant categorization with the *sequential touching* paradigm (Mandler *et al.*, 1991; Mandler & Bauer, 1988). In this task, infants ranging from 14 to 30 months of age are presented with eight toy models drawn from two categories (e.g. four different cars and four different dogs) and the systematicity of successive touches reveals the extent to which they are categorizing. For example, if an infant touches three cars and then three dogs this would indicate that they are treating the members of each category as equivalent in some way. In one study (Mandler & Bauer, 1988) infants at 16 and 20 months of age were successful in forming categories from different superordinate domains — that is, they categorized animals as different from vehicles. In contrast, only the 20-month-olds formed basic level categories within the same superordinate domain — that is, by categorizing dogs as different from horses. Similarly, Mandler *et al.* (1991) found that 18-month-old infants categorized animals as different from vehicles but did not categorize as different basic-level contrasts within these domains when the contrast between the object sets was low or moderate (e.g. dogs vs. horses, dogs vs. rabbits). In related work, Pauen (2002) found that 11-month-olds in an object-examining task responded on the basis of category membership rather than between-category perceptual similarity.

Mandler *et al.* (1991; see also Pauen, 2002) concluded from these results that infants' categorization behaviour was based on conceptual knowledge of the *meaning* of the animals and vehicles (e.g. one group was animals that can start to move on their own), with properties perceptible in the immediate input playing only a subsidiary role. Their reasoning was as follows. The members of the category of animals have different exterior appearances, as do the members of the category of vehicles. If infants can group together objects that look different it must be because they understand that they are alike in some other, less obvious way. Similarly, if infants do not categorize dogs as different from horses — even though dogs look similar to one another and so do horses — it must be that they understand that the members of these categories are alike in some nonobvious way (e.g. dogs and horses are both animals). Recall that in both cases, the claim is that infants use conceptual, declarative knowledge to form these categories and therefore they do so consciously (Mandler, 2004).

There are, however, a number of reasons to cast doubt on a conceptually rich explanation that involves attributing infants with access consciousness. Most notably there is no direct evidence from these data that infants employed conceptual knowledge about the meaning of animals or vehicles to categorize. Mandler and colleagues inferred that infants could not categorize animals and vehicles on the basis of surface appearances and therefore relying on conceptual knowledge was the only alternative explanation. An alternative interpretation of infants' behaviour in the task, however, is that surface perceptual features — which are represented as procedural knowledge — are sufficient to explain categorization. Rakison and Butterworth (1998), for example, argued that superordinate categorization in the experiments by Mandler *et al.* (1991) and Mandler and Bauer (1988) could be explained by infants' attention to one or more object features or parts (e.g. legs, wheels, eyes). Although members of superordinate categories often possess a number of different features they also generally share a few important features, and exemplars of two basic-level categories from within the same superordinate category generally share the same features. In other words, infants may successfully categorize animals as different from vehicles or cars and different from dogs because they attend to specific object features and not because they have knowledge of category relations that exist among animals or among. Similarly, infants' failure to categorize at the basic level may be attributable to the fact that both dogs and horses have many shared features.

To test this question empirically, Rakison and Butterworth (1998; see also Rakison & Cohen, 1999) used the sequential touching technique to present 14-, 18- and 22-month-olds with two kinds of superordinate contrasts. In one kind of contrast, infants were tested with two categories of objects that shared a single large feature; for instance, they were presented with varied animal exemplars and varied furniture exemplars — which all possessed legs. In the other kind of contrast, infants were presented with two categories of objects that were characterized by different parts; for example, they were presented with varied animal exemplars that possessed legs and varied vehicle exemplars that possessed wheels. The results revealed that 14-, 18-, and 22-month-old infants successfully categorized the different-part contrasts, but only at 22 months were infants able to categorize the same-part contrasts.

In a second experiment, the features of objects were manipulated so that they no longer confounded category membership (Rakison & Butterworth, 1998, Experiment 2). Infants at 14, 18 and 22 months of age were presented with objects in four conditions, each with animals and vehicles. In one condition, the objects had ordinary parts (e.g. cow with legs); in a second condition, the object parts were removed (e.g. cow with no legs); in a third condition, the objects possessed both kinds of parts (e.g. cow with legs and wheels); and in a fourth condition, the objects were altered so that objects of the same category did not share the same parts (e.g. two animals with legs and no wheels and two with wheels and no legs). This final trial pitted category membership against part relations so that infants were presented with a choice to group together objects on the basis of parts or category membership. The results showed that infants were attending to parts, and not using conceptual knowledge, when they categorized animals as different from vehicles. In the condition when object parts were left unmodified, infants at all three ages categorized the animals as distinct from the vehicles. But, when object parts no longer defined the categories — the conditions in which exemplars possessed no parts and the one in which exemplars possessed both parts — infants failed to categorize the animals as different from the vehicles. More revealing, perhaps, in the final condition infants at 14 and 18 months of age, but not those at 22 months of age, categorized on the basis of parts, grouping together 'things with legs' and 'things with wheels' rather than categorizing animals as different from vehicles.

Together, these results suggest that until at least between 18 and 22 months of age, perceptual features may be sufficient to explain infants' ability to form categories at the superordinate level without positing the existence of conceptual knowledge that is accessible to conscious awareness. The key point is that if, as Mandler (2004) argued, conceptual categorization implies the presence of consciousness, then it must be demonstrated rather than assumed that infants rely on declarative knowledge to group the objects and entities in the world around them. In the absence of such evidence, it is somewhat of a mental leap on the part of the researcher to attribute infants with the ability to access consciously their knowledge in the same way that we, as adults, are able.

Inductive inference in infancy

Another line of research that Mandler (2004) used to support the view that infants can be attributed with access consciousness involved the study of early inductive inference. Whereas categorization is the treatment of discriminable entities — properties, objects or events — as similar by an equivalence rule (i.e. if X_1 is a P then X_2 is also a P), induction is generalization based on observed instances (i.e. if X_1 has property P then X_2 has property P). That is, we use our concepts to generalize or make inductive inferences about the properties, characteristics and behaviours of novel things. We can make inferences about the properties and behaviours of novel cats and other mammals, for example, based on our experience with a select population of cats.

The *inductive generalization* or *generalized imitation* technique has been developed to study concept and inductive inference development (Mandler & McDonough, 1996, 1998). This task, which is suitable for infants between 10 and 24 months of age, exploits their tendency to imitate what they have observed. Typically the task involves three phases: (1) a baseline phase during which infants are presented with two exemplars (e.g. a cat and a truck) and a prop (e.g. a key) and their spontaneous play is observed; (2) a modelling phase during which the experimenter performs an appropriate action with the prop and a novel exemplar (e.g. 'starting' a car with the key) while making a vocalization that is suitable for the action (e.g. making a 'broom broom' noise for the car); (3) a test phase during which infants are again given the three objects presented during baseline and are encouraged to repeat the action modelled by the experimenter.

Mandler and McDonough (1996, 1998) reasoned that if infants have represented — in a conceptual, declarative and accessible form — information about the actions typical of animals and vehicles, they will generalize an action to the appropriate novel exemplar (the truck in the previous example) rather than the inappropriate one (the cat). Consistent with this prediction, infants between 9 and 14 months of age generalized drinking from a cup and going to bed to animals, and they generalized starting with a key and giving a ride to vehicles. Moreover, when infants were provided with two members of the same category in the baseline and generalization phase of the task (e.g. dog and cat for drinking) they were just as likely to repeat the action with both the available exemplars (Mandler & McDonough, 1998). According to Mandler and McDonough such findings support the conclusion that '. . . conceptual control of inductive generalization begins early in life. There does not seem to be a period in which infants respond only on the basis of physical appearance or are restricted in their generalizations to objects that look alike' (Mandler & McDonough, 1998, pp. 230–1). Clearly, then, Mandler's view is that within the first year of life infants are able to make inductive inferences on the basis of conceptual knowledge which is available or accessible to consciousness. Infants, according to this view, observe the action performed by the experimenter and consciously refer to their knowledge about the property displayed (e.g. drinking) which specifies which category of things in the world exhibits such a property.

Once again, however, there are reasons to doubt whether infants in these tasks possess conceptual, declarative knowledge about the actions they observe. One issue relates to whether infants' behaviour is generated on-line during the task or is based on conceptual knowledge of the specific actions in the task. The appropriate test object or objects for each action tend to have similar surface characteristics as the model exemplar (Rakison, 2003). It is conceivable that infants come to the task with no knowledge of the actions they are shown and simply imitate with the object(s) they perceive as most similar to the exemplar manipulated by the experimenter. This explanation — which eliminates the need to invoke consciousness on the part of the infants — would explain why animals were chosen — including cats, anteaters, fish and birds — rather than vehicles when the dog was the model and why vehicles were chosen — including trucks, forklifts, motorcycles and aeroplanes — when the car was the model. True enough, the animals and vehicles listed are perceptually diverse, but the animals are more similar to each other than they are to the vehicles and vice versa.[3]

In support of this line of reasoning, studies by Rakison (2003) with the inductive generalization procedure found that 14- and 18-month-old infants will repeat an observed motion with an exemplar from the same category as the model even if the exemplar is inappropriate for the motion. For example, if an experimenter modelled a cat

---

[3] There are a number of possible counterarguments to this view. For example, Mandler and McDonough (1998) found that when infants are tested with domain-general tasks they use both of the test exemplars to imitate the action (e.g. cats and cars both go inside buildings). Careful analysis of Mandler and McDonough's data revealed, however, that infants in the task tended first to imitate with the same category member as that used during the modelling phase; that is, their first action was driven by the similarity of the exemplar they saw used to model the action to the two available test exemplars. It could also be argued that infants in the inductive generalization task must use their memory to remember what they have seen so that they can then imitate it. Yet this argument fails to consider that infants' imitation occurs approximately 10 to 20 seconds after they have seen the action modelled by the experimenter, which suggests that information about the event was stored and retrieved from working memory rather than long-term memory.

going up a set of stairs, 14- and 18-month-olds repeated the action with a novel animal rather than a novel vehicle; but if the experimenter modelled a car going up a set of stairs, infants will repeat the action with a novel vehicle rather than a novel animal.

Another possible problem for Mandler's (2004; Mandler & McDonough, 1996, 1998) view is that infants may have brought to the laboratory some knowledge about the actions or motions of animals and vehicles but that this knowledge is perceptually bound and inaccessible to consciousness. For example, if infants' concept for drinking did not involve a 'meaning' but was instead an association between two perceptual cues (e.g. things with mouths drink) then according to Mandler (2004) it would not be accessible to consciousness. One potentially fruitful avenue to disentangle empirically these two views is to provide infants with a choice of more than two objects with which to demonstrate the modelled actions and to observe which of those objects are chosen. To this end, Rakison (2005) used the generalized imitation procedure to study 18- and 22-month-olds' inductions for simple motions such as walking and rolling. Infants in one condition, for example, were shown a cat moving non-linearly (i.e. walking) in an up-and-down fashion and then given four test objects that varied in their appropriateness for the motion and their membership in a common category with the target object. Thus, when the cat was observed 'walking' one test exemplar was a similar category member (i.e. a dog), a dissimilar category member (i.e. a dolphin), an exemplar from another category but with similar parts (e.g. a bed), and an exemplar from another category with dissimilar parts (e.g. a truck).

The results of the experiment showed that younger infants demonstrated the action with objects that had the appropriate features for the motion (i.e. they 'walked' the dog and the table). In contrast, the older infants demonstrated the action with objects from the appropriate category (i.e. the dog and the dolphin). A discerning reader may wonder whether these behaviours may have been driven by imitation and matching rather than any perceptually bound representation of walking or rolling. That is, infants at 18 months of age may have chosen the dog and table to repeat the action they observed modelled with the cat because they observed during the task that they all possess legs. To address this issue, the first experiment was repeated with an ambiguous block as the model exemplar; in this case, infants' choice of object with which to imitate could not be based on matching to the model exemplar. Results of the experiment matched that of the first one in that 18-month-olds chose objects that possessed the appropriate parts for the motion (e.g. legs for walking or wheels for rolling) whereas 22-month-olds chose the objects from the appropriate category.

Recall that according to Mandler (2004), infants possess a mechanism called perceptual analysis that leads to the emergence of knowledge that is available to consciousness by the end of the first year of life and can be used to make inductive inferences. The findings outlined here cast serious doubt on this view. Instead, they suggest that infants at least as old as 18 months may have concepts that embody how things move but that these concepts are perceptually-based and are not accessible to conscious awareness. The evidence also suggests that by 22 months infants may start to generalize motion properties, at least, on the basis of category membership (e.g. animals walk and land vehicles roll). Thus, it may be between 18 and 22 months of age that infants start to develop concepts that are more available to consciousness.

Summary of the literature on infant concepts and consciousness

According to one view, infants are precocious concept formers who possess declarative knowledge that allows them to subtract and add, categorize and make inductive inferences. These abilities, it is argued, are possible in such young preverbal infants because their concepts are freely available for use in reasoning and for the rational control of action; in other words, conceptual categorization allows infants to 'reason', 'compute' and 'analyse' objects, entities and events in the world (Mandler, 2004). The brief evaluation of the literature provided here suggests an alternative interpretation of infants' behaviour however. Close inspection of research in the domains of mathematics, categorization and inductive inference reveals that infants' behaviour can be explained without the need to invoke such conceptually rich representation; instead, empirical work shows that infants' behaviour is governed by perceptually-based concepts, which do not involve consciously exploiting theoretical knowledge but rather rest upon sensitivity to perceptible features.

Note that although only three areas of research were discussed here, there are a number of other domains in which comparable arguments (and data) exist. For example, findings on support, solidity and a naïve theory of rational action that putatively show that infants possess conceptually rich representations have all been called into question both theoretically and empirically (e.g. Bogartz *et al.*, 2000; Cicchino & Rakison, 2006; Cohen, Gilbert & Brown, 1996).

How does Concept Development Facilitate the Emergence of Consciousness?

If we reject the notion that infants younger than 18 months of age can be attributed with access consciousness, an important question remains: when and how does such consciousness emerge? In my view (and I am certainly not alone in this), the available data on concept development in infancy points to the emergence of language as a crucial turning point in this regard. Recall that in the experiments on categorization and induction, it is only after 18 months of age that infants begin to show evidence that their behaviour is based on category relations (Rakison, 2005; Rakison & Butterworth, 1998). For example, 22-month-olds, but not 18-month-olds, categorized and made inductive inference on the basis of whether an object belonged to the animal or vehicle category rather than on the basis of its surface appearance.

I suggest that it is no coincidence that this change in behaviour co-occurs with the period that infants begin to learn and produce labels at a more rapid rate, an change known as the *naming spurt* (see also Nelson, 1996). Once infants have learned that a label is shared between category exemplars and is a perfect predictor of the category (e.g. all dogs are labelled 'dogs'), learning labels for categories results in more compact and robust category representations that can be accessed by consciousness (Rakison & Lupyan, in press). One prediction of this view is that infants who have reached the vocabulary spurt should improve in their categorization skills, and indeed there is evidence that is consistent with this prediction (Gopnik & Meltzoff, 1987; cf. Gershkoff-Stowe *et al.*, 1997). This developmental change in behaviour is believed to result from the emergence of basic behavioural and neurological executive functions, which is grounded in the development of the lateral prefrontal cortex as well as the frontal cortex (Diamond, 1991). Due to this higher level of executive control, infants are able to use represented declarative knowledge rather than current information to make decisions and to act.

I propose, then, that concepts prior to approximately 18 months are grounded in perceptual associations of surface features (e.g. legs), motion properties (e.g. moves non-linearly) and psychological properties (e.g. is goal-directed); however, once infants learn a label for a category, these disparate associations are representationally drawn together under one word which causes knowledge that was perceptual and procedural to become conceptual and declarative. It is unlikely that this mechanism causes all knowledge that was previously procedural to become declarative because as adults there are a number of motor skills and perceptual abilities that we are unable to verbalize. More probable is that some knowledge remains procedural, some becomes declarative, and some becomes both procedural and declarative.

I suggest that information about animates and inanimates falls into the last of these categories. For example, as adults we group a cat and a dog together because they are 'the same kind of thing'; yet we cannot explain exactly what it is about them that allows us to infer that they are the 'same kind of thing'. We know that they are land mammals, animals, they are alive, and they have hearts, brains, legs, and are furry. But we cannot verbalize which of these cues we use to categorize them as equivalent in some way. To be clear, in this view it is not that the emergence of word learning makes early perceptually-based concepts available to consciousness because it provides the apparatus to verbally reflect on this knowledge; instead, it is that the acquisition of labels for specific categories causes a change in the way that knowledge is represented. Evidence to support this idea was recently found by Lupyan (2006) who showed that labelling objects caused a shift in the way that objects within categories were represented and subsequently recalled. According to this perspective, then, consciousness is not a prerequisite for concept formation; instead it is an emergent property of concept formation (cf. Mandler, 2004).

Objections to the language = consciousness view

Clearly, this view is not in accordance with that of Mandler (2004). It is also incongruent with that of Bermudez (1998) who argued that infants are conscious at least insofar as they are capable of voluntary actions. Bermudez questioned the notion that consciousness cannot be attributed to entities without language — what he called the 'Thought-Language Principle' — and proposed that infants' early attentional preferences, as well as their behaviours in responses to changes in their environment, are confirmation that they are self-conscious at least in some basic sense. According to this view, consciousness 'involves a recognition of oneself as a perceiver, an agent, and a bearer of reactive attitudes against a contrast space of other perceivers, agents, and bearers of reactive attitudes' (Bermudez, 1998, pp. 252–3). In other words, Bermudez claimed that when infants recognize that they are individual entities that are capable of responding to external stimuli then they can be attributed with a form of consciousness. Crucially, Bermudez' claim is that there is a three-stage process involved such that consciousness emerges during the final stage at the point when infants have learned many stimulus-response behaviours and must 'choose' between them in any given situation.

In support of this view, Bermudez cited a wide range of developmental research with infants in the first year of life. Included in this list is evidence that infants in the first months of life adjust how they reach for an object based on the distance between themselves and the object (Field, 1976), that neonates can discriminate their mother's voice and face to that of a stranger and imitate facial movements such as tongue protrusion (DeCasper & Fifer, 1980; Field et al., 1982; Meltzoff & Moore, 1977), and that 9-month-olds follow the direction of an individual's gaze or pointing (Scaife & Bruner, 1975). All of these behaviours, however, can be explained without the need to invoke the notion of self-consciousness on the part of the infant: reaching can be adjusted through classical condition; preferences for certain familiar stimuli (e.g. mother) and facial imitation are adaptive, procedural mechanisms that help early parental bonding; and gaze following can be explained by associative learning. Regardless of the philosophical argument, then, the empirical evidence that Bermudez relies upon does not support the conclusion that infants in the first year of life are making self-conscious choices between a range of behaviours.

Bermudez is not alone, however, in concluding that preverbal infants' behaviours suggest a form of self awareness. Reddy (2003) argued that infants around 2 months of age react to attention towards them by responding with a variety of emotions (e.g. smiles, distress, indifference). She claimed that these responses to engagements early in life imply that young infants 'show an awareness of others as attended beings, as well as an awareness of self as an object of others' attention' (p. 397). These early affective reactions, however, could be based on a procedural mechanism of facial imitation (e.g. you smile, I smile) as well as influences from infants' physical state (e.g. tired, uncomfortable). Moreover, as Reddy (2003) pointed out, it is entirely possible that 2-month-olds' affective responses, though appearing like the behaviour of older children, could be driven by different processes and in the absence of metacognitive awareness of having them.

Finally, it is worth pointing out that I have confined the discussion here to the emergence of concepts in a tightly limited sense and have not touched on evidence that comes from a consideration of emotional and interpersonal development. This is not to say that the concepts that arise from social and emotional interactions should be regarded as orthogonal to the issues outlined here. It is, unfortunately, beyond the scope of this paper to take account of such a considerable database of research. Nonetheless, it is important to acknowledge that a fully integrated understanding of infant concepts and consciousness needs to include research on the development of playfulness and fun, for instance, or of the kind of awareness of other people that leads infants and young children to comply or maybe to comfort them (for a full discussion of this issue see Hobson, 2002).

Concluding Remarks

The study of consciousness in infancy is an important but as yet uncharted area. In this article, I have used the extant literature on concept development in the first years of life to examine whether infants have theoretical conceptual knowledge that is available for free use in cognitive tasks and for the control of action. To achieve this aim, I have used the distinction between procedural and declarative knowledge as a marker for the presence of access consciousness. A number of researchers assume, either implicitly or explicitly, that early concepts involve declarative knowledge and that infants consciously use this knowledge to 'reason' and 'think' about the world around them (e.g. Baillargeon *et al.*, 1992; Mandler, 2004). I have presented evidence that suggests otherwise from research with infants on mathematics, categorization and inductive inference. In each case in which infants are purported to apply declarative knowledge there is strong counter-evidence that suggests that their behaviour is based on perceptual, procedural knowledge.

I also proposed that the onset of labelling around 18 months of age is the catalyst for the emergence of accessible declarative knowledge. In contrast to previous formulations that argue for the importance of language in the development of consciousness, this proposal stresses the effects of labelling on already established perceptually-based concepts rather than the faculty to 'think using language'. Given the dearth of research that has directly investigated infant consciousness, this proposal is clearly speculative. However, these issues are open to empirical testing, and it is only a matter of time before researchers start to address them more directly and the issue of consciousness in infancy is in a position to be resolved.

Acknowledgements

The author would like to thank three anonymous reviewers and Jose Bermudez for constructive feedback on this manuscript. He would also like to extend special thanks to Rocco Gennaro for his continued support and help throughout the review process.

References

Baillargeon, R. (1987), 'Object permanence in 3.5- and 4.5-month-old infants', *Developmental Psychology*, **23**, pp. 655–64.

Baillargeon, R. (1998), 'Infants' understanding of the physical world', in *Advances in Psychological Science: Vol. 2. Biological and Cognitive Aspects*, ed. M. Sabourin, F. Craik & M. Robert (East Sussex: Psychology Press).

Baillargeon, R., Needham, A. & DeVos, J. (1992), 'The development of young infants' intuitions about support', *Early Development and Parenting*, **1**, pp. 69–78.

Baillargeon, R., Spelke, E.S. & Wasserman, S. (1985), 'Object permanence in 5-month-old infants', *Cognition*, **20**, pp. 191–208.

Bauer, P. (2005), 'Developments in declarative memory: Decreasing susceptibility to storage failure over the second year of life', *Psychological Science*, **16**, pp. 41–7.

Bermudez, J.L. (1998), *The Paradox of Self-Consciousness* (Cambridge MA: MIT Press).

Block, N. (1995), 'On a confusion about a function of consciousness', *Behavioral and Brain Sciences*, **18**, pp. 227–47.

Bogartz, R.S., Shinskey, J.L. & Schilling, T.H. (2000), 'Object permanence in 5.5-month-old infants', *Infancy*, **1**, pp. 403–28.

Bomba, P.C. & Siqueland, E.R. (1983), 'The nature and structure of infant form categories', *Journal of Experimental Child Psychology*, **35**, pp. 294–328.

Butterworth, G.E. (1992), 'Origins of self-perception in infancy', *Psychological Inquiry*, **3**, pp. 103–11.

Cashon, C.H. & Cohen, L.B. (2000), 'Eight-month-old infants' perception of possible and impossible events', *Infancy*, **1**, pp. 429–46.

Clearfield, M.W. & Westfahl, S.M.C. (2006), 'Familiarization in infants' perception of addition problems', *Journal of Cognition and Development*, **7**, pp. 27–43.

Cohen, L.B. & Marks, K.L. (2002), 'How infants process addition and subtraction events', *Developmental Science*, **5**, pp. 186–201.

Cohen, L.B., Gilbert, K.M. & Brown, P.S. (1996), 'Infants' understanding of solidity: Replicating a failure to replicate', Poster session presented at the International Conference on Infant Studies, Providence, RI.

Collie, R. & Hayne, H. (1999), 'Deferred imitation by 6- and 9-month-old infants: More evidence for declarative memory', *Developmental Psychobiology*, **35**, pp. 83–90.

Cicchino, J.B. & Rakison, D.H. (2006), 'Do infants have a theory of rational action?', unpublished manuscript.

DeCasper, A.J. & Fifer, W. (1980), 'Of human bonding: Newborns prefer their mother's voices', *Science*, **208**, pp. 1174–6.

Dennett, D.C. (1991), *Consciousness Explained* (New York, NY: Bay Back Books).

Diamond, A. (1991), 'Neuropsychological insights into the meaning of object concept development', in *The Epigenesis of Mind: Essays on Biology and Cognition*, ed. S. Carey & R. Gelman (Hillsdale, NJ: Erlbaum).

Edelman, G.M. & Tononi, G.A. (2000), *Universe of Consciousness: How Matter becomes Imagination* (New York, NY: Basic Books).

Fagan, J.F. & Singer, L.T. (1979), 'The role of simple feature differences in infants' recognition of faces', *Infant Behavior and Development*, **2**, pp. 39–45.

Field, J. (1976), 'Relation of young infants' reaching behaviour to stimulus distance and solidity', *Developmental Psychology*, **12**, pp. 444–8.

Field, T.M., Woodson, R., Greenburg, R. & Cohen, D. (1982), 'Discrimination and imitation of facial expression by neonates', *Science*, **218**, pp. 179–81.

Gallup, G.G. (1970), 'Chimpanzees: Self-recognition', *Science*, **167**, pp. 86–7.

Gelman, R. & Williams, E.M. (1998), 'Enabling constraints for cognitive development and learning: Domain specificity and epigenesis', in *Handbook of Child Psychology: Vol. 2. Cognition, Perception, and Language* (5th edn.), Series Ed. W. Damon, Vol. Eds. D. Kuhn & R.S. Siegler (New York, NY: Wiley).

Gershkoff-Stowe, L., Thal, D.J., Smith, L.B. & Namy, L.L. (1997), 'Categorization and its developmental relation to early language', *Child Development*, **68**, pp. 843–59.

Gopnik, A. & Meltzoff, A. (1987), 'The development of categorization in the second year and its relation to other cognitive and linguistic development', *Child Development*, **58**, pp. 1523–31.

Hobson, P. (2002), *The Cradle of Thought: Challenging the Origins of Thinking* (New York: Oxford University Press).

Langlois, J.H., Roggman, L.A., Casey, R.J., Ritter, J.M., Rieser-Danner, L.A. & Jenkins, V.Y. (1987), 'Infant preferences for attractive faces: Rudiments of a stereotype?', *Developmental Psychology*, **23**, pp. 263–369.

Lewis, M. & Brookes-Gunn, J. (1979), *Social Cognition and the Acquisition of Self* (New York, NY: Plenum Press).

Lupyan, G. (2006), 'From chair to "chair": a representational change account of object naming effects on memory', manuscript under review.

Mandler, J.M. (1992), 'How to build a baby: II. Conceptual primitives', *Psychological Review*, **99**, pp. 587–604.

Mandler, J.M. (2003), 'Conceptual categorization', in *Early Category and Concept Development: Making Sense of the Blooming, Buzzing Confusion*, ed. D.H. Rakison & L.M. Oakes (New York, NY: Oxford University Press).

Mandler, J.M. (2004), *The Foundations of Mind: Origins of Conceptual Thought* (New York: Oxford University Press).

Mandler, J.M. & Bauer, P.J. (1988), 'The cradle of categorization: Is the basic level basic?', *Cognitive Development*, **3**, pp. 247–64.

Mandler, J.M., Bauer, P.J. & McDonough, L. (1991), 'Separating the sheep from the goats: Differentiating global categories', *Cognitive Psychology*, **23**, pp. 263–98.

Mandler, J.M. & McDonough, L. (1996), 'Drinking and driving don't mix: Inductive generalization in infancy', *Cognition*, **59**, pp. 307–35.

Mandler, J.M. & McDonough, L. (1998), 'Studies in inductive inference in infancy', *Cognitive Psychology*, **37**, pp. 60–96.

Margolis, E. (1994), 'A reassessment of the shift from classical theory of concepts to prototype theory', *Cognition*, **51**, pp. 73–89.

Meltzoff, A.N. & Moore, M.K. (1977), 'Imitation of facial and manual gestures by human neonates', *Science*, **198**, pp. 75–8.

Mix, K. (2002), 'Trying to build on shifting sand: Commentary on Cohen and Marks', *Developmental Science*, **5**, pp. 205–6.

Moscovitch, M., Goshen-Gottstein, Y. & Vriezen, E. (1994), 'Memory without conscious recollection: A tutorial review from a neuropsychological perspective', in *Attention and Performance 15: Conscious and Nonconscious Information Processing*, ed. C. Umilta & M. Moscovitch (Cambridge, MA: MIT Press).

Needham, A. & Baillargeon, R. (1993), 'Intuitions about support in 4.5-month-old infants', *Cognition*, **47**, pp. 121–48.

Nelson, K. (1996), *Language in Cognition: The Emergence of the Mediated Mind* (Cambridge University Press).

Pauen, S. (2002), 'Evidence for knowledge-based category discrimination in infancy', *Child Development*, **73**, pp. 1016–33.

Piaget, J. (1952), *The Origins of Intelligence in Children* (New York: International University Press).

Quinn, P.C., Eimas, P.D. & Rosenkrantz, S.L. (1993), 'Evidence for representations of perceptually similar natural categories by 3-month-old and 4-month-old infants', *Perception*, **22**, pp. 463–75.

Rakison, D.H. (2003), 'Parts, categorization, and the animate-inanimate distinction in infancy', in *Early Category and Concept Development: Making Sense of the Blooming, Buzzing Confusion*, ed. D.H. Rakison & L.M. Oakes (New York, NY: Oxford University Press).

Rakison, D.H. (2005), 'Developing knowledge of motion properties in infancy', *Cognition*, **96**, pp. 183–214.

Rakison, D.H. & Butterworth, G. (1998), 'Infants' use of parts in early categorization', *Developmental Psychology*, **34**, pp. 49–62.

Rakison, D.H. & Cohen, L.B. (1999), 'Infants' use of functional parts in basic-like categorization', *Developmental Science*, **2**, pp. 423–32.

Rakison, D.H. & Lupyan, G. (in press), 'Developing object concepts in infancy: An associative learning perspective', *Monographs of SRCD*.

Reddy, V. (2003), 'On being an object of attention: Implications for self–other-consciousness', *Trends in Cognitive Science*, **7**, pp. 397–402.

Rivera, S.M., Wakely, A. & Langer, J. (1999), 'The drawbridge phenomenon: Representational reasoning or perceptual preference?', *Developmental Psychology*, **35**, pp. 427–35.

Rovee-Collier, C. (1997), 'Dissociations in infant memory: Rethinking the development of implicit and explicit memory', *Psychological Review*, **104**, pp. 467–98.

Schacter, D.L. (1987), 'Implicit memory: History and current status', *Journal of Experimental Psychology: Learning, Memory, and Cognition*, **13**, pp. 501–18.

Scaife, M. & Bruner, J.S. (1975), 'The capacity for joint visual attention in the infant', *Nature*, **253**, pp. 265–6.

Smith, E.E. (1995), 'Concepts and categorization', in *Thinking: An Invitation to Cognitive Science*, Vol. 3, ed. E.E. Smith & D.N. Osherson (Cambridge, MA: MIT Press).

Spelke, E.S., Breinlinger, K., Macomber, J. & Jacobson, K. (1992), 'Origins of knowledge', *Psychological Review*, **99**, pp. 605–32.

Tulving, E. (1990), 'Memory and consciousness', *Canadian Journal of Psychology*, **26**, pp. 1–12.

Wynn, K. (1992), 'Addition and subtraction by human infants', *Nature*, **358**, pp. 749–50.

Wynn, K. (1995), 'Infants possess a system of numerical knowledge', *Current Directions in Psychological Science*, **4**, pp. 172–7.

Wynn, K. (2002), 'Do infants have numerical expectations or just perceptual preferences?', *Developmental Science*, **5**, pp. 207–9.

Younger, B.A. & Cohen, L.B. (1986), 'Developmental change in infants' perception of correlations among attributes', *Child Development*, **57**, pp. 803–15.

Zelazo, P.D. (2004), 'The development of conscious control in childhood', *Trends in Cognitive Sciences*, **8**, pp. 12–17.

John Beeckmans

Can Higher-Order Representation Theories Pass Scientific Muster?

Abstract: *Higher-order representation (HOR) theories posit that the contents of lower-order brain states enter consciousness when tracked by a higher-order brain state. The nature of higher-order monitoring was examined in light of current scientific knowledge, primarily in experimental perceptual psychology. The most plausible candidate for higher-order state was found to be conceptual short-term memory (CSTM), a buffer memory intimately connected with a semantic engine operating in the medium of the language of thought (LOT). This combination meets many of the requirements of HOR theories, although falling short in some significant respects, most notably the inability of higher-order states to represent more than a small fraction of the information contained in primary states, especially in vision. A possible way round this obstacle is suggested, involving the representation of visual detail by means of ensemble concepts.*

Introduction

Although its detailed working is only poorly and partially understood, the brain is known to contain numerous tightly linked functional modules. It is thus coherent to speak of regional brain states, with their conjunction constituting the state of the brain as a whole at a given instant. Consciousness is also structured, with distinct sensory modalities as well as somatic, cognitive and emotional dimensions. The experimental evidence suggests that the disparate dimensions of consciousness are mediated by anatomically and functionally separate regions of the brain. Indeed, the linking of aspects of consciousness to specific geographical areas of the brain (the identification of the neural correlates of consciousness) is an on-going research objective. Nevertheless, although it is universally accepted that all aspects of consciousness are mediated by occurrences within the brain, not every brain event is reflected within consciousness. In fact, the mind has been likened to an iceberg, with most of its activity hidden from consciousness. Which raises the question: What distinguishes brain events that are expressed in consciousness from those that are not?

It has been proposed in response that a brain state becomes conscious only when monitored by a higher-order brain state. In a way, the higher-order state plays a role reminiscent of the much-ridiculed homunculus, a sort of mini-mind within the brain. Thus we are conscious only of what the homunculus is 'aware of' and blind to the rest of the brain's goings-on. Of course no one denies that higher-order states exist. Indeed, consciousness implies awareness, which in turn implies an ability to report; and reports are cognitive, and hence are drafted by higher-order mental states. So it follows that higher-order mental states are necessary for consciousness, or at least essential adjuncts. But whether they are sufficient is another question altogether. Some philosophers argue that they are, while others disagree and yet others sit on the fence. But let me make it clear that this particular issue is not on the agenda. Instead, the focus will be on a critical examination of the relationship between higher- and lower-order brain states in light of the empirical findings of cognitive and perceptual psychology, and of neuroscience, and the implications of these findings in connection with the merits of HOR theories

Articulations on the theme have produced a variety of HOR theories. The main division is between higher-order thought theories (HOT) and higher-order perception theories (HOP) (sometimes called higher-order experience theories). They differ in that in HOT theories the higher-order states are purely conceptual, whereas in HOP they are deemed to be quasi-perceptual. Different versions have been advanced within the two main divisions, as well as a theory involving a blend of HOT and HOP (Carruthers, 2000). Despite their differences, higher-order theorists agree on two things (beyond the essential role of higher-order mental states). The first point of agreement is that the higher-order states must themselves be predominantly unconscious. This is to avoid regress, since conscious higher-order states would themselves require yet-higher-order states, with no end to the number of orders of representation if all were to be conscious. This

restriction may nevertheless be partially contravened during introspection, which is posited to involve conscious HOTs that are in turn
monitored by other, unconscious, higher-order thoughts. (Which explains
the requirement that higher-order states be *predominantly* unconscious). The second point of agreement is that the consciousness-
causing higher-order representations must be non-inferential. That is
to say, they must be arrived at directly and intuitively rather than by a
process of deliberate, conscious inference. The visual impairment
known as akinetopsia (Zeki, 1983) illustrates nicely why this restriction is needed. Sufferers from this debilitating condition cannot perceive motion, which is such a severe handicap that they are unable to
cross a street safely or fill a cup without overflowing it, despite having
otherwise normal vision. Yet they can consciously *infer* motion
because they can see changes in the position of objects; however this
doesn't suffice to induce consciousness of motion and hence they are
unable to interact effectively with their environment. In what follows
the principal HOR theories will be scrutinized in turn, the empirical
evidence relevant to each theory will be identified and described, and
the strengths and weaknesses of the respective theories that this process reveals will be discussed.

Higher-Order Thought Theory

Standard higher-order thought theory

The leading exponent of standard HOT theory is David Rosenthal
(e.g. 1986; 2000; 2005), who propounds that the contents of lower-
order states become conscious when *conceptualized* within a higher-
order state that is itself generally unconscious. Rosenthal stipulates
that the higher-order thoughts must occur within the context of an
assertoric mental attitude that expresses a belief that the subject is perceiving or feeling or thinking whatever the HOTs are about. A purely
conceptual and propositional higher-order state of this kind has no
analogic component, implying that since we only have a limited reper-
toire of recognitional concepts pertaining to the senses most qualitative content can only be conceptualized by interpolation. Thus we
could, for instance, describe a particular shade of colour as 'slightly
orangey yellow'. While it may seem far-fetched that the brain should
have the ability to rapidly represent arbitrary colours in this manner, it
should be remembered that this occurs unconsciously; and HOT
theorists can argue that conscious, verbalized interpolations do not
mirror the underlying unconscious processes. The principal tests of
plausibility for HOT theory are, rather, the following: (1) can it be

shown experimentally that the brain has the ability to conceptualize incoming sensory percepts extremely rapidly (since conscious states can change very rapidly); and (2) is there plausible neurobiological evidence for the existence of higher-order states of the kind posited by HOT theory?

Conceptual short-term memory

HOT theory requires a buffer memory capable of representing a rich, occurrent, *conceptual* representation of the contents of lower-order sensory brain states. Rosenthal (2000, p. 206) is explicit that the informational content of the first-order mental states that are rendered conscious must be represented in HOT:

> So it must be that we are conscious of our conscious states by having suitable thoughts about them. These thoughts will represent the states they are about in respect of the information content those states have or, in the case of sensory states, in respect of their sensory quality.

It could be argued that this doesn't mean that *all* of the information in the primary states must be represented. In fact, in some circumstances we can be completely unconscious, both phenomenally and conceptually, of information represented in primary cortical areas. This is especially evident in inattentional blindness (Mack & Rock, 1998), when subjects are oblivious to the presence of certain objects or features (even at the fovea) located outside a region of focused attention, and in binocular rivalry, when subjects are conscious of only one of the images presented; and it is certainly plausible that information that does not appear at all in consciousness should lack higher-order represention. That is one side of the coin; the other side is that it is difficult to dispute that we can experience chromatically cluttered visual percepts, which suggests that at least a certain level of detailing is represented in phenomenal consciousness, and by implication also in higher-order thoughts. For instance, a glance at an intricately patterned Persian carpet *feels* (in the phenomenal sense) very different from the feel of a cloudless blue sky: one percept feels profusely polychromatic, the other monochromatic. We must therefore conclude that HOT theory requires that our brains have the capacity to simultaneously conceptualize substantial numbers of concurrently perceived objects and features (such as colours), a tall order indeed. Nevertheless, a buffer memory that appears promising as a representational vehicle with the desired attributes has been proposed and backed up by a wealth of experimental evidence. Termed conceptual short-term memory (CSTM) by its proponent, Mary Potter, it is distinct from short-term (or working) memory (STM) and from iconic memory, which is held to be purely pictorial. CSTM and STM are quite distinct in that the former is intimately connected to cognitive processing whereas the latter is a passive store for phonological and articulatory information, as well as for visuospatial properties. The reader is referred to Potter's reviews (Potter, 1993; 1999) for a full discussion of CSTM, since only a curtailed overview can be given here.

The genesis of CSTM came from experiments showing that a target image of a scene embedded within a sequence of distractor images can be efficiently detected when shown at rates as high as 8 images/s (Potter, 1975; 1976). The conceptual nature of the target image identification process follows from the fact that detection rates were similar for previously described targets and for previously viewed targets. Indeed, targets defined by a logical criterion (e.g. does *not* contain a food) can also be identified, albeit not as accurately, at these rates of presentation (Intraub, 1981). Characterization of a scene involves not only identification of the objects that define the scene's meaning, but also verification that their placement is semantically appropriate. The resulting global concept must then be compared with the target concept to see if they match, all this occurring in slightly over 100 ms. The semantic processing capability revealed in these relatively simple experiments demonstrates the involvement of more than a simple flash memory. CSTM should properly be seen as merely a scratchpad for a powerful semantic engine operating unconsciously and at blazing speed. However, since the two are so closely interconnected it is convenient to refer to them simply as CSTM. It has long been recognized that unconscious semantic processing underpins thought and its expression in language. The vehicle for this processing is alternatively called the language of thought (LOT) or Mentalese (see Aydede, 2004, for a review).

Potter proposes that a brief perception of a scene generates a primary percept consisting of numerous categorical concepts that are fleetingly and concurrently activated within CSTM. The primary percept is then cognitively processed (presumably in the LOT, although Potter doesn't explicitly refer to the LOT), resulting in the identification of a meaningful structure. Only the latter is retained in explicit memory, while the concepts that were activated but don't form part of the structure are immediately forgotten. The memorized structure is called a gist, and it captures the semantically most important features of the image. It may be regarded as the secondary, or consolidated, percept. A gist will also contain some global concepts, such as a theme concept (e.g. STREET SCENE), as well as object concepts. Because we can generally report at least a few colours (Luck & Vogel, 1997), it will also contain concepts identifying some salient colours. Finally, some ensemble concepts will also usually be retained (Beeckmans, 2004). These represent directly apprehended qualitative or quantitative general properties of collections of identifiable particulars contained in a complex image, or in a region thereof. They include, but are not limited to, statistical properties. That the latter can be intuitively perceived has been amply demonstrated. For instance, the average direction of motion (Watamaniuk *et al.*, 1989) or velocity (Watamaniuk & Duchon, 1992) of assemblies of moving dots, or the average diameter of a set of heterogeneously sized circular spots (Ariely, 2001), can, without conscious deliberation or calculation, be accurately estimated following a very brief presentation. Recently, Chong & Treisman (2005) showed that subjects can intuitively perceive the respective mean diameters of two sets of intermingled, heterogeneously distributed, briefly displayed circles, the members of each set being distinguishable by their colour. For the brain to estimate a mean property of a set its members must first be individually identified; and since the apprehension of such means is both rapid and effortless, the entire process must be automatic and unconscious.

Potter's results with the rapid serial visual presentation paradigm suggest that the brain surreptitiously perceives far more than it is consciously aware of, or than is conserved in explicit memory. Additional evidence for rich primary perception is provided by a series of studies on fast categorization performed at the Centre de Recherche Cerveau et Cognition in Toulouse, France. Subjects in the first study were required to push a button as rapidly as possible if they perceived that a natural scene flashed for 20 ms contained an animal (which could be a mammal, fish, insect, bird, or any other type of animal, could be partially occluded, or be in a herd, and appear anywhere in the image) (Thorpe *et al.*, 1996). The median reaction time was 445 ms, with 94% correct responses. Potentials at several scalp locations were also recorded (yielding so-called event-related potentials, or ERPs). Differences were found within about 150 ms in the ERPs from scenes with and without animals, indicating that categorization occurred within that time frame. This is quite remarkable, given that the subjects' visuo-cognitive system first had to identify and categorize all objects (animal and non-animal) appearing anywhere in the image,[1] then to determine whether or not the recognized objects belong to the

[1]   Although it should be pointed out that some scenes can be partially categorized on the basis of low-level features, without prior object categorization (e.g. Rousselet *et al.*, 2005, Renninger & Malik, 2004).

super-ordinate category 'animals', and finally to decide on the appro-priate response to the task. Similar results were obtained in a follow-up study using rhesus monkeys and human subjects, with 'foods' or 'animals' as target categories (Fabre-Thorpe *et al.*, 1998). Monkeys were on average 100–180 ms faster than humans, although the reader may perhaps draw solace from knowing that humans made slightly fewer mistakes. Even shorter latencies (as low as 120 ms) were observed using a protocol in which the subject had to saccade to the image containing an animal when presented with two side-by-side images flashed for 20 ms (Kirchner & Thorpe, 2006). Fabre-Thorpe *et al.* (1998, p. 307) stated that

> The implication is that object recognition and visual categorization of complex natural images relies essentially on massively parallel pro-cessing, and not on processes in which individual objects in the scene are checked and compared sequentially with internally stored sets of information.

Indeed, a parallel processing model can account for results of an animal/ no animal categorization task with up to four images flashed concur-rently for 26 ms (Rousselet *et al.*, 2004), albeit with some loss of accu-racy. There are nevertheless limits to parallel processing. VanRullen *et al.* (2004), using up to 16 images exposed simultaneously for 200 ms at random locations within a 15° x 10° visual angle box, found that response latency and accuracy in animal/no animal categorization tasks declined as the number of images increased. However, in this case the images were necessarily quite small (3.5° x 2.5°), which may partly explain the apparent discrepancy with the results of the Rousselet *et al.* (2004) study.

Because gists contain only stripped-down semantic summaries they can't perform the function demanded of Rosenthal's HOTs. But could the content of CSTM prior to the rapid erasure of (unconscious) infor-mation that occurs immediately after gist formation be sufficiently complete to perform this function? If so, we may have found the holy grail of HOT theory, because CSTM appears to go a long way towards meeting all but one of the theory's essential requirements: it is uncon-scious, it is not consciously inferential, it operates at the enormous speed needed to represent fast-changing sensory contents (if for no other reason than to accommodate scene changes induced by involun-tary saccades, which occur on average every 300 ms), and it accepts information in parallel mode, so that it is ideally suited for represent-ing synchronous perceptual information in cognitive form. The only requirement that is not explicitly satisfied is that the concepts be expressed within the context of an assertoric mental attitude. However, the contents of CSTM become raw inputs to an LOT semantic engine with access to the mind's full cognitive resources, including its standing beliefs; and this LOT thought factory is doubtless capable of generating an assertoric thought for every recognitional concept activated in CSTM, or of tagging recognitional concepts with an assertoric intention. For instance, perception of a prominent red colour would activate the concept RED, which could immediately be translated into the assertoric LOT thought: 'I am experiencing red'. So it appears that CSTM might fit the bill; and moreover it seems most implausible that the brain should contain a second, parallel cognitive system with the desired attributes. For these reasons, unless a better candidate is proposed it seems logical to identify CSTM as the vehicle for the higher-order states posited by HOT theory.

The picture that emerges is thus preliminarily encouraging. The evidence we have reviewed suggests that the brain continuously parses the entire visual field in parallel, with relatively promiscuous representations appearing in a conceptual, higher-order form within CSTM. Furthermore, there is evidence that the brain recognizes simple features such as shapes and colours even more rapidly than it characterizes objects. Thus, Van Rullen and Thorpe (2001) found average differential ERP latencies of only 75–80 ms between pictures with animals and pictures illustrating modes of transport, as opposed to 150 ms for go/no go decisions in categorization tasks, a discrepancy which they attributed to differences in low-level cues between these two image categories. This suggests at least the possibility that low-level features of the visual field, including colour, may be even more richly represented in CSTM than objects.

Difficulties with standard HOT theory

The evidence reviewed in the previous section is at least consistent with automatic, occurrent conceptualization of objects and of at least a few sensory qualities. However, notwithstanding that several colour concepts can be simultaneously activated and memorized (Luck & Vogel, 1997), it is inconceivable that the myriad chromatic details within complex stimuli are fully represented within CSTM. There are about a million nerve fibres connecting each eye with the visual cortex, with a correspondingly large information transmission capacity that allows complete representation of retinal information in V1, the primary visual area. But there are good reasons, based on the functional architecture of the brain, to resist the notion that every chromatic detail within complex visual percepts is *conceptually* represented in CSTM. Indeed, there is no evidence that detailed chromatic information is represented in the frontal and prefrontal lobes (where presumably the higher-order centres postulated by HOR theories are located), although information about a limited number of salient, concurrently perceived colours must reach cognitive centres, since they can be reported. Both the problem of conceptual representation of chromatically detailed percepts and the problem of conceptual representation of arbitrary colours are serious difficulties for Rosenthal's version of HOT theory, as critics have pointed out. For instance, Carruthers (2000) put forward his dispositionalist HOT theory primarily to evade the problem of 'cognitive overload'; and Byrne (1997) has suggested that conceptualization of complex scenes would necessitate inexpressible and unthinkable thoughts.

HOT theorists may counter that the richness of our visual phenomenal percepts is illusory, and I have argued (Beeckmans, 2004) that until we understand the ontology of phenomenal consciousness this assertion cannot be rigorously refuted. But the reality of rich visual phenomenality may nevertheless be defended on the ground of 'inference to the best explanation' (Harman, 1965). This is essentially the tack taken by Block (2001), citing various lines of evidence. It may also be noted that it has been shown that naïve subjects exposed very briefly (95 ms) to complex abstract patterns containing large numbers (either 66 or 200) of coloured circular spots can subsequently report surprisingly detailed information, including relatively accurate estimates of the number of spots perceived (Beeckmans, 2001). More to the point, they were convinced they had experienced many more specific colours than they could report, implying that inability to report details may be due to limitations of memory rather than to sparse phenomenology. Block (2001, p. 209) calls this 'phenomenality without access', and cites Sperling's iconic memory experiments in support (Sperling, 1960). Subjects in these experiments briefly viewed a matrix of letters and were convinced they saw all the letters, although only able to recall a few. Ensemble concepts also strongly suggest that our phenomenality can represent far more information than we are able to report. But a problem looms for HOT theory with even the weakest (and most plausible) claim:[2] simply that we are capable of experiencing *numerous* shades of colour in parallel (i.e. significantly more than the 3–4 that can be recalled following a brief exposure to a

[2] Stronger claims would be that we can experience in parallel all of the shades of colour represented throughout the retina, or that we can experience both the colours and the metric in visual percepts.

chromatically rich stimulus). Lastly, one additional challenge for HOT theory should be mentioned: it doesn't suffice that multiple colours in scenes be represented conceptually as HOTs in CSTM, since each colour must also be indexed to a specific location within the visual field. This difficulty is a version of the well-known binding problem.

But HOT theory also has potential difficulties with conscious thoughts. As we saw earlier, when a scene is briefly viewed a conceptual gist is generated and memorized. The fact that gists are available for subsequent conscious examination may give the impression that their contents (which are entirely cognitive) were all synchronously conscious at the time the image was perceived. But this must be an illusion, since despite the fact that numerous concepts can be *un*consciously activated in parallel it is unlikely that we have the ability to be *conscious* of multiple concepts concurrently. In fact, natural-language based conscious thinking is inherently sequential, and even conscious intuitive thinking probably involves serial attentional focusing on individual thoughts. If this is correct, then the fact that CSTM can contain multiple simultaneously activated concepts is not an unalloyed plus for HOT theory. Indeed, only concepts with lower-level intentional objects (such as colours) that can be multiply *experienced* in parallel appear to be completely compatible with HOT theory. Concepts that are activated in CSTM and that don't concern sensa, for instance object categorization concepts, don't have lower level intentional (mental state) objects and so must be regarded as first-order. Two questions arise concerning such concepts: (1) how a single concept, or possibly the very few concepts, that is (are) conscious at a given instant is (are) selected from the (generally large) set of concepts active at a given moment in CSTM; and (2), where the corresponding higher-order thought(s) required by HOT theory to render it (them) conscious is (are) located. HOT theorists might respond by suggesting that the semantic engine generates a higher-order thought (cast in the requisite assertoric format) in connection with categorization concepts arising during perception, with *both orders* of concepts activated simultaneously within CSTM. Selection for higher-order tracking would be from amongst those concepts already selected for inclusion in a gist, presumably on the basis of semantic saliency as determined by the LOT machine. This is a tempting solution, but it involves duplicate activation of certain concepts within CSTM, which seems on the face of it to be odd and inefficient. But perhaps the neural substrates of higher-order thoughts about concepts that are activated in CSTM are located within a so-called 'propositional attitude box', such as a 'belief box', which could be apart, both functionally and geographically, from the neural substrates of lower-order thoughts activated in CSTM and which HOT theory suggests they render conscious. CSTM (and its implied LOT engine) was put forward by Potter to account for the results of her rapid serial visual presentation experiments, but she didn't speculate about its location or its internal structure. There is therefore no inconsistency in proposing that CSTM may encompass multiple functionally and anatomically distinct regions. Finally it should be pointed out that duplication is apparently called for not only in connection with deliberative thinking but also with involuntary conscious phenomenal judgments and with the conscious object and feature categorizations that arise continually during perception.

Dispositionalist HOT theory

Peter Carruthers (2000) has advanced a dispositionalist HOT theory in which a lower-order mental state is rendered conscious in virtue of being disposed to (non-inferentially) cause an activated belief to occur, within a higher-order mental state, that it (the lower-order state) is being experienced. Cognitive overload is thereby avoided, since higher-order states need not *actually* represent the full contents of their targeted lower-order mental states in order to make them conscious; all that is required is that the detailed contents of the lower-order state be *potentially* available for targeting. That a mere availability for targeting by a higher-order mental state should cause a lower-order state to become conscious is of course controversial; however, as previously mentioned, the issue of consciousness rendering is off-limits in this article. Instead, I will discuss some of the theory's psycho-neural aspects.

Carruthers proposes that incoming sensory signals are sent to a short-term buffer memory he calls C, defined by the availability of its contents to a higher-order state with access to a theory of mind. As regards vision, it seems that C should be identified with early parts of the cortical pathway (since only these areas have the small receptive fields needed for representing chromatic details), although Carruthers seems to believe that C's neural substrate is located in the temporal lobes (Carruthers, 2000, p. 311). But aside from this quibble, of greater interest for our purpose is the nature and quantity of information about C's contents that *is* transmitted to the higher-order state. On the one hand, the threat of cognitive overload suggests that only a small fraction of C's information should be transmitted. But on the other hand, sufficient information must be sent to generate appropriate beliefs within the higher-order state about the lower-order state's condition. Carruthers states that the selection of material in C for sending on to the higher-order state can be done by 'a variety of processes determining salience, including goals and interests which are active elsewhere in the system' (*ibid.*, p. 311). This fits well with what we know about the generation of concepts in CSTM, which also appears to be governed by saliency (e.g. size of objects, and bottom-up processes that identify features of potential interest), generally modulated by attention, which may in turn be affected by the organism's goals and interests. Ensemble concepts appear to be singularly apt in connection with dispositional HOT theory because they permit the higher-order state to be parsimoniously informed about pertinent group attributes of the undisciplined hordes of chromatic particulars storming the ramparts of the visual system. Thus could the organism become *cognizant* of chromatic richness without incurring cognitive overload, while at the same time *experiencing* the C-buffer's cornucopia in all its glory. Unfortunately this happy outcome may not convince critics who are not persuaded that mere dispositionality for targeting by a higher-order state suffices for arousing phenomenal consciousness of the contents of a primary mental state.

Other versions of HOT theory

Several other versions of HOT theory have been advanced, notably by Gennaro (1996), van Gulick (2000), and Rolls (2004). Rolls's higher-order syntactic thought theory is similar to Rosenthal's theory, but places greater emphasis on the importance of conscious and unconscious syntactic thought. He suggests that evolution encouraged the formation of goal-directed syntactic reasoning capabilities as a more effective means of practical problem solving in many situations than simple conditioned responses. His theory inherits the same problems as Rosenthal's. The theories of Gennaro and van Gulick posit that both the lower-order states and the higher-order metastates are components of a single complex state, the difference between the theories being that van Gulick proposes a global complex state whereas Gennaro's complex states are more localized. The meta-states are thereby intrinsically a part of the states that are rendered conscious, rather than being extrinsic to them as is the case with Rosenthal's theory. This stratagem naturally raises the question of the ontological difference between a complex state and a simple conjunction of interconnected primary and higher-order states. Gennaro addresses this issue (Gennaro, 2006) and suggests, *inter alia*, that the components of complex mental states have causal interdependencies, such as feedback loops and perhaps synchronization (Kriegel, 2003), that differentiate them from simply connected separate states. Be that as it may, this issue is quite separate from the difficulties discussed earlier relating to the content of higher-order representations, and these are equally applicable to the complex states advocated by Gennaro and van Gulick.

Higher-Order Perception Theory

Higher-order states as sensational sentences

HOP theories of consciousness posit that the higher-order meta-state is quasi-perceptual, and has the attributes of an 'inner sense' that purposefully introspects lower-order states. The currently most active advocate of HOP theory is Lycan (1987; 1996; 2004), who stresses the importance of voluntary control of attention even in passive perception (1996, p. 102):

> Here again, that introspec*ting* is a highly voluntary activity does not entail that ordinary passive representation of first-order states is as well. But it seems to show that the introspectors, the monitors or scanners, are there to be mobilized and that they may function in a less deliberate way under more general circumstances. I contend, then, that the high-order representations that make a first-order state conscious are (etiologically) more like perception than they are like thoughts. They are characteristically the outputs of an attention mechanism that is under voluntary control; thoughts are not that.

But the supposed importance of attention seems inconsistent with evidence from experiments involving tachistoscopic presentations, which points to massively parallel processing of the entire visual field. Furthermore, abbreviated presentations don't allow sufficient time for either voluntary or involuntary control of attention, yet subjects are nevertheless immediately conscious of colours and shapes in the stimuli. This isn't of course to deny that *focused* attention can profoundly influence perception (*vide* inattentional blindness [Mack & Rock, 1998]).

While it is difficult to say exactly what defines a higher-order quasi-perceptual state (this issue is thrashed out in Güzeldere, 1995, and in van Gulick, 2000), it is evident they cannot simply be literal re-representations of their targeted lower-order states. In fact, Lycan (1996, p. 60) views a higher-order representation as '. . . a token in the subject's language of thought . . .', and that (*ibid.*, p. 64):

My mental reference to a first-order psychological state of my own is a tokening of a semantically primitive Mentalese lexeme. My mental word is functionally nothing like any of the complex expressions of English that in fact refer to the same (neural) state of affairs; certainly it is neither synonymous with, or otherwise semantically related to, any of them. And since no one else can use that mental word or even any functionally or syntactically similar word of their own to designate that state of affairs, of course no one can explain in English or in any other language why that state of affairs feels like [*that* or *Semantha*] to me. Introspection involves a very special mode of presentation, primitive and private in the senses I have described.

This view seems to require that the higher-order representations posited by HOP theories be instantiated in the CSTM/LOT system. Several other philosophers (Rey, 1997; Leeds, 1993, 2002; Vinueza, 2000) support the notion that phenomenal experiences are indeed describable by sentences in the LOT. However, 'sensational sentences' in the form proposed by Leeds and Rey involve only 'atomic'[3] experiences, such as a particular colour experienced at a specific location in the visual field. Complex visual experiences would then presumably require instantiation of correspondingly complex sentences consisting of massive conjunctions of 'atomic' sentences. In effect, such LOT sentences would encode visual experiences in somewhat the same fashion as digitized images are stored in a computer memory, i.e. using a form of mental quasi-pixelization, and the specification of each quasi-pixel's qualitative properties. Thus it appears that what Lycan refers to as a semantically primitive lexeme or mental word in the LOT others view as a highly complex sentence. Since the LOT as originally proposed by Fodor (1975) gets its productivity and systematicity from the combinatorial power derived by operating with atomic symbols possessing simple syntactic and semantic properties, it seems that Lycan's lexemes don't qualify as basic LOT units. But this is only a terminological issue; what is important is that if higher-order percepts are assumed to be represented by LOT sentences then the difference between HOT and HOP theories vanishes and we are free to identify CSTM as the locus of the higher-order state for both types of theory.

The imagistic dimension in cognition

Notwithstanding Lycan's position, there are no *a priori* reasons requiring HOP theorists to accept that operations in higher-order

---

[3] Leeds (1993, p. 324) suggested that the atomic sentences as here defined would need to be conjunctions of even more primitive sentences that specify features such as colour relationships, as specified in the so-called colour solid, and presumably also a depth-of-field parameter.

mental states are restricted to syntactic operations on symbolic representations (i.e. concepts). Although the LOT hypothesis deals exclusively with the cognitive aspects of mind, this doesn't mean that cognitive and sensory (analogical) representations cannot interact. On the contrary, they are intimately linked. Incoming sensory information is automatically cognized (at least up to a point) and, conversely, mental images can be generated from cognitive specifications. Even completely novel images (e.g. Adolph Hitler in a ballet costume) can easily be conjured upon cognitive command. There are in fact ample grounds for believing that cognition has an imagistic dimension, with evidence coming from the work of, *inter alia*, Paivio (summarized in Paivio, 1991), Kosslyn (summarized in Kosslyn, 1994), Baddeley (summarized in Baddeley, 2003), and Potter (Potter *et al.*, 2004).

Paivio proposed a dual coding theory involving two parallel and interconnected memory encoding systems, one verbal and the other imagistic. The two systems contribute additively to memorization, so that, for instance, concrete words, which tend to evoke images, are more easily remembered than abstract words, which don't. Similarly with pictures that are easily labelled or described as opposed to those that are not. Dual coding of memories is supported by much empirical evidence pointing to the existence of a purely imagistic component.

Kosslyn's extensive studies involving the manipulation of mental images led him to conclude that they require an inherently geometric medium of representation. He proposed that mental images are 'ordered up' by higher centres from information stored in a format he calls 'deep representations', which is neither depictive nor propositional. When recalled, this information travels backward toward the early parts of the visual cortex (which Kosslyn terms the visual buffer), where a pattern of activation is created which is subsequently processed by the brain as though it was incoming visual information. Kosslyn suggests that since the geometric properties of the primary cortices will inhere in the patterns in the visual buffer, they will also obtain in the resulting mental image. Presumably the geometric properties in question are topological rather than metrical, since metrical properties are not fundamental to neural networks (which can in principle be physically distorted without affecting their functioning).

Further evidence for the existence of an imagistic dimension to cognition comes from the work of Baddeley (2003), who developed a model of working memory containing a visuospatial sketchpad and a phonological loop connected to a central executive, and from Potter and her collaborators (2004), who demonstrated the existence of a pictorial short-term memory with a span of 2–3 sec.

But the question of the nature of the representations underlying mental images and imagistic memories is very disputatious. On one side are the depictionists, who defend the view that these representations have an analogic, depictive component; on the other side are the descriptionists, led by Pylyshyn (Pylyshyn, 1981), who insist that images are propositionally encoded (in the LOT, needless to say). Geometry is then not explicitly represented, just as a digitally encoded image is not geometrically represented in the computer's memory. This dispute has now festered for almost a quarter of a century, with no resolution in sight (Pylyshyn, 2003; Kosslyn, 2005), and it will not be settled here. But does it have any bearing on HOP theory? If the descriptionists are right, this would accord with the preliminary conclusion reached at the end of the previous section, namely that in both HOT and HOP theory the higher-order state is propositionally encoded in the LOT. But would HOP theory be distinguishable from HOT theory should the depictionists prevail? One possibility is to regard HOP as HOT supplemented with links to non-cognitive representations such as Kosslyn's 'deep representations'. However, both long- and short-term imagistic memories are very sketchy (although this may be less true in the case of the rare individuals gifted with an eidetic memory), and so are incapable of fully representing the contents of lower-order states. For instance, Baddeley (2003) acknowledges that visual working memory has only a very limited capacity, typically for about three or four objects. Likewise with long-term imagistic memories which, although usually possessing ample content for recognitional purposes, lack the fine details needed for veridically recreating chromatic details. Moreover it seems unclear that memories, whose function is information storage for future recall, can be regarded as suitable agents for real-time monitoring of first-order states for consciousness-rendering purposes. So we conclude that while at a stretch it may be possible in principle to differentiate HOP theory from HOT theory on this basis, HOP theory still inherits most of the criticisms levelled at pure HOT theory, and furthermore is vulnerable to the charge that degraded, purely analogical memories are implausible facilitators for on-line monitoring.

Discussion

During perception the brain snatches potentially useful information, on the fly, from a chaotic torrent of sensory inputs. The perceptual process may be viewed as a pyramid in which incoming analogical signals enter at the base and information flows upwards in ever-decreasing volume towards a decision-making executive at the apex able to cope with only a limited amount of synchronous information. Various specialized modules, whose outputs are sent to cognitive modules in the anterior cortex, process signals received from the primary cortices. The outputs of these intermediate-level regions indicate the presence of significant features in the visual field, such as objects, motion, salient colours, and statistical and other general properties within segmented regions. At this point there are signs that the limits of parallelism are being stretched and that information about only the most significant features is extracted and transmitted on (Rousselet *et al.*, 2004). Indeed, the function of the early cortices is not to forward the complete inventory of incoming information to the cognitive centres but rather to abstract for decision-making purposes an abridged précis, in a cognitive (conceptual) form, of the organism's environmental situation. This raises a knotty issue for higher-order theories, since it implies that only a tiny fraction of the information contained in first-order states actually reaches the higher-order states. Given the radical transformation, content reduction and abstraction of incoming sensory information on its journey to the cognitive areas, it seems fair to ask HOR theorists to define more explicitly exactly what they understand by higher-order monitoring of lower-order states.

If higher-order brain states are informationally impoverished, how is it that we appear to be able to experience chromatically rich percepts? One possibility open to actualist HOT theorists to explain away the feeling of chromatic richness is to invoke ensemble concepts. To illustrate, suppose an observer is briefly exposed to an image of a tree in leaf. Then the following collection of ordinary and ensemble concepts, all relating to a specific region of the visual field, might be activated simultaneously within the subject's CSTM and subsequently be retained in a gist (i.e. this information would be memorized): GREEN$_{11}$; GREENS; BROWN$_{15}$; BROWNS; TREE; NUMEROUS EDGES AT VARIOUS ANGLES; BRANCHES; TWIGS; LEAVES. Colour words with a numerical subscript denote a specific, salient hue. Colour terms in the plural are ensemble concepts signalling the presence of potpourris of related shades chromatically clustered around the dominant (i.e. subscripted) colour, and contained within a naturally segmented region of the visual field (e.g. the foliage on a specific branch). The subject would then be able to report having experienced certain salient colours, but that these were dappled with numerous related shades (although of course unable to specify them individually). The last four items are also examples of ensemble concepts, as indicated by their plural form. They signify to the perceiver (i.e. the self) that an unspecified number of leaves were seen, as well as branches and twigs oriented at various angles; although many of these items may individually have been briefly unconsciously cognized simultaneously in CSTM, they were too numerous and/or insufficiently salient to be memorized in the ensuing gist. Other regions of the visual field that segment naturally would also be categorized analogously. In this economical manner a higher-order belief could be engendered that numerous details about the tree as well as countless chromatically distinct areas had been experienced. This raises an interesting question for HOR theorists, to wit, should activated ensemble concepts qualify in their own right as causal agents of consciousness-raising? A concept such as GREEN clearly qualifies as a phenomenal belief and is eligible under HOR theories to 'conscify' the corresponding bit of the first-order state. But does an assertoric thought such as 'I'm experiencing a variegated green' also qualify as an occurrent phenomenal belief? It is a phenomenal belief of sorts, since it is informative about the corresponding phenomenal experience. The subject will believe (correctly) that she is perceiving a variety of intermingled greens within a patch of her visual field, although unable to describe details. It should be noted that some philosophers *identify* qualia with their associated phenomenal beliefs. For instance, to quote Leeds (1993, p. 317):

> . . . we will have no reason to distinguish between having a (conscious) impression and having a phenomenal belief: impressions are needed, if at all, to make phenomenal beliefs true, but the event of having the phenomenal belief already does that. So impressions are beliefs. (More carefully: the having of an impression is the having of a belief; I shall often use the looser formulation.)

If so, the 'impression' (quale) will have an indefinite chromatic content (although constrained to being predominantly green), since a virtual infinity of stimuli could instigate the phenomenal belief 'I'm experiencing a variegated green'. So the question arises: is the corresponding quale veridical (i.e. does it contain and truly represent all the greens actually present within a certain region of the stimulus and veridically represented in a primary mental state, say in cortical region V1), or is it partly fictitious (i.e. an indefinitely mottled green, a sort of half-truth that nevertheless contains enough information for practical purposes)? The first alternative means that the quale faithfully represents *all* of the chromatic information in the first-order state, although the latter was tracked by a higher-order state in which only a single dominant colour was represented, plus some abstract knowledge about the textural and statistical properties of the area in question. The second alternative implies that the contents of complex qualia are grossly under-specified with respect to the information represented in both the corresponding first-order state and in the stimulus. It is tempting to believe that this loss of information is akin to blurring, but this won't do because a brief presentation of an image of a tree would induce a belief that fine chromatic details were experienced, not that a blurred percept was experienced. It is as though a fictitious detailed filling-in occurred, something that in fact does happen during mental imaging of chromatically complex objects (fictitious because the brain can't provide information too detailed to have been memorized). I leave it to HOT theorists to decide which of these alternatives, if either, to endorse. This dilemma doesn't arise with dispositionalist HOT theory because in that theory qualia are unambiguously deemed to be accurate representations of the content of the (first-order) C-buffer while at the same time the higher-order state is not required to fully represent all this information. But it should be pointed out that ensemble concepts furnish an alternative mechanism, one not relying on the dispositionality hypothesis, for enabling higher-order brain states to track information-rich first-order states without having to accommodate the latter's detailed contents.

Conclusions

HOT theories face severe difficulties in explaining how higher-order, purely conceptual representations of complex visual percepts are feasible. At best, only a limited number of particulars plus some generalities seem capturable in higher-order form, the latter through the device of ensemble concepts. Conceptual short-term memory was identified as the most plausible locus for higher-order conceptual representations of perceptual events, but it seems geared to the identification and representation of objects and salient features. This creates a challenge for HOT theory inasmuch as while there is no evidence that chromatic details are monitored individually in CSTM we nevertheless appear able to experience chromatically profuse percepts. Other difficulties include the problem of conceptual specification of arbitrary colours and the binding problem. One final problem is that HOP theory demands that every conscious thought (including involuntary ones such as phenomenal judgments and object identifications that accompany perception in some profusion) must be monitored unconsciously at a higher-order level. But thoughts are by nature cognitive and hence their neural substrates are located outside the primary cortical areas. So in this case the neural substrates of both orders of thought must be located in the brain's cognitive regions, yet there is no scientific evidence that I am aware of for the existence of such a hierarchy. The Achilles heel of HOP theory is the inability of its defenders to explain exactly how non-conceptual higher-order tracking is realized in the brain (unless they deem relatively degraded pictorial and auditory memories to be acceptable realizers for this role), given that the entire perceptual process seems designed to conceptualize incoming information for decision-making purposes. Perhaps this difficulty is implicitly recognized by some proponents of HOP, since the quotation from Lycan cited earlier seems to imply that at bottom HOP is a form of HOT theory, although other proponents of HOP may disagree.

References

Ariely, D. (2001), 'Seeing sets: Representation by statistical properties', *Psychological Science*, **12**, pp. 157–62.

Aydede, M. (2004), 'The language of thought hypothesis', *Stanford Encyclopedia of Philosophy* (http://plato.stanford.edu/entries/language-thought/).

Baddeley, A. (2003), 'Working memory: Looking back and looking forward', *Nature Reviews Neuroscience*, **4**, pp. 829–39.

Beeckmans, J.M. (2001), 'Generation of gists of abstract patterns', *Cognitive Sciences Eprint Archive* (http://cogprints.org/1173/).

Beeckmans, J.M. (2004), 'Chromatically rich phenomenal percepts', *Philosophical Psychology*, **17**, pp. 27–44.

Block, N. (2001), 'Paradox and cross-purposes in recent work on consciousness', *Cognition*, **79**, pp. 197–219.

Byrne, A. (1997), 'Some like it HOT: Consciousness and higher-order thought', *Philosophical Studies*, **86**, pp. 103–29.

Carruthers, P. (2000), *Phenomenal Consciousness: A Naturalistic Theory* (Cambridge: Cambridge University Press).

Chong, S.C. & Treisman, A. (2005), 'Statistical processing: Computing the average size in perceptual groups', *Vision Research*, **45**, pp. 891–900.

Fabre-Thorpe, M., Richard, G. & Thorpe, S.J. (1998), 'Rapid categorization of images by rhesus monkeys', *NeuroReport*, **9**, pp. 303–8.

Fodor, J.A. (1975), *The Language of Thought* (Cambridge, MA: Harvard University Press).

Gennaro, R.J. (1996), *Consciousness and Self-Consciousness* (Amsterdam/Philadelphia: John Benjamins).

Gennaro, R.J. (2006), 'Between pure self-referentialism and the (extrinsic) HOT theory of consciousness', in *Self-Representational Approaches to Consciousness*, ed. U. Kriegel & K. Williford (Cambridge, MA: MIT Press).

Güzeldere, G. (1995), 'Is consciousness the perception of what passes in one's own mind?', in *Conscious Experience*, ed. T. Metzinger (Paderborn: Imprint Academic/Schöningh).

Harman, G. (1965), 'The inference to the best explanation', *Philosophical Review*, **74**, pp. 88–95.

Intraub, H. (1981), 'Rapid conceptual identification of sequentially presented pictures', *Journal of Experimental Psychology: Human Perception and Performance*, **7**, pp. 604–10.

Kirchner, H. & Thorpe, S.J. (2006), 'Ultra-rapid detection with saccadic eye movements: Visual processing speed revisited', *Vision Research*, **46**, pp. 1762–76.

Kosslyn, S.M. (1994), *Image and Brain: The Resolution of the Imagery Debate* (Cambridge, MA: MIT Press).

Kosslyn, S.M. (2005), 'Mental images and the brain', *Cognitive Neuropsychology*, **22**, pp. 333–47.

Kriegel, U. (2003), 'Consciousness, higher-order content, and the individuation of vehicles', *Synthese*, **134**, pp. 477–504.

Leeds, S. (1993), 'Qualia, awareness, Sellars', *Noûs*, **27**, pp. 303–30.

Leeds, S. (2002), 'Perception, transparency, and the language of thought', *Noûs*, **36**, pp. 104–29.

Luck, S.J. & Vogel, E.K. (1997), 'The capacity of visual working memory for features and conjunctions', *Nature*, **390**, pp. 279–81.

Lycan, W.G. (1987), *Consciousness* (Cambridge, MA: MIT Press).

Lycan, W.G. (1996), *Consciousness and Experience* (Cambridge, MA: MIT Press).

Lycan, W.G. (2004), 'The superiority of HOP to HOT', in *Higher-Order Theories of Consciousness: An Anthology*, ed. R.J. Gennaro (Amsterdam/Philadelphia: John Benjamins), pp. 93–114.

Mack, A. & Rock, I. (1998), *Inattentional Blindness* (Cambridge, MA: MIT Press).

Paivio, A. (1991), *Images in Mind* (Hemel Hempstead: Harvester Wheatsheaf).

Potter, M.C. (1975), 'Meaning in visual search', *Science*, **187**, pp. 965–6.

Potter, M.C. (1976), 'Short-term conceptual memory for pictures', *Journal of Experimental Psychology: Human Learning and Memory*, **2**, pp. 509–21.

Potter, M.C. (1993), 'Very short-term conceptual memory', *Memory & Cognition*, **21**, pp. 156–61.

Potter, M.C. (1999), 'Understanding sentences and scenes: The role of conceptual short-term memory', in *Fleeting Memories*, ed. V. Coltheart (Cambridge, MA: MIT Press), pp. 13–46.

Potter, M.C., Staub, A. & O'Connor, D.H. (2004), 'Pictorial and conceptual representation of glimpsed pictures', *Journal of Experimental Psychology: Human Perception and Performance*, **30**, pp. 478–89.

Pylyshyn, Z.W. (1981), 'The imagery debate: Analog media versus tacit knowledge', *Psychological Reviews*, **88**, pp. 16–45.

Pylyshyn, Z.W. (2003), 'Return of the mental image: Are there really pictures in the brain?', *Trends in Cognitive Sciences*, **7**, pp. 113–18.

Renninger, L.W. & Malik, J. (2004), 'When is scene identification just texture recognition?', *Vision Research*, **44**, pp. 2301–11.

Rey, G. (1997), *Contemporary Philosophy of Mind* (Cambridge, MA: Blackwell Publishers).

Rolls, E.T. (2004), 'A higher-order syntactic thought (HOST) theory of consciousness', in *Higher-Order Theories of Consciousness: An Anthology*, ed. R.J. Gennaro (Amsterdam/Philadelphia: John Benjamins), pp. 137–72.

Rosenthal, D.M. (1986), 'Two concepts of consciousness', *Philosophical Studies*, **49**, pp. 329–59.

Rosenthal, D.M. (2000), 'Consciousness, content, and metacognitive judgments', *Consciousness and Cognition*, **9**, pp. 203–14.

Rosenthal, D.M. (2005), *Consciousness and Mind* (Oxford: Oxford University Press).

Rousselet, G.A., Joubert, O.R. & Fabre-Thorpe, M. (2005), 'How long to get the "gist" of real-world natural scenes?', *Visual Cognition*, **12**, pp. 852–77.

Rousselet, G.A., Thorpe, S.J. & Fabre-Thorpe, M. (2004), 'Processing of one, two, or four natural scenes in humans: The limits of parallelism', *Vision Research*, **44**, pp. 877–94.

Sperling, G. (1960), 'The information available in brief visual presentations', *Psychological Monographs*, **74**, pp. 1–29.

Thorpe, S.J., Fize, D. & Marlot, C. (1996), 'Speed of processing in the human visual system', *Nature*, **381**, pp. 520–2.

Van Gulick, R. (2000), 'Inward and upward: Reflections, introspection and self-awareness', *Philosophical Topics*, **28**, pp. 275–305.

VanRullen, R. & Thorpe, S.J. (2001), 'The time course of visual processing: From early perception to decision-making', *J. of Cognitive Neuroscience*, **13**, pp. 454–65.

VanRullen, R., Reddy, L. & Koch, C. (2004), 'Visual search and dual tasks reveal two distinct attentional resources', *J. of Cognitive Neuroscience*, **16**, pp. 4–14.

Vinueza, A. (2000), 'Sensations and the language of thought', *Philosophical Psychology*, **13**, pp. 373–92.

Watamaniuk, S.N.J. & Duchon, A. (1992), 'The human visual system averages speed information', *Vision Research*, **32**, pp. 931–41.

Watamaniuk, S.N.J., Sekuler, R. & Williams, D.W. (1989), 'Direction perception in complex dynamic displays: The integration of direction information', *Vision Research*, **29**, pp. 47–59.

Zeki, S. (1983), 'Cerebral akinetopsia (cerebral visual motion blindness)', *Brain*, **114**, pp. 811–24.

Georges Rey

Phenomenal Content and the Richness and Determinacy of Colour Experience[1]

In a seminal article that has shaped much discussion in the philosophy of mind for the last twenty years, Joseph Levine (1983) called attention to a serious 'explanatory gap' that persists between physical explanation and the 'qualia' of our conscious, phenomenal experience. In a number of earlier pieces I have tried to develop a strategy for accounting for this gap that combines a narrow representationalist account of phenomenal *experience* with a projectivist, eliminativist (or 'fictionalist') account of those *qualia*.[2] Roughly, the view is that our phenomenal experience consists in our standing in a specific causal/computational relation to specially restricted 'sensational' sentences and/or predicates or other representations that are the outputs of sensory modules. The stability of this relation, and the associated stability of our idiosyncratic representations of ourselves and our conspecifics (and of things that look and act like them), leads us to

[1]   Previous versions of some of this material were delivered at a conference on subjectivity
      in Dubrovnik, August 2003, and at a symposium on Joseph Levine's *Purple Haze* at the
      Pacific APA, March 2004. I'm grateful to audiences there, but especially to Levine, both
      then and over many years, for extended discussions of the issue, and to Cynthia Haggard
      for forcing me to clarify some distinctions.
[2]   See Rey, 1988/96; 1992; 1995; 1998; 2004; I provide a summary of the view in Rey
      (1997), as well as more briefly below (§1). I emphasize that I regard it as a 'strategy', not
      anything like an adequate theory, since, as I will discuss below, there is (to put it mildly) a
      great deal about the view that still needs to be spelt out — here, as of course in the rest of
      psychology. Note that for purposes of this paper I will follow Levine in describing my
      view as 'fictionalist', though to avoid the association with deliberate *fiction*, I prefer
      'eliminativist'.

project phenomena, 'qualia', corresponding to these predicates, but there is no non-tendentious evidence for their actual existence: they play no causal/explanatory role in any true account of either ourselves or other people. Consequently there is no reason to believe they exist; indeed, there is good reason to do without them. I thereby join a number of other philosophers (e.g. Loar, 1990/2002; Tye, 1995; Lycan, 1996) in thinking that the explanatory gap is therefore not a metaphysical gap in *the world*, but, rather, a certain sort of epistemic gap between physical and phenomenal *concepts* (and/or non-conceptual contents; the distinction won't be significant for purposes here). I differ from these other philosophers in the details about how those concepts should be understood. Unlike Lycan and Tye, I think their content needs to be construed relatively narrowly;[3] unlike Loar, I think the internal representations need to have a more substantial 'projected' content than his mere 'recognitional concepts' seem to me to possess; and, unlike nearly everyone else,[4] I think there are no actual phenomena corresponding to these contents.

Levine (2001, hereafter '*Haze*') has responded at length to my proposal, setting it out with admirable clarity and raising an important problem for it that deserves extended discussion. In this paper, I want to distinguish this right problem from what seems to me to be Levine's erroneous diagnosis of it. In §1 of what follows I briefly summarize my view (§1.1) and some arguments on its behalf (§1.2). One of my more controversial arguments involves my requirement for non-tendentious data (§1.3), Levine's rejection of which seems to me to be based on a conflation of properties with contents (§1.4). I argue that, as 'irresistible' as Levine finds the postulation of qualia properties, he is not entitled to such a highly theoretical claim on the basis of his introspectible experience alone. Moreover, I argue, the qualia properties do no real work for him, nor for other 'qualiaphiles' like Chalmers (1996), who

[3]   Lycan and Tye join many others, e.g. Dretske (1988), Millikan (2000) and Fodor (1990), in presuming what I call 'Strong Externalisms' according to which the contents of primitive terms are 'wide', constituted by genuine phenomena in the external world to which they are in various ways causally related. In Rey (2005b; 2006) I argue against such views, provisionally endorsing only a 'weak externalism': *some* contents of *some* psychological states depend in *some way or other* upon *some* phenomena external to an agent's brain. A moment's reflection shows that it is only this weaker view that the stock (e.g. twin earth) examples for externalism support: the rest is speculative and, I think, pretty dubious theory. My defence (Rey, 1998) of the 'narrow' content of sensational sentences (and my use of 'narrow' throughout the present discussion) should be read as allowing for this weaker view, and consequently is only of 'relatively' (or 'weakly'?) narrow content.

[4]   Except radical eliminativists such as Quine (1960, p. 264) and Dennett (1988/2002; 1991; 1995). Since they are eliminativist (or, anyway, instrumentalist) about the *whole* of mental ascription, and 'superficialist' about its evidence, their denial of qualia differs from mine in a number of ways (see Rey, 1994; 1995; 1997 and §1.3 below).

insist upon them in even more ontologically rich ways. As Wittgenstein (1953/68, §271) put it, they are 'wheels that turn but nothing turns with them'. What does do the work are our *representations* of these properties, with their intentional content, work that in general can be performed without there being in fact any actual properties represented.

But Levine doesn't rest his belief in qualia on ontological appearances alone. He also claims that the specific intentional contents of experience can't in fact be explained without reference to actual qualia, an issue to which I turn in §2. He provides two arguments. The first is an argument about the semantics of identity statements generally that rests on an externalist theory of content that seems to me rash (§2.1). The second is an argument about how specifically the 'rich and determinate' content of experiences of colour can't be had by representations alone, but require real qualia (§2.2). Now, I think he is importantly right to call attention to this richness and determinacy, especially of colour experience, and how it is a problem for my view. I think he is mistaken in supposing that it is the *qualia themselves* that provide the solution to this problem, by serving, themselves, as their own mode of presentation (§2.3). I consider a proposal of Papineau (2002) and Balog (ms.) in this regard that assimilates phenomenal to quotation concepts. The proposal seems to me both phenomenologically dubious — one frequently entertains phenomenal concepts, mercifully without having the associated experience — and theoretically problematic: unlike the case of quotation, we have no idea how even a (facsimile of a) quale instanced in its own representation could be *read*. Indeed, as Levine himself acknowledges, we not only have no account of how qualia properties themselves could properly serve as the content of internal representations, we have no good account of phenomenal content at all.

But if we have no account of phenomenal content, then, there is no reason for Levine to insist that any account will require the postulation of qualia. I conclude (§3) that, while the problem of understanding the content of particularly the rich and determinate colour experience is a problem for my view, it is in fact a problem for *any* view, computationalist, physicalist or dualist alike. The further *ontology* is of no use, whatever it may be. What is needed is a better psychology of phenomenal content. Despite what seems to be their immediate availability — and even how much vision theory can already tell us about them — there is something about the content of our own colour experiences that seems peculiarly difficult to capture in any theoretically satisfying way.

1. Summary of 'Sensational Sentences'

1.1. CRTQ

My treatment of qualitative experience tries to locate it within the framework of a causal-computational theory of thought (CRTT),* for which I believe there is considerable independent evidence. Let me emphasize, however, that I view CRTT not so much as a serious 'theory', but as a promising research programme, within which, however, quite independently of qualitative experience, there are plenty of serious explanatory gaps. As Fodor (1983, 2000) has argued for some time, although CRTT may well be *necessary* for a theory of thought, no one yet has a serious idea about how it actually explains such basic processes as ordinary abductions and confirmation. Moreover, as Levine (1987), himself, has rightly pointed out, Quine's argument for the indeterminacy of translation is simply a way of raising an explanatory gap for intentionality, quite apart from consciousness. Despite all this, I still think Fodor (1975) is right in claiming that CRTT is 'the only president we've got'.

My proposal within the framework of CRTT is to treat qualitative experiences as involving causal-computational relations to specially restricted representations, the specialness of the representations consisting in, *inter alia*, their serving only as the output of sensory modules. They don't freely combine, as other predicates standardly do, into logical complexes other than perhaps conjunctions — in this way they are 'non-conceptual' representations expressing the same content as unrestricted, conceptual ones like 'looks red'. Moreover, unlike unrestricted ones, they can't be entokened in describing the states of other people, just as (the internal equivalent of) 'I' can't be used for that purpose either. The best we can do is to infer that other people themselves have such predicates, and consequently the subjectivity and experiences to which these restricted representations give rise. The narrow content of representations is determined by features of this special role, which provides the content of our sensory experience, analogously to the way that the role of a first-person indexical

---

* An explanation of the origin of these acronyms is in order. 'CRTT' is the acronym I've used in a quite a few places over the last fifteen years or so, originally for 'Computational Representation Theory of Thought'. More recently, I've come to realize the importance of the causal aspect of the account, and how the computational aspect is just a special case, in which certain rational processes can be causally realized. Indeed, I surely wasn't committed, e.g., to blushing being a computational process! So I've taken to adding the 'causal' prefix, but it seems too confusing to change the standing acronym. *Mutatis mutandis* for 'CRTQ'.

provides the similarly narrow content of our first-person ('I') thoughts. The difference between the colour-sighted and a colour-blind person unaware of his lack is that the former can express the proposition [It looks red] using (what we can indicate in English by the pseudo-sentence:) 'It's R-ing', whereas the latter has to use some other device, e.g. 'It's F-ing', which might encode merely reflectances.

Sensational sentences also have something like a wide content — at any rate, a content that would be genuinely external were it real — but this wide content is a mistaken projection of their narrow content, a positing of peculiar 'qualia' properties separate from the corresponding secondary properties, rather in the way, again, that the peculiar content of 'I' thoughts often leads to a projection of 'souls' separate from bodies. This sort of projection *needn't* be mistaken — I see no reason to regard our ordinary projections of material objects from our sensory evidence as seriously mistaken. But, unlike the case of material objects, I see no non-tendentious reasons for believing in qualia. Indeed, their postulation seems as peculiar and otiose as Hume and Parfit have found the postulation of a soul.

Note that I diverge from other 'representationalists' who claim that experience represents, 'transparently', *only* the external secondary properties, such as colours, themselves. I agree with Levine (*Haze*, p. 179 n. 5) that experience also can represent 'phenomenal' properties (think of them as what Jackson's (1982) 'Mary' might notice about *herself* when she first sees something red; I follow Levine in using the '-ish' suffix to indicate such properties). It's just that, unlike Levine and other *non*-representationalists, I think we have no reason to believe that these projected, phenomenal properties actually exist — nor, for that matter, the projected external, secondary properties either. Both secondary and phenomenal properties are mere 'intentional properties', just as the soul is a mere 'intentional object'.[5]

---

[5] By which I don't mean that they must be reckoned in one's ultimate ontology. While they are often the 'objects' of our thoughts, *pace* Brentano and Meinong, purely intentional objects don't exist, nowhere, nohow (cf. Cartwright, 1960/87). Talk of them seems to me best regarded as simply an odd 'projected' way we have of talking about intentional content: thus, x thinks about *Zeus* is just a way of saying that x has a thought with the content [Zeus] (I refer to contents by placing phrases that express them in brackets.) Note that [Zeus] is not the same as *Zeus*, since the latter, but not the former, is supposed to have, e.g. a beard. In Rey (2006) I argue that talk of intentional inexistents pervades cognitive science, e.g. in theories of vision and phonology.

1.2. Brief arguments for CRTQ

Why believe such a (even to my mind!) peculiar view? My main reasons are, very briefly, the following (see the references in fn. 2, above, for a fuller discussion).

1. It offers a clear way to integrate qualitative experience into an independently motivated and promising research programme.
2. It allows a consistent treatment of the apparent qualities of experience with the more obviously representational aspects of, e.g. pains, itches and visual qualia seeming to have 'location' and variable intensities.
3. It avoids the needless and problematic metaphysics and epistemology of real 'qualia'. Just what sort of physical properties are they? How do they interact with the brain? How come no one else can enjoy my reddish experiences by inspecting my brain?
4. It explains the 'subjectivity' of the first-person by the restrictions on the relevant predicates, which cannot be used for the states of others any more than a first-person indexical can be. Each person would have available to them representations that only they can enjoy when they are receiving the output of certain perceptual modules, which they presumably self-ascribe using a first-person indexical, thus achieving a specific first-person perspective on the world.
5. It avoids unwanted possibilities of these special properties being detached from the rest one's cognitive structure, as in the case of zombies, arbitrarily divergent qualia, or of some 'anaesthetic' that severed the connection between qualia and cognition.
6. It explains what seems to me the important problem in this area, what I call 'the mind/body problem problem', which is why there is a mind/body problem at all (why aren't we happy scientists, taking psychophysical hypotheses in our stride, as we do the discovery that glass is a liquid?). For example, it avoids Levine's problem of 'gappy identities' (*Haze*, §3.6), since no such identities are being claimed about the projected qualia themselves. What we have instead are identifications of *experiences* of some qualia, x, with some computational processes that have the content [x], which in turn can be identified with physical states of the brain in the way that states in a computer can be identified with physical states in it.[6]

---

[6] Some gappiness may still attach to these identities, given the gaps that arguably attach to CRTT. These may be substantial: unlike Chalmers (1996), and despite widespread

1.3. Non-tendentious data

Another of the arguments I provided for my position is that the qualiaphile can provide no non-tendentious, or non-question-begging reasons for believing in qualia. Typically, all the qualiaphile does is insist that he just knows 'immediately' that he has qualia. Of course, he might also try appealing to various bits of behaviour and perhaps cranial phenomena on their behalf: wincing in the case of pain, scratching in the case of an itch, idiosyncratic activity in the visual cortex in the case of visual qualia. But all such evidence seems to me better explained merely by appeal to *representations* of qualia than by the notoriously problematic qualia themselves. Thus, on my account, someone winces because they have a sensational representation with the content [pain], and scratches because of such a representation with the content [itch], and even her introspections and reports about these sensations — about how 'ineffable', 'categorical', entirely 'private' they seem — can be explained by those self-same representations. Rejecting this account on the basis of introspective claims that one is 'directly aware' of the qualia over and above processing the representations simply begs the question.[7]

Indeed — and this is my main reason for believing the view — were qualia to be posited independently of one's representations of them, we would be faced not only with the usual 'problem of other minds', wondering whether anyone else had them, but with even more worrisome first-person doubts: it would seem nomologically possible to be clearly and unhesitatingly convinced one was in excruciating pain, as a result of representing oneself to be so in the above restricted ways, and yet still fail in fact to be — perhaps many of us would turn out to have the real qualia only half the time: only your physicalist or dualistic neurosurgeons would know for sure![8] This possibility strikes me as pointless and personally intolerable: having all the intentional

---

optimism among many, I think intentionality continues to be a really 'hard' problem. But it seems to be a very different one from the one that concerns Levine here, and one informed by more ample non-tendentious reasons to take it seriously.

[7]   I hasten to point out that this situation with regard to qualia is dramatically different from that of positing intentional states themselves (as Levine notes, *Haze*, pp. 143–4). *Pace* Quine and the Churchlands, these *are* needed to explain a wide variety of phenomena that can be specified independently of a theory of mind (my favourite examples are jokes: how could one hope to explain regularities in people laughing at jokes without adverting at least sometimes to their content?).

[8]   In Rey (1995) I argue that this is this most profitable way to read the notorious passages of Wittgenstein (1953/68, §§240–308), which he (to my mind) needlessly burdens with his dubious argument against a 'private language'. Note that, so understood, the issue here is not merely *epistemic*, concerning how we *know* we're in pain, but *metaphysical*, concerning

attitudes of someone in pain — noticing it, hating it — is surely every bit as bad as being in pain. As Levine observes, 'If qualia, or the qualitative characters of conscious experiences, entered the game only as theoretical posits, then of course they would be more trouble than they're worth' (*Haze*, p. 133).

Levine thus aims 'to challenge the status of theoretical posit to which conscious experience is relegated, instead treating it as a basic datum that itself requires explanation' (*Haze*, p. 133). He supports this by a criticism of what would superficially appear to be a view similar to mine advocated by Daniel Dennett (1988/2002, 1991), whereby the 'theory of consciousness ought to be constrained by everything we are tempted to say about our experience' (*Haze*, p. 133). Levine claims:

> I maintain, however, that conscious experiences themselves, not merely our verbal judgments about them, are the primary data to which a theory must answer. — (*Haze*, p. 134)

Now I actually agree with Levine about this latter claim. For I agree that, understanding 'judgment' in the ordinary way that Dennett does, it's not enough merely to produce a theory that agrees with our ordinary judgments. There seems to me every reason to think there are phenomena of *really seeming* that exist apart from merely the phenomena of merely *judging* one way or the other (at least as this is ordinarily understood by Dennett); and, moreover (*pace* Dennett) things can seem to seem a certain way, and yet not seem that way at all. For example, as against Dennett's (1991) claims about there being no fact of the matter about whether it's the taste of beer or our preferences for it that have changed since childhood, it seems to me this could be settled by investigation of a person's gustation module, about which his superficial introspective judgments are perhaps hopelessly confused, mistaken or undecided (see Rey, 1994, for discussion). So, on my view, unlike Dennett's, there is a question about the character of experience, one that is not always settled merely by asking people what they think their experience is like.

But, of course, none of this implies that Levine's own characterization of his experience in terms of the experience of *qualia* is correct. It may be true that, contrary to Dennett, there's a distinction to be made between 'judgments' and what we regard as 'conscious experience', and perhaps we can know *that* without much theory. But to take the presentations of experience as *veridical*, as about genuine properties, is not something experience alone can decide. The dispute between

---

the possibility of having all the attitudes with the content [pain], but not the pain experience itself.

representationalists and qualia realists is a fairly abstract *theoretical* dispute, which it's hard to see how introspection alone could settle — as Brian Loar (1990/2002, p. 308) notes, 'there is no introspective guarantee of *anything* beyond mere appearance'. But to see the specific issue here, we need to be perhaps a little clearer than the literature generally is about the distinction between properties and intentional contents.

1.4. Properties vs. contents

Expressions such as 'experience of' (like 'concept of' and 'representation of') are *intentional*, in the 'logical' sense that someone can have an experience of something, x, even though x doesn't exist. Thus one can have an experience of a hallucinated dagger without there being a dagger: the experience simply has [dagger] as its *intentional content*, which specifies what the experience is 'about', especially in cases in which the thing it is about doesn't exist (see fn. 5, above). Thus, it's at least logically possible that there are experiences (and concepts and representations) of qualia without there being any qualia.

This latter claim can be obscured by an unfortunate, widespread tendency in philosophy to not distinguish talk of intentional content from talk of *properties*. Particularly for purposes here, it's important to resist what I call *property profligacy*, which simply presumes without argument that there is a property for every predicate. Ontological postulations have to earn their explanatory keep, and I see no explanatory purpose served by supposing that, e.g., there actually are properties in the world corresponding to perfectly meaningful predicates like 'round square' or 'magical'. Thus there is no contradiction in my supposing that there can be experiences that have qualia as their content, despite there being no actual (or even possible) qualia properties.

Levine, himself, agrees one should not be profligate about properties:

> Realism about a domain means thinking of it as ontologically independent of how we conceive it. It must always be open to claim that though we think of the world as containing such-such properties, in fact it doesn't. — (*Haze*, pp. 11–12)

Nevertheless, he consistently thinks of his experience as disclosing the existence of *phenomenal* properties. For example, when he introduces 'the second important dimension [besides subjectivity] that requires explanation', he refers to it as:

> qualitative character itself: . . . reddish or greenish, painful or pleasurable and the like. From within the subjective viewpoint I am presented with these qualitative features of experience, or 'qualia' as they're

called in the literature . . . In fact, as will emerge in the course of my argument, the explanatory gap between physical properties and qualitative properties is a symptom of the subjectivity of consciousness.

— (*Haze*, p. 7)

Apparently he finds the belief in properties here 'irresistible':

> The temptation to believe that there has to be some genuine distinction in properties corresponding to the representations of reddishness and its physical correlate is cognitively irresistible. — (*Haze*, p. 91)

Indeed, in re-phrasing the problem as one about whether some alien had qualitative experiences, he insists it must be understood in terms of properties:

> I'm not asking whether or not to extend my use of the term 'reddishness' . . . to the alien . . . I want to know whether or not it has this sort of experience, whether or not it instantiates a certain property . . . If one feels there really is a contrast here, as I do, then it seems to commit one to the claim that reddishness is a genuinely independent property.
> — (*Haze*, p. 89; see also p. 91)

Now, I quite agree that whether an alien has a certain qualitative experience is not in general a matter for merely verbal decision. But this doesn't entail that it must be a matter of metaphysically independent properties. For a narrow representationalist, it can be a matter simply of whether the alien is in a state with the same intentional content, whether or not that content picks out a genuine property.[9]

2. Levine's Arguments

In the course of his book, Levine does provide two arguments for thinking that qualitative experience must involve experience of actual qualia properties. The first, made quickly in passing, is a general semantic argument that involves an implicit but, I think, insufficiently critical appeal to a theory of content, which I address in §2.1. The second argument is the one I take to be the more important one, regarding the richness and determinacy of qualitative experience, which I address

---

[9] In conversation, Levine has pointed out to me that in quoting these specific passages here, I am slightly misconstruing the structure of his argument, which, at this point, was simply taking for granted the postulation of qualia properties, postponing discussion of the eliminativist option until later (see *Haze*, pp. 146 ff., discussed in §2.2 below). Fair enough; but I think it is nevertheless worth quoting just how 'irresistible' Levine does find that postulation, especially in view of how widely this lack of resistence is shared in the field.

Note that the eliminativist could, of course, agree that the predicate 'x is an experience with content [y]' itself picks out a genuine (e.g. a CRTT) property. The issue here is whether the content [y] itself picks out a property, such as the 'reddishness' with which Levine is concerned in this passage.

in §2.2. In §2.3 I consider his and others' further claims about the 'substantive content' of phenomenal concepts, but will conclude, with Levine, that we actually haven't any account of how such substantive content would be, or, *pace* Levine, how it would really do any good.

2.1. Rash theories of content

According to Levine's 'semantic' argument, qualia properties are needed to explain the explanatory gappiness of claims that would identify qualia with physical states:

> The point is that an intelligible request for explanation seems to entail a distinction in properties of the one thing we're representing on both sides of the identity sign . . . What other account of conceptual difference is there, except to appeal to distinct ascriptive modes of presentation, which brings with it appeal to distinctive properties?
>
> — (*Haze*, p. 87)

In a footnote to this passage, he does consider the possibility of invoking the concept/property distinction in turn for the 'ascriptive' terms, so that the identity might express the fact that two concepts pick out the same property, but he replies that this 'only pushes the question back to the identity claims involving those properties, so no real progress is made' (*Haze*, p. 188 n. 9).[10]

Levine seems to be presupposing here a certain view about intentional content of identity claims, viz., all modes of presentation must ultimately be explained by reference to different, actual worldly properties. Now, to be sure, the current philosophical world is largely on his side: according to strongly externalist theories of content (see fn. 3, above), there needs to be a property for every primitive predicate we can think. But, aside from semantic desperation, I see no reason to think these theories are true. Indeed, providing we resist property profligacy, there are plenty of (even necessarily) non-referring but perfectly contentful terms and predicates: e.g. 'Zeus', 'angel', 'magic', 'soul', 'phlogiston'.[11] Of course, a strategy for some externalists is to claim that all such empty terms must ultimately be 'analysed' into

---

[10] This is just a development of the 'distinct property model' of identities that Levine discusses from Smart (1959); see *Haze*, p. 47.

[11] Indeed, if recent theories of vision and phonology are to be believed, some of the basic contents deployed by the visual and phonological systems, e.g. [circle], [cone], [consonant] may not apply to anything at all; they may be the result simply of tractable computations in the brain (see Rey, 2006). Note that these strong externalist theories are not entailed by the 'weak externalism' I endorsed in fn 3, above.

terms that do refer.[12] But such a claim, familiar from the empiricists, Russell and the Positivists, has yet to be shown to be plausible, especially in view of the attacks upon it by Quine (1956/76), Kripke (1972) and Fodor (1998). If this is the source of Levine's worries about qualia, it seems to me he would be wiser to hold out for a better theory of content.

A brief methodological aside about such a theory. For reasons that are increasingly obscure to me the more I've thought about it, it seems to have been a presumption of modern philosophy that a theory of content (or meaning) should be relatively easy to come by, say, by mere philosophical reflection. Thus, when Quine (1960, ch. 2) raised his famous conundra about translation, readers thought it was not unreasonable for him to proceed to declare translation (and the whole of mentalistic psychology!) 'indeterminate'.[13] Similarly, philosophers such as Dretske, Millikan and Fodor are prepared to commit themselves to theories of mental content of astounding generality, usually on the basis of relatively few examples, driven, I think, by the fear that, without such a theory, we would not be entitled to insist upon the reality of our minds. Such a presumption and its attendant fears seem to me inappropriate. Although it would be terrific to have a satisfactory theory of content — and much of what these authors say are valuable ideas along the way — there is no special rush: intentional psychology and our mental lives are not holding their breath. They are supported well enough by the vast (again, non-tendentious) evidence of at least some intelligent activity in the world. If the last century has taught us anything, it is that the provision of an adequate theory, either of the mind or of intentionality, is stunningly more difficult than has been supposed. In particular, understanding the nature of concepts is probably at least as difficult as understanding the principles of a Chomskyan grammar (see Rey, 2005b). This, at any rate, seems to me the presumption one should bring to the difficulties of understanding our concepts of the phenomenal.

Returning to Levine's worry, it is, in any event, a mistake to suppose that rich differences between intentional states require genuine worldly properties: two ideas of non-existent properties — say, [magical] and [dephlogistonated] — may occasion enormous differences in

---

[12] Two other strategies are either simply to indulge in property profligacy (as in Fodor, 1990) or to resort to the even more desperate measure of denying that such empty terms have any content at all, as in Millikan, 2000, and Taylor, 2003. I criticize these strategies in Rey, 2005b.

[13] Kim (1993, pp. 194–6) explicitly draws such a conclusion from Davidson's gloss on a Quinean semantics.

the experiences of thinking them. It's not the real, existent objects of our thoughts that explain the differences they make to our experience: it's presumably something about the way we encode or otherwise incorporate them into our mental lives, and once one has specified these different ways then it would seem that any actual properties drop out, at least as a way of internally distinguishing the experiences.[14]

2.2. Richness and determinacy

Levine raises a second, more troublesome argument, specifically against my view that qualia properties should be regarded as having no more reality than magic (for which, he and I agree, there is a concept but no property):

> The fundamental problem I see with treating reddishness like magic derives from the very source of the explanatory gap itself: the determinateness and substantiality of our conception of qualitative content. It is the richness and determinacy of the mode of presentation of my concept of reddishness that causes the problem in the first place, since it is this factor that makes any purported identity with physical or functional properties gappy . . . On Rey's view the difference [between reddish and greenish qualia] has to consist in the difference between the two representations. But I don't see how you can get the representational difference to do the work it has to do without there being a difference in the properties represented . . . — (*Haze*, pp. 146–7)

Richness and determinacy are recurring themes of his discussion from the beginning:

> By saying that the conception is 'determinate,' I mean that reddishness presents itself as a specific quality, identifiable in its own right, not merely by its relation to other qualities. — (*Haze*, p. 8)

He nicely contrasts this richness and determinacy with the 'thinness' of demonstrative concepts, like [this] and [that]:

> I point blindly in front of me and say 'I wonder what that is.' I have no more substantive idea of what I'm pointing at than that it's an object occupying space . . . [W]ith phenomenal concepts, such as our concept of a reddish quale, there is a 'thick' substantive mode of presentation. We are not just labeling some 'we know not what' with the term 'reddish,' but rather we have a fairly determinate conception of what it is for an experience to be reddish. — (*Haze*, pp. 82, 84)

Now, I think Levine is right to press the case that phenomenal concepts are richer and more determinate than mere *demonstrative* ones.

---

[14] I realize that current 'disjunctivists' (e.g. Snowdon, 1980–1; Campbell, 2002) don't share this view, but I'm unpersuaded by their reservations. See Rey (2005a) for discussion.

But the question is how to explain this difference. On my view, part of the character of an experience will be provided by the structure of the sensational sentences themselves: unlike pure demonstratives, the restricted predicates of vision, for example, are presumably parameterized for hue, saturation and tone, as well as relative position in a 2-1/2D retinocentric grid. I also assume that many such predicates also give rise to what I call a certain 'characteristic processing' that is constitutive of having an experience of a specific sort. Thus, sensational representations of an itch at a certain location involve a desire to scratch at that location; of a sour taste, a disposition to pucker; of pitches, associations with different degrees of bodily tension; of pain, serious aversion. It is this further processing that I presume provides the basis for the narrow content that, on my view, distinguishes one kind of experience from another.

Levine (*Haze*, p. 147) notes my recourse here to such processing, but worries that it papers over the problem. After all, at least one of the things that motivates my eliminativist (or fictionalist) view is the difficulty of identifying qualia with physical, functional roles. But, Levine asks:

> If characteristic processing, essentially functional role . . . captures what seems present to us in our experience of reddishness, then why bother with the fictionalism? — (*Haze*, pp. 147–8)

This, however, mistakes my motivation. The fictionalism doesn't serve to identify qualia with some *better* candidate than functional role; rather, as I indicated in §1.2 (6), it serves to explain Levine's own observation of the 'gappiness' of such identifications, i.e. *why we are so reluctant to accept them*. It is because they are an illusory *projection* of simple, categorical properties in an 'inner world' from stabilities in our experience that we are puzzled, and unwilling to identify them with a certain functional role. The *fictionalism* addresses not the *mind/body* problem — what addresses *that* is my *functionalism* (i.e. CRTT); the fictionalism addresses, rather, 'the *mind/body problem* problem': why we resist being simply good scientists and accepting a CRTT account.

However, it would be glib to leave things at that. Although I've suggested some plausible examples of characteristic processing that may begin to capture the content of many conscious experiences, I think Levine is right to worry that I haven't directly addressed how they might capture the content of colour ones. It's one thing to point out that itches are connected to desires to scratch, and pains with serious aversion, quite another to say what distinguishes an experience of red from one of green. Levine doubts that this difference can be captured merely by differences in the representations alone, and I think what's bothering him about my further reliance on 'characteristic processing' is that, at least in the case of colour, it's extremely hard to see what to cite.

I think it's no accident that colour experiences have figured so prominently in the philosophical discussions of qualia, and especially in Levine's discussion of the explanatory gap. Colour experiences do seem to display a richness and determinacy not shared to the same degree by most other experiences. Arbitrary portions of a continuous spectrum of external differences are perceived as dramatically different properties: indeed, there seems to be nothing about red, green, yellow and blue experiences *by themselves* that even suggests they are related on any sort of continuum with one another. Of course, we know this is due at least in part to the particular structure of retinal sensitivity, with its special cells responsive to different ranges of wave-lengths. But how does that fact alone explain just how *dramatic* the differences are? Why shouldn't the differences be as relatively innocuous as the step-wise differences in pitch on a piano? Why the extraordinary display of the rainbow? Why shouldn't the difference between red and green be no more vivid than the distinction between an experience of middle C and G?

What's additionally troublesome about this richness of at least these colour experiences is that they are at the same time peculiarly *passive*. Unlike the itches, tickles, pains, bitter tastes and high pitches that I mentioned above, *they don't seem to involve any constitutive connections with any other states.*[15] At any rate, there don't seem to be any specific associations, responses or desires that seem peculiar to each of the distinctive (un-mixed) colour experiences that would come close to capturing their individual richness, in the way that a desire to scratch comes close to capturing an itch. Doubtless there are further, as yet unknown, constitutive connections with other states of the visual system, and, though it's not hard to imagine these being the source of *some* sort of richness, it's extremely hard to imagine how such connections would explain the *determinate* richness of, e.g., red and green. Of course, there are the connections with *judgment*, e.g. that one is indeed having a colour experience of a certain sort; but, on pain of circularity, those connections alone can't provide the *content*

---

[15] It is this striking richness and passivity of colour experiences, and the serious possibility that colour experiences might be symmetrical in colour space, that gives rise, of course, to the problem of 'inverted qualia', so much more plausible in the case of colours than in that of, say, itches and tickles

of a colour experience (the content of [reddish] can't be specified merely in terms of a disposition to judge that an experience has that very content). If one doubts, as I and many do, the reality of such 'secondary' properties as colours themselves, then one can't rely on the content being supplied externally. So what provides the content of rich, passive experiences like those of colour?

I don't mean to suggest that something like these same problems don't arise for other sensations, many of which, such as those of musical timbre (e.g. a trumpet vs. a flute), have an undeniable richness and determinacy that is also not obviously connected to other states. But the colour cases are striking in this regard, and it's a merit of Levine's discussion to focus our attention on them. Another merit is that it invites us to focus on these rather more specific features somewhat independently of other features — 'consciousness', 'privacy', 'subjectivity' — that, I think, can unnecessarily confound the discussion (as it occasionally does even Levine's (*Haze*, pp. 7, 9, 165–7)). Richness and determinacy seem to me particularly difficult problems that would persist even if the problems surrounding these other features were solved.

2.3. 'Substantive' content

Levine believes that it is this richness and determinacy that requires the existence of qualia. The passage I quoted at the beginning of the last section continues:

> But I don't see how you can get the representational difference to do the work it has to do without there being a difference in the properties represented, which there can't be if the properties don't exist. In other words, how can there be a difference between reddish and greenish if there weren't any reddish and greenish in the first place? — (*Haze*, pp. 146–7)

Well, again, there is the logical point that there can, of course, be differences in properties represented without the properties existing, as with [magical] and [dephlogistinated]. But perhaps, nevertheless, the actual properties would help in capturing the difference between colour experiences.

This, at any rate, is a suggestion Levine seems initially to endorse:

> When I think of what it is to be reddish, the reddishness itself is somehow included in the thought; it's present to me. This is what I mean by saying it has a 'substantive' mode of presentation. In fact, it seems the right way to look at it is that reddishness itself is serving as its own mode of presentation. — (*Haze*, p. 8)

It is an idea advanced by a number of authors. Loar (1990/2002, p. 300) mentions it in passing, and Papineau (2002, pp. 116–25) and Balog (ms.), for example, propose modelling phenomenal concepts on quotational ones: just as a representation of the word 'apple' — e.g. ' "apple" ' — arguably contains the word 'apple' as a proper part, so would a (canonical?) representation of a phenomenal state contain that state.

There are, however, at least two serious problems with this latter proposal. In the first place, it is phenomenologically implausible. Phenomenal concepts seem to be deployed all the time without a trace of the corresponding experience, as I might do right now as I entertain various such concepts — [turquoise], [itch], [nausea], [ecstasy] — which, I assure the reader, do not in the least appear to be true of my experience at the moment. Indeed, the proposal would seem to have the extraordinary consequence that one couldn't coherently deny one was having a certain experience: my claim, for example, that I'm presently not experiencing intense pain would nevertheless involve my, quotationally, experiencing intense pain![16]

More importantly, the analogy with the quotation convention presupposes the very answer to the question we are seeking, viz., what is the content of a phenomenal concept? Understanding how to use 'mention' quotes involves understanding their roughly demonstrative content — [the string of symbols enclosed by these marks] — and having a fairly good purchase on their intended referents: letters, symbols, strings.[17] But the questions raised by Levine's discussion are precisely how to understand the corresponding content of a phenomenal representation, and the qualia being represented. Which properties of the representation are picked out by this corresponding demonstrative of a phenomenal representation? How are those properties appreciated, incorporated into our mental lives? It is not hard to imagine a machine programmed to process quotation marks and read off the

[16] Papineau (2002, pp. 118–21) claims that at least in *imagining* phenomenal states one is instantiating 'faint copies' that 'resemble' the original state. But how could a faint copy of an intense pain serve as any sort of instance of *intense* pain? In any case, it would then be self-vitiating to claim that one wasn't even experiencing a *faint* copy of an intense pain. Balog (ms.) acknowledges the problem and hopes in future work to handle it by distinguishing 'direct' from 'indirect' phenomenal concepts, the latter depending upon the former. I'm sceptical, but I think I should hold my reasons until the proposal is spelt out in detail. In any case, her view would need to answer my second objection.

[17] This is easily exaggerated. Just what *words* or other standard linguistic items are is a topic of considerable controversy. At the risk of damaging my credibility beyond repair, I should mention that in Rey (2006) I argue that these sorts of things don't exist either: they are just as much intentional inexistents as are qualia (see fn 11 above). But I ignore these issues for the present.

symbols enclosed by them. But how might a machine read the qualia? What are qualia that they could be even sufficiently well specified to be read in this way?

Although Levine feels partial to this view, he recognizes its problems:

> The mere fact that a representation of a sensory experience involves recreating a facsimile of the experience in order to represent it doesn't explain how the facsimile itself makes a cognitive difference — how it enters into the cognitive significance, or the content of the representation. — (*Haze*, p. 86)

Reflection on this problem seems to me to raise an even more fundamental one: *why think that putting the qualia property itself into the representation would do any good?* The passive richness and determinacy of colour experience won't be explained by the qualia property unless we have an account of *its* richness and determinacy, as well as an account of how that richness and determinacy could be so passively appreciated by the mind. But then we would need an account of how that richness and determinacy get *represented*; i.e. we'd need an account of phenomenal concepts in addition to an account of these qualia properties and, as Levine himself concludes, 'that's something we don't have' (*Haze*, p. 86).

But, of course, if we don't have an account of the content of phenomenal concepts, then why think there is no way to 'get the representational difference to do the work it has to do without there being a difference in the properties represented' (*Haze*, p. 147)? Why isn't it an open question?

3. Conclusion

Indeed, I think it is by and large still an open question, and the value of Levine's discussion consists in his forcing us to see that it is. My only reservation about his discussion is that he, like many others, keeps burdening this question with the 'irresistible' postulation of qualia properties that, for the reasons I've indicated here, seems gratuitous.

The problem of characterizing particularly the richness and determinacy of the content of our colour experience turns out to be a lot harder than I think many of us have supposed. This is perhaps unsurprising, given how much harder the problems of characterizing concepts in general have turned out to be. But it's important to see that this is a problem not only for my CRTT proposal, but for all existing proposals, physicalist and dualist alike. Postulating qualia properties, whether in the brain or in some special realm, will be of no help unless we have an account of how those properties are assimilated into a person's cognitive life; and it's hard to see how they could be assimilated without being *represented*. But, if we have an account of how they can be represented, then we would have an account of phenomenal concepts; and if we had that, then, I submit, we'd have no more need of actual qualia properties than would an account of the content of Greek theology have a need of any actual Greek gods. As I think we find with many other questions in this area, ontology is no substitute for psychology — and not much help in it either.

References

Balog, K. (ms.), 'Acquaintance and the mind-body problem'.

Campbell, J. (2002), *Reference and Consciousness* (Oxford University Press).

Cartwright, R. (1960/87), 'Negative existentials', in R. Cartwright, *Philosophical Essays* (Cambridge, MA: MIT Press).

Chalmers, D. (1996), *The Conscious Mind* (Oxford University Press).

Chalmers, D. (ed. 2002), *Philosophy of Mind: Classical and Contemporary Readings* (Oxford University Press).

Dennett, D. (1988/2002), 'Quining qualia', in Chalmers (2002), pp. 226–46.

Dennett, D. (1991), *Consciousness Explained* (Boston: Little Brown & Co).

Dennett, D. (1995), 'Superficialism vs. hysterical realism', *Philosophical Topics*, **22**, (1-1), pp. 530–6.

Dretske, F. (1988), *Explaining Behavior: Reasons in a World of Causes* (Cambridge, MA: MIT Press).

Fodor, J. (1975), *The Language of Thought* (New York: Crowell).

Fodor, J. (1983), *The Modularity of Mind* (Cambridge, MA: MIT Press).

Fodor, J. (1990), *A Theory of Content* (Cambridge, MA: MIT Press).

Fodor, J. (1991), *A Theory of Content and Other Essays* (Cambridge, MA: MIT Press).

Fodor, J. (1998), *Concepts: Where Cognitive Science Went Wrong* (Cambridge, MA: MIT Press).

Fodor, J. (2000), *The Mind Doesn't Work That Way: The Scope and Limits of Computational Psychology* (Cambridge, MA: MIT Press).

Kim, J. (1993), *Supervenience and Mind: Selected Philosophical Essays* (Cambridge University Press).

Kripke, S. (1972), 'Naming and necessity', in *Semantics of Natural Language*, ed. D. Davidson and G. Harman (Dordrecht: Reidel), pp. 253–355

Levine, J. (1983), 'Materialism and qualia: the explanatory gap', *Pacific Philosophical Quarterly*, **64**, pp. 354–61.

Levine, J. (1987), 'Quine on psychology', in *Naturalistic Psychology: A Symposium of Two Decades*, ed. A. Shimony and D. Nails (Dordrecht: Reidel), pp. 259–90.

Levine, J. (2001), *Purple Haze* (Oxford University Press).

Loar, B. (1990/2002), 'Phenomenal states (second version)', in Chalmers (2002), pp. 285–310.

Lycan, W. (1996), *Consciousness and Experience* (Cambridge MA : MIT Press).

Millikan, R. (2000), *On Clear and Confused Ideas* (Cambridge University Press).

Papineau, D. (2002), *Thinking About Consciousness* (Oxford University Press).

Quine, W. (1956/76), 'Carnap and logical truth', in W. Quine, *Ways of Paradox and Other Essays* (2nd edn., Cambridge, MA: Harvard University Press).

Quine, W. (1960), *Word and Object* (Cambridge, MA: MIT Press).

Rey, G. (1988/96), 'A question about consciousness', with postscript, in *The Nature of Consciousness*, ed. Block, N., Flanagan, O. and Guzeldere, G. (Cambridge, MA: NIT Press, 1996), pp. 461–82.

Rey, G. (1991), 'Sensations in a language of thought', in *Philosophical Issues I: Consciousness*, ed. E. Villaneuvo (Atascadero: Ridgeview Press), pp. 73–112.

Rey, G. (1992), 'Sensational sentences', in *Consciousness*, ed. M. Davies and G. Humphreys (Oxford: Blackwell), pp. 240–57.

Rey, G. (1994), 'Dennett's unrealistic psychology', *Philosophical Topics*, **22** (1–2), pp. 259–89.

Rey, G. (1995), 'Wittgenstein, computationalism and qualia', in *Philosophy and the Cognitive Sciences*, ed. R. Casati, B. Smith and G. White (Vienna: Hölder-Pichler-Tempsky), pp. 61–74.

Rey, G. (1995), 'Annaherung an eine projektivistische Theorie bewussten Erlebens' ('Towards a projectivist account of conscious experience') in *Bewusstsein* (Paderborn: Ferdinand-SchöninghVerlag, 1995); English version, *Conscious Experience*, ed. T. Metzinger (Thorverton: Imprint Academic, 1996), pp. 123–42.

Rey, G. (1997), *Contemporary Philosophy of Mind: A Contentiously Classical Approach* (Oxford: Blackwell).

Rey, G. (1998), 'A narrow representational account of qualitative experience', in *Philosophical Perspectives 12: Language Mind and Ontology*, ed. J. Tomberlin (Atascadero: Ridgeview Press), pp. 435–57.

Rey, G. (2004), 'Why Wittgenstein ought to have been a computationalist (and what a computationalist can learn from Wittgenstein)', *Croation Journal of Philosophy*, **3** (9), pp. 231–64.

Rey, G. (2005a), 'Explanation, not experience: Commentary on John Campbell, *Reference and Consciousness*', *Philosophical Studies*, **126**, pp. 131–43.

Rey, G. (2005b), 'Philosophical analysis as cognitive psychology: The case of empty concepts', in *Handbook of Categorization in Cognitive Science*, ed. H. Cohen and C. Lefebvre (Dordrecht: Elsevier), pp. 71–89.

Rey, G. (2006), 'The intentional inexistence of language — but not cars', in *Debates in Cognitive Science*, ed. R. Stainton (Oxford: Blackwell).

Smart, J.J.C. (1962), 'Sensations and brain processes', *Philosophical Review*, **LXVIII**, pp. 141–56

Snowdon, P. (1980–1), 'Experience, vision and causation', *Proceedings of the Aristotelian Society*, **81**, pp. 175–92.

Taylor, K. (2003), *Reference and the Rational Mind* (Stanford: CSLI Publications).

Tye, M. (1995), *Ten Problems of Consciousness: A Representational Theory of the Phenomenal Mind* (Cambridge, MA: MIT Press).

Wittgenstein, L. (1953/68), *Philosophical Investigations* (Oxford: Blackwell).

Arthur B. Markman, W. Todd Maddox,
Darrell A. Worthy and Grant C. Baldwin

Using Regulatory Focus to Explore Implicit and Explicit Processing in Concept Learning

Abstract: *Complex cognitive processes like concept learning involve a mixture of redundant explicit and implicit processes that are active simultaneously. This aspect of cognitive architecture creates difficulties in determining the influence of consciousness on processing. We propose that the interaction between an individual's regulatory focus and the reward structure of the current task influences the degree to which explicit processing is active. Thus, by manipulating people's motivational state and the nature of the task they perform, we can vary the influence of conscious processing in cognitive performance. We demonstrate the utility of this view by focusing on studies in which people acquire new perceptual concepts by learning to classify them. This technique will allow us to better tease apart the roles of explicit and implicit processing in a variety of cognitive tasks.*

As Cognitive Psychologists, we are often led astray by the labels we place on our phenomena. We study processes like attention, concept formation and memory. By giving each of these processes a label, we reify it and thereby give it more unity than it may deserve. What research is beginning to make plain, however, is that the traditional labels used by cognitive psychologists refer to input-output relationships that may be served by many underlying cognitive and motivational processes (Uttal, 2001). For example, memory involves encoding information about some experience in a manner that permits it to influence later processing. The general consensus within the memory literature is that this ability is served by multiple memory systems (Ashby & Waldron, 1999; Packard & Cahill, 2001; Roediger, 2003).

Two aspects of this situation complicate the study of cognitive processing. First, the suite of mental systems that serve different functions all operate simultaneously. Thus people's performance in a task is a reflection of multiple systems operating together. At times these systems may lead to the same response, and at times they may suggest different responses (Sloman, 1996). Teasing apart the contribution of these systems is a difficult process. Second, these systems differ in their conscious accessibility. Some systems are explicitly mediated, while others operate only implicitly.

So, a complete model of a task requires understanding the component cognitive processes, their relationship to conscious processing and the factors that engage these processes. In this article we describe a research programme designed to address this question by focusing on the interaction of motivation and cognition in perceptual classification learning. This domain is particularly apt because we understand a lot about the component processes involved in classification learning. In addition, our research on motivation suggests that different motivational conditions can affect the relative use of implicit and explicit processes in learning.

In the next section we discuss our framework for perceptual category learning. Then we present a motivational framework that addresses the role of implicit and explicit systems in learning. Next we illustrate the utility of this framework with studies in which people acquire new perceptual concepts by learning to classify them. Finally we demonstrate how this framework can be extended to other cognitive processes.

Perceptual Classification

We are interested in classification learning because it is known to involve a mix of conscious and unconscious processes. Classification is the ability to take a set of items and to determine the category to which they belong. Thus, classification learning requires learning an underlying representation (or concept) that binds together members of the same category. There is a long history of using people's ability to learn to classify new items as the empirical basis for models of categorization

(Medin & Schaffer, 1978; Nosofsky, 1986; Posner & Keele, 1970). Although there are many tasks one might use to study category representations (see e.g. Markman & Ross, 2003), classification learning has the advantage that the processes involved in acquiring new perceptual categories are reasonably well understood (Ashby & Maddox, 2005). Furthermore, there are good mathematical modelling tools that can be used to characterize the performance of individual subjects and how that performance changes over the course of a study (Maddox & Ashby, 2004).

In a typical perceptual classification task, two classes (or groups) of simple perceptual stimuli are constructed by the experimenter with one class of items being associated with category A and the second with category B. On each trial of a typical task, one stimulus is sampled randomly from the set of all stimuli and is presented to the subject. The subject studies the item and assigns it to one of the two categories by pressing either the key associated with category A or the key associated with category B. Following the response the subject receives feedback regarding the correctness of their response.

Over the past several years, there has been much research supporting the notion that different category structures are learned by different systems, each of which has a unique neurobiological underpinning. Empirical support comes from a wide range of research areas including animal learning, neuropsychology, functional neuroimaging and cognitive psychology (see Ashby & Maddox, 2005; Keri, 2003, for a review).

One multiple-systems model that has stimulated much research is the COmpetition between Verbal and Implicit Systems (COVIS) model of perceptual classification learning (Ashby, *et al.*, 1998; Ashby, Isen & Turken, 1999). This model postulates two systems that compete throughout learning. One system is an explicit, hypothesis-testing system that uses working memory and executive attention to select and test specific hypotheses. This system is mediated predominantly by frontal brain regions. The second system is an implicit, procedural-based learning system that learns to associate a category response with a region of perceptual space. A critical brain structure in this system is the striatum (a subcortical structure) that is assumed to provide a low-resolution map of the perceptual stimulus space. This system learns to associate sub-regions of perceptual space with category assignments through a gradual and incremental learning process. Of particular interest to the current discussion is the fact that processing in the explicit hypothesis-testing system is available to conscious awareness, whereas processing in the implicit, procedural-based learning system is not.

The hypothesis-testing system is assumed to mediate the learning of rule-based categories. *Rule-based* classification learning tasks are those in which the category structures can be learned via some explicit reasoning process. Frequently, the rule that maximizes accuracy (i.e. the optimal rule) is easy to describe verbally. For example, Figure 1a presents a scatter-plot of stimuli from a rule-based condition with two categories. Each point in the plot denotes the length and orientation of

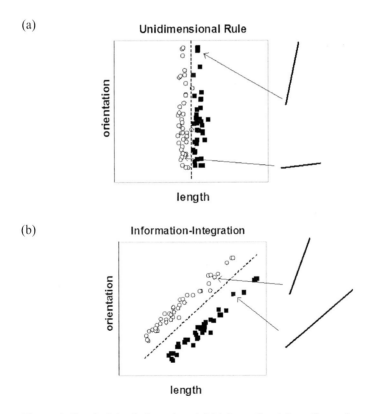

Figure 1. Simple (a) rule-based and (b) information integration category structures using two-dimensional stimuli. The dimensions are the length and orientation of a single line. The figure shows a sample of stimuli from two regions of space. The rule-based structure is unidimensional because only one of the two stimulus dimensions is relevant. Open circles denote stimuli from category A and filled squares denote stimuli from category B.

a single line stimulus, with different symbols denoting different categories. A sample stimulus from each category, along with its associated point representation in the scatterplot, is also displayed. The broken line denotes the optimal decision bound. In this example, the rule is to give one response to 'short' lines and a second to 'long' lines.

The procedural-based learning system is assumed to mediate the learning of information-integration categories. *Information-integration* category learning tasks are those in which accuracy is maximized only if information from two or more stimulus components (or dimensions) is integrated at some pre-decisional stage (Ashby & Gott, 1988). For example, Figure 1b presents a scatter-plot of stimuli from an information-integration condition with two categories. The broken line denotes the optimal decision bound. It has no verbal or rule-based analogue because length and orientation are measured in different units. Although one can certainly state the rule as, 'respond A if the orientation is greater than the length; otherwise respond B', it is unclear how to interpret the term 'greater than' because the dimensional values are measured in different units, so this type of decision rule makes no sense to naïve participants.

An advantage of the perceptual classification learning task is that a large amount of data is collected from each subject, and thus all analyses can be performed at the individual-subject level. Two levels of analyses are always conducted. First, accuracy-based analyses that include estimating learning curves and performing ANOVA are conducted. Second, a series of quantitative models are applied that provide useful insights into the types of decision strategies that subjects are using. The model-based analyses are important because qualitative differences in strategy are not always identifiable at the level of accuracy. This follows because it is often the case that two qualitatively different models can yield identical accuracy rates (see e.g. Maddox, Markman & Baldwin, 2006). In our modelling approach we fit a number of different decision bound models to each subject's responses on a block by block basis. Decision bound models are a standard and very useful tool in classification research (e.g. Ashby, 1992; Ashby & Gott, 1988; Maddox & Ashby, 1993). Decision bound models assume that the subject partitions the perceptual space into response regions. On each trial, the subject determines which region the percept is in, and then emits the associated response.

Two classes of decision bound models are generally applied. One class of models assumes that the subject uses an explicit hypothesis-testing strategy. Using the Figure 1a condition as an example, these include a model that assumes that the subject uses the optimal decision criterion along the length dimension, a model that assumes that the subject uses a sub-optimal decision criterion (where the decision criterion is freely estimated from the data) along the length dimension, and a model that assumes that the subject uses a sub-optimal decision criterion along the orientation dimension. The same models might be applied to the Figure 1b conditions, but in addition models that instantiate conjunctive rules might also be applied. For example, the subject might set a criterion along the length dimension (whose value is estimated from the data) and a criterion along the orientation dimension (whose value is estimated from the data) and might respond 'A' to short, steep lines and respond 'B' to all other lines. The second class of models assumes that the participant uses an implicit procedural-based learning strategy (see Maddox & Ashby, 1993 for details).

Although a number of these strategies are possible, we focus on models that assume a linear decision bound of arbitrary slope and intercept (freely estimated from the data). Each model also has one 'noise' parameter that captures the variability in the memory for, or application of, each rule. Well-understood statistical procedures exist for determining how to select the best-fitting model from among a set of competitors (Ashby, 1992; Wickens, 1982).

Regulatory Focus and Cognitive Processing

Research on cognition has typically focused on information processing in a variety of tasks. Motivational factors — those that drive individuals to action — are not typically explored. It is becoming clear in a variety of domains, however, that motivational processes are crucial for understanding cognitive processes. Without motivation, people will not act at all (Carver & Scheier, 1998). Furthermore, behaviour changes radically under different motivational circumstances. For example, many observed cultural differences in reasoning may be attributed to motivational factors that differ across cultures (Briley & Wyer, 2002; Hong & Chiu, 2001; Kim & Markman, 2006). Furthermore, changes in motivational states can alter the choices people make and the processes they use to reach decisions (Higgins et al., 2003; Loewenstein, 1996).

We are particularly interested in regulatory focus theory as a motivational framework (Higgins, 1997; 2000). This view builds from the observation that organisms have two psychologically distinct kinds of goals: *approach* goals and *avoidance* goals. Approach goals are desirable states of the world that the individual desires to achieve. Avoidance goals are undesirable states of the world that the individual desires to avoid. In addition to the pursuit of specific approach and avoidance goals, Higgins (1997) suggests that the motivational system may be tuned to a state of readiness for potential gains or losses in the environment. In particular, an individual may have a *promotion focus*, which involves sensitivity to potential gains and nongains in the environment, or an individual may have a *prevention focus*, which involves sensitivity to potential losses and nonlosses in the environment.

There are two ways that these regulatory foci can be engaged. First, individuals have a chronically accessible regulatory focus. That is, they have a predisposition to be in either a promotion of a prevention focus (Higgins, 1987). In addition, situations may induce a regulatory focus. In particular, when people are pursuing a particular approach goal, they often have an active promotion focus. Similarly, when people are pursuing an avoidance goal, they often have an active prevention focus. The goals that lead to active regulatory foci can be pursuits of external rewards and punishments, social rewards and punishments, or the desire to achieve particular internal states (e.g. to reduce anxiety).

Of particular interest is that regulatory focus interacts in an interesting way with the feedback people receive while performing a task. The tasks that we give people in the laboratory have a reward structure. For example, in many psychology experiments people are given points or have points taken away from a score over the course of the task. The total score someone achieves is frequently related to performance bonuses. At a minimum, participants are told to do their best, and so there is a social contract between the participant and the experimenter. Thus, gains of points are a mild reward and losses of points are a mild punishment on each trial of the study.

Just from this analysis, we can see that the overall regulatory focus of a participant may fit or mismatch with the reward structure of the task. Specifically, if someone has a promotion focus, then there is a regulatory fit if they receive points (or are rewarded) while performing the task, but a regulatory mismatch when they lose points (or are punished) while performing the task. Conversely, if someone has a prevention focus, then there is a regulatory fit if they lose points (or are punished) while performing the task, but a regulatory mismatch if they gain points (or are rewarded).

What are the consequences of a regulatory fit? Higgins and colleagues (Higgins, 2000, 2005; Higgins *et al.*, 2003) suggest that regulatory fit induces a feeling of fluency that enhances people's preferences. In our research, we have expanded this proposal (Maddox, Markman &

Baldwin, 2006; Markman *et al.*, 2005). We draw a parallel between the circumstances of regulatory fit and those that induce positive affect (Ashby, Isen & Turken, 1999; Isen, 2001; Isen & Labroo, 2003). Often, in studies of positive affect, participants get an unexpected reward that matches their promotion focus. Neuropsychological theories of positive affect suggest that positive affect increases dopamine release from the ventral tegmental area (VTA) into frontal brain areas, in particular the anterior cingulate (Ashby, Isen & Turken, 1999).

Dopamine release in these frontal areas is thought to promote more flexible cognitive processing. One finding consistent with this view comes from work using the Remote Associates Task (RAT) (Mednick & Mednick, 1967), a test in which people are given three words that are all related to a fourth word, typically in a distant way. Subjects must find the related word. For example, the words ENVY, GOLF and BEANS are all related to the word GREEN. Ashby, Isen & Turken (1999) report data in which people given a manipulation of positive affect solved more of these problems than did those who did not receive this manipulation. We obtained a parallel result using a manipulation of regulatory fit. We drew our items from three previous studies and we selected seven items designed to be easy, seven designed to be of moderate difficulty, and seven designed to be hard (Bowers *et al.*, 1990; Dorfman *et al.*, 1996; Mednick & Mednick, 1967).

For the purposes of this task, we assume that finding a remote associate is intrinsically rewarding, and so the task itself gives positive feedback for correct responses. Thus, the RAT should lead to a regulatory fit for subjects with a promotion focus and a regulatory mismatch for subjects with a prevention focus. We added the RAT to an unrelated study that manipulated regulatory focus by having subjects perform a task with the prospect of obtaining an entry into a draw to win $50. In our study, seventeen subjects were given a promotion focus. They were told that if they performed well on the unrelated task, they would get an entry. In addition, nineteen subjects were given a prevention focus. They were given an entry ticket when they arrived at the lab and were told that they could keep the ticket if they performed well on the unrelated task. This manipulation has been used successfully in previous studies of regulatory focus (Shah & Higgins, 1997).

The mean proportion of items correctly solved by subjects with a promotion and prevention focus is shown in Table 1. Of interest, participants solve about the same proportion of the items overall in the promotion ($M = 0.20$) and prevention ($M = 0.19$) focus conditions. Where these groups differ is in the difficulty of the items they solve.

We contrasted the proportion of items solved within each type using
t-tests. The only reliable difference is that promotion subjects solved a
significantly higher proportion of the hard items ($M = 0.10$) than did
the prevention subjects ($M = 0.02$), $t(34) = 2.27$, $p < 0.05$. There was,
however, a tendency for subjects with a prevention focus to solve
more of the easy items ($M = 0.50$) than did subjects with a promotion
focus ($M = 0.40$). These data are consistent with the suggestion that
people are more strategic and flexible in their processing when they
have a regulatory fit than when they have a regulatory mismatch,
although obviously this task shows only the regulatory fit between
promotion focus and tasks with positive rewards.

Table 1. Proportion of items solved in the Remote Associates Task as a
function of Regulatory Focus

Regulatory Focus	Easy Items	Medium Items	Hard Items
Promotion Focus	0.40	0.21	0.10
Prevention Focus	0.50	0.20	0.02

To be clear, however, we are not arguing that regulatory fit induces
positive affect, which in turn produces greater cognitive flexibility.
Rather, we think that most prior studies of positive affect have induced
a promotion focus that interacts with the reward structure of the task
being performed. Often this task has a gains reward structure, so many
studies of positive affect examine subjects in a state of regulatory fit.
We do not think that subjects with a prevention focus in a task with
losses will necessarily experience positive affect, but we do think they
will show similar effects of regulatory fit to subjects with a promotion
focus in a task with a gains reward structure.

The frontal systems implicated in these results are also associated
with consciously accessible cognitive processes. Thus, an alternative
way to look at these results is that conditions of regulatory fit lead to
relatively greater involvement of explicit conscious processing than
do conditions of regulatory mismatch. From our standpoint, then, this
framework provides a method for changing the mix of explicit and
implicit processes brought to bear on a task. In this way we can begin
to tease apart the role of consciously accessible cognitive processes in
normal thinking. In the next section, we review studies of perceptual
classification that demonstrate the utility of this technique.

Studies of Regulatory Fit in Classification

Classification learning provides a good domain for testing the regulatory fit framework, because classification involves both explicit and implicit processes. As discussed above, the COVIS framework suggests that there are two distinct strategies that people use to learn new sets of categories. The hypothesis-testing system is clearly associated with consciously accessible processes. The system itself involves generating and testing explicit hypotheses, and subjects are able to report the rules they are using to classify with great accuracy. In contrast, the procedural-based learning system involves a more implicit similarity-based classification process. Learning is slow in this system. Furthermore, subjects cannot report the basis of their classification accurately. That is, while many subjects using a procedural-based learning strategy will state a rule that they are using to classify the items if asked, they are unable to do so accurately. This hypothesis seems broadly consistent with other neuropsychological approaches to consciousness (e.g. Crick & Koch, 1998).

We know from the research sketched above that normal individuals are able to use both of these strategies, and that both of them are typically brought to bear on a classification task. Indeed, information-integration tasks may be learned initially by the hypothesis-testing system and later performance may be supported by the procedural-based learning system.

If we are correct, and regulatory fit increases the involvement and effectiveness of hypothesis-testing processes in classification, then sets of categories that require learning complex explicit rules should be acquired more easily under conditions of regulatory fit than regulatory mismatch. Thus, if we examine people's responses in a complex rule-based learning task, they should be more accurate when there is a regulatory fit than when there is a regulatory mismatch. In addition, people should find the more complex rule that distinguishes among categories more quickly when there is a fit than when there is a mismatch.

Regulatory fit should not always lead to better performance, however. There are two conditions under which participants with a regulatory mismatch may outperform those with a regulatory fit. First, there are cases in which people are learning rule-based categories for which the task requires refining the application of the rule rather than a search for a complex rule. In this case, elaborate hypothesis testing will interfere with refining a simpler rule. Thus, when there is a regulatory fit, we should observe people trying a number of different rules, but when there is a mismatch, people should focus on a single strategy.

Second, when people are learning true information integration categories, then rules will not support accurate performance. In this case, people with a regulatory mismatch will learn faster and more accurately, because they will be less prone to try (sub-optimal) explicit rules, and will abandon the explicit hypothesis-testing system in favour of the procedural-based system earlier. Thus, when looking at the strategies that characterize people's performance, people with a regulatory mismatch should shift from the use of explicit rules (which will dominate early in processing) to the use of implicit procedural--based learning strategies. Because explicit processing is less prominent with a regulatory mismatch, this shift to procedural-based learning strategies should occur earlier in learning when there is a mismatch than when there is a match.

We have explored this set of predictions in a series of studies that provides basic support for the framework outlined here. First, we conducted studies with a complex rule-based task to test whether regulatory fit promotes explicit rule-based processing (Maddox, Baldwin & Markman, 2006). Stimuli for this study were lines varying in length, orientation and the horizontal position of the line on the screen. The items were divided into two categories (see Figure 3a). The items were set up so that good performance could be achieved by forming a rule along any one dimension. However, the learning criterion for this task was 90% accuracy. This level of accuracy could only be achieved by forming a conjunctive rule that combined the length and orientation dimensions. This pair of dimensions was chosen for the conjunctive rule, because pilot research with these items suggested that the position of the line on the screen was most salient. Thus, we expected that many subjects would begin by trying a simple rule based on the position of the line. In order to exceed the learning criterion, participants would eventually have to abandon this rule and form a different rule involving two other dimensions.

We manipulated regulatory focus in this task using an overall incentive for performance. Subjects given a promotion focus were brought to the lab and told that they would have a chance to win a ticket into a raffle for a one-in-ten chance to win $50. They were shown the raffle ticket they could win. They were told that they would be given this ticket if the number of points they had at the end of the last block of the learning task exceeded a criterion. This criterion was set to require 90% accuracy in responding across the last forty-eight trials of the experiment. Subjects given a prevention focus received similar instructions, except that they were given a raffle ticket for a draw to win $50 when they entered the lab and were told that they could keep the ticket provided their performance in the last block of trials exceeded the criterion.

Items were presented on a computer display as shown in Figure 2. The stimulus is presented in the window. Along the right side of the screen is a 'Point Meter' showing the subject the current number of points that they have obtained. This scale also shows the bonus criterion. The region above the criterion is labelled 'Yes' and the region below is labelled 'No' to make clear whether participants have exceeded the criterion. When participants make a correct response, the number of points given for a correct response is awarded and the sound of a cash register plays over the computer speakers. When the participants make an incorrect response, the number of points given for an incorrect response is awarded, and the sound of a buzzer plays. In addition, verbal feedback (the word 'Correct' or 'Incorrect') is shown at the bottom of the screen after each trial.

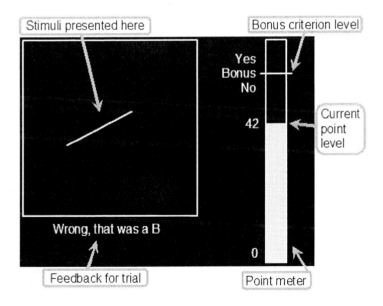

Figure 2. Annotated screen shot showing the computer interface used in the experiments.

(a)

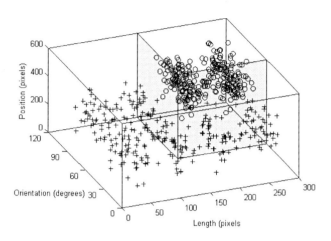

(b)

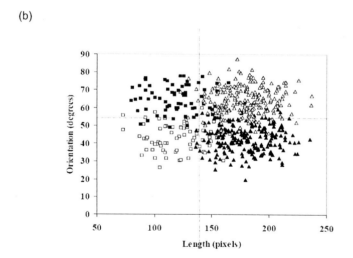

Figure 3. Category structures used in studies of regulatory fit. (a) A three-dimensional rule-based category structure with a low-salience conjunctive rule that requires flexibility to be learned. Open circles denote stimuli from category A and plus signs denote stimuli from category B. (b) A two-dimensional rule-based structure with categories that required less flexibility to learn. Open squares denote stimuli from category A, filled squares denote stimuli from category B, filled triangles denote stimuli from category C, open triangles denote stimuli from category D.

In the first version of the task that we ran, participants received points for correct responses. They were given two points for a correct response, and zero points for an incorrect response. They had to achieve a bonus criterion of eighty-six points in the last block in order to qualify for the raffle. Thus, for this version of the task, participants with a promotion focus had a regulatory fit and those with a prevention focus had a regulatory mismatch.

The data supported the prediction that regulatory fit promotes the use of explicit hypothesis-testing. Participants with a promotion focus were more accurate in their classification performance than were those with a prevention focus. This difference in accuracy was most prominent in the last few blocks of the study. Furthermore, a higher proportion of participants reached the learning criterion when they had a promotion focus than when they had a prevention focus. Finally, a variety of models were fitted to each subject's performance in each block. Typically, subjects' data were best fit by either unidimensional models or conjunctive models, indicating that everyone was using rules of some type. The difference is that subjects with a promotion focus began to use a conjunctive rule earlier in the study than did subjects with a prevention focus.

This pattern of data alone is ambiguous, because it could either reflect that promotion and prevention focus differ in their effects on cognitive processing, or it could reflect differences between regulatory fit and regulatory mismatch. To distinguish between these possibilities we ran a second study that was identical to the one just described, except that participants lost points on each trial (Maddox, Baldwin & Markman, 2006). Participants lost three points for an incorrect response but only one point for a correct response. In this case they started the study with zero points. The point meter moved downward as points were lost. The performance criterion in this case was –58 points. Thus, for this version of the study, subjects with a prevention focus have a regulatory fit and those with a promotion focus have a regulatory mismatch.

As predicted by regulatory fit, the results of this study are the mirror image of those just described. In this study, participants with a prevention focus were more accurate than were those with a promotion focus. Similarly, participants with a prevention focus were more likely to reach the learning criterion than were those with a promotion focus. Finally, participants with a prevention focus found a conjunctive rule faster than did those with a promotion focus. Thus, regulatory fit appears to engage explicit rule-based processing more strongly than does regulatory mismatch.

We have also identified situations in which a regulatory mismatch is advantageous for performance. In one study, we gave participants a task for which extensive hypothesis testing is disadvantageous. In this task, participants were asked to learn to distinguish between four categories. Once again, the stimuli were lines that differed in their length and orientation (all stimuli were presented centred on the screen and thus did not differ in position). As shown in Figure 3b, the categories were distinguished by values on a conjunction of length and orientation with each category occupying a different quadrant of stimulus space. These categories overlapped, so that optimal accuracy was only 77%. Thus, what made this task difficult was not finding a rule, but rather sticking with the set of rules long enough to establish good performance.

To enhance the need to stick with the rules, we ran subjects under two between-subjects conditions. For one group, the criterion was fairly easy to achieve. For the second group, the criterion was actually impossible to achieve. Thus, for this second group, participants had to work hard to optimize performance, although they would never actually exceed the performance criterion. To date, we have run this experiment only with a gains reward structure in which participants get points for correct answers and get no points for incorrect answers (Maddox, Baldwin & Markman, in press).

The results of this study are consistent with the predictions of regulatory fit. Participants do about equally well when the performance criterion is fairly easy to achieve. However, when the criterion is unattainable participants with a promotion focus (who have a regulatory fit) are significantly less accurate than are those with a prevention focus (who have a regulatory mismatch). When we fit models to participants' data, we find that there is more variability in the decision criterion for people with a promotion focus than for people with a prevention focus. This finding suggests that those with a promotion focus are trying a variety of different rules, while those with a prevention focus are sticking with a single rule and trying to refine it. Thus this pattern of data is also consistent with the proposal that a regulatory fit engages explicit processing more strongly than does a regulatory mismatch.

Converging evidence for this point comes from a comparison of learning rule-based and information-integration categories (Markman *et al.*, 2006). We performed a new study using a somewhat different manipulation of motivation than we used previously. In this study, in order to connect with research on 'choking under pressure' (e.g. Beilock & Carr, 2005; Beilock *et al.*, 2004; Gray, 2004; Masters,

1992), we created a social manipulation that creates a prevention focus and compared that to a control condition with no motivational manipulation. For this social manipulation, subjects are told that they and a partner are both performing the task and that if both of them exceed the performance criterion then both will receive a $6 monetary bonus. Furthermore, they are told that their partner has already performed the task and has exceeded the criterion. Thus the onus is on them to exceed the criterion as well. This manipulation creates a prevention focus, because participants typically perceive that their partner has achieved the bonus, and it is theirs to lose. This regulatory focus contrasts with the reward structure for the task, in which people receive positive points on each trial. Thus participants in the pressure condition have a regulatory mismatch. In contrast, the participants in the control condition are just told to 'do their best', and so they have a mild promotion focus that creates a regulatory fit with the gains reward structure of the task. Thus we expect the participants under pressure to have relatively less influence of explicit processes than participants with no pressure.

Participants are then given either a simple rule-based or information-integration category structure to learn. The rule-based task involves focusing on one of two stimulus dimensions. The information-integration task involves a conjunction of two dimensions that is not verbalizable. We expect that the control condition will be more likely to promote explicit processing because it leads to a regulatory fit, whereas the pressure condition leads to a regulatory mismatch. Conditions that promote explicit processing will yield relatively good performance on the rule-based task but relatively poor performance on the information-integration task, where the attempt to form rules will interfere with information-integration learning.

Consistent with our expectations, there was a reliable interaction between the category structure and the motivational state of the participants. When learning the rule-based categories, participants' performance was significantly worse when they were under pressure than when they were not. Furthermore, the data from participants in the low-pressure control condition were more likely to be fit by a rule-based model than were the data from participants in the pressure condition. These results reflect that the regulatory mismatch induced by the pressure manipulation impaired rule-based learning. In contrast, when learning the information-integration categories, participants' performance was significantly better when they were under pressure than when they were not. In addition, data from participants in the high-pressure condition were more likely to be fit by a procedural-based learning model than were data from participants in the low pressure control condition. This result reflects that the regulatory mismatch was advantageous in this situation, because participants were less likely to form rules in this case.

Taken together, the data reviewed in this section suggest that regulatory fit promotes explicit processing. Participants with a regulatory fit are more likely to use rule-based processes than are participants with a regulatory mismatch. When the task being performed requires learning complex rules, then a regulatory fit leads to better performance than does a regulatory mismatch. In contrast, when rule-based learning impairs performance, then participants perform more poorly when they have a regulatory fit than when they have a regulatory mismatch. Before we look at the broader implications of this view, we examine the influence of regulatory fit in another domain in order to assess the generality of the phenomena presented here.

Regulatory Fit and Choice

So far we have focused on the influence of regulatory focus and reward structure on concept learning. However, we are arguing that participants should be more likely to engage explicit processes when there is a regulatory fit than when there is a mismatch in general. Thus it would be useful to demonstrate another influence of regulatory fit. Recently we have begun to explore motivational factors in choice, and we present the results of a pilot study here.

We ran a group of thirty-eight subjects on a variant of the Iowa Gambling task (Bechara *et al.*, 1994), a decision-making task that has been used to examine how people come to associate good and bad valence to choice options. In our version of the task, participants are shown two decks of cards on a computer screen. They are told that they can select cards from the decks and that the cards will have point totals on them. For half of the subjects, the point totals are positive and for the other half, the point totals are negative. For those given decks with positive point totals, their task is to draw eighty cards from the decks in a way that allows them to exceed a criterion point total to reach a bonus. For those given decks with negative point totals, their task is to select the eighty cards in a way that allows them to keep their point total above the criterion point total in order to reach a bonus. Subjects are shown the point total on the card after each draw.

Regulatory focus is manipulated in this study as well. The promotion focus involves the opportunity for subjects to get a raffle ticket for an entry to win $50 if they exceed the bonus criterion. In the prevention focus, subjects are given a raffle ticket for the draw and are allowed to keep it if their point total exceeds the criterion at the end of the study.

The two decks are constructed so that the initial impression of the decks is not consistent with their long-run value. The first few cards in one deck have high positive point totals (or low negative point totals), but the remaining cards have lower positive point totals (or higher negative point totals). We call this deck the 'bad' deck, because choosing it for the entire study will not allow the subject to reach the bonus criterion. The other deck has the opposite structure, and so it creates a bad impression at first, but ultimately subjects need to draw primarily from this deck to achieve the criterion. We refer to this deck as the 'good' deck. Thus, in order to succeed in this task, subjects need to recognize that the deck that looked good initially is in fact the bad deck, and that the deck that looked bad initially is in fact good. We hypothesized that succeeding in this task quickly would require explicit monitoring of performance, and so we expected that people would perform better if they had a regulatory fit than if they had a regulatory mismatch. In this study, a regulatory fit involves either a promotion focus and decks with positive point totals, or a prevention focus and decks with negative point totals.

The data support this hypothesis. Subjects given the decks with gains obtained significantly more points on average when they had a promotion focus ($M = 446$) than when they had a prevention focus ($M = 422$), $F(1,18) = 6.05$, $p < 0.05$. In contrast, subjects given the decks with losses showed the opposite pattern. In this case, subjects with a prevention focus lost fewer points on average ($M = -419$) than did subjects with a promotion focus ($M = -444$), $F(1,16) = 7.16$, $p < 0.05$. Thus participants with a regulatory fit performed better than did subjects with a regulatory mismatch. Ongoing research is exploring this phenomenon in more detail. In particular, we are examining the strategies people use in this task and people's ability to use these strategies flexibly.

These data allow us to extend our approach beyond simple perceptual learning. The decision-making task we gave people here required explicit monitoring of the items to recognize when an initially good item turned bad and when an initially bad item turned good. People were better able to recognize this shift when they had a regulatory fit than when they had a regulatory mismatch, suggesting greater involvement of explicit processing in this task.

Conclusions and Future Directions

Understanding the role of conscious processing in cognitive processing will be a difficult task, because normal cognition involves a mix of explicit and implicit processes. We believe that the research on the motivation-cognition interface described here in concept learning and other domains presents an interesting opportunity to help us learn more about the contributions of implicit and explicit processes in a variety of tasks. Regulatory fit appears to turn up the gain on explicit processes, while regulatory mismatch appears to turn down this gain. This method, then, provides us with a way of affecting the amount of conscious processing involved in task performance.

There are many techniques for trying to influence the contribution of explicit processing to cognitive processing, though we believe the manipulation of regulatory focus has advantages over all of them. For example, psychologists have long used dual-task paradigms to engage explicit resources in processing (Waldron & Ashby, 2001; Zeithamova & Maddox, 2006). While we have learned much about cognitive processing from dual-task studies, they place subjects in an unnatural situation and they often require significant training. Furthermore, performance in the tasks trades off depending on the degree of effort subjects place on the two tasks.

Other research has manipulated anxiety as a way of dampening available working-memory resources (e.g. Tohill & Holyoak, 2000). This manipulation is also expected to decrease the involvement of explicit processing in a task. In our view, manipulations of anxiety are a subcomponent of the framework described here. Anxiety is a state that is associated with avoidance goals (Higgins, 1987). People are anxious in situations in which they are attempting to avoid a potential negative outcome. There are two potential difficulties with research using anxiety to manipulate the degree of explicit processing in a task. First, this research generally attributes the effects of anxiety manipulations to anxiety rather than to the regulatory mismatch caused by activating a prevention focus in a task that (typically) rewards good performance. Second, this research does not recognize that activation of a prevention focus can actually lead to greater involvement of explicit processes when the task itself has losses.

The manipulations of regulatory fit described in this article also hold promise for future studies of brain imaging. Because the manipulation itself does not require any additional responses on the part of subjects, we can induce this manipulation and then examine task performance using imaging techniques like fMRI. Recent research by

Cunningham, Raye and Johnson (2005) found that manipulations of regulatory focus influence patterns of blood flow in evaluation tasks, suggesting that there is potential for these manipulations to further illuminate our understanding of brain regions involved in explicit processing.

Regulatory Fit and Consciousness

So far, we have suggested only that regulatory fit is associated with brain regions that are thought to promote conscious thought. In this section we give one speculation about why a regulatory fit would lead to greater conscious processing than a regulatory mismatch. Promotion and prevention foci are expectations about the projected state of the world. A promotion focus prepares an individual for a world in which there are potential gains and nongains in the environment. Likewise, a prevention focus prepares an individual for a world in which there are potential losses and nonlosses. When the reward structure of the environment matches individuals' expectations, then they should bring their full cognitive resources to bear on problems to be solved in that environment. However, when the reward structure mismatches individuals' expectations, then a reasonable initial response is to engage fast-acting (and probably unconscious) cognitive strategies until the environment can be better understood.

This possibility is sensible, because in most situations the regulatory focus is aligned with the task being performed, and so the reward structure of that task often helps to create the active regulatory focus. In the world in which the human cognitive system evolved, mismatches probably occurred when individuals had mistaken expectations about the nature of a task or environment. In cases in which expectations have been violated, it is important to be reactive to stimuli in the environment. However, the modern world contains a number of socially-defined incentive systems for which our motivational apparatus may not be optimized. Thus it is important to have a better understanding of what situations do and do not engage conscious processing in order to create social scaffolding that engages appropriate motivational states for the tasks we ask people to perform.

Future Research

In any study of cognitive processing there is a tension between gaining control of the stimuli and task so that it can be modelled accurately and the exploration of tasks that have the complexity of those pursued by people outside the laboratory setting. So far we have focused primarily on simple concept learning tasks in which we have fine control over both the stimuli and the processes people bring to bear on the task. This control has been useful in allowing us to discover the complex interaction underlying regulatory fit. Now that the structure of this interaction has become clear, however, we wish to broaden our focus to explore a wider range of cognitive tasks to better understand the interplay of explicit and implicit processes.

One important line of research that we plan to continue is the study of performance under pressure. The existing literature on pressure suggests that under some circumstances expert performance is hurt by using explicit processes when a highly-learned skill should be carried out implicitly (Gray, 2004; Masters, 1992). In contrast, other research suggests that performance may be harmed under pressure by constricting the availability of conscious resources (Beilock & Carr, 2005; Beilock et al., 2004). The research described above suggests that the regulatory fit framework presented here will be useful for exploring this situation in more detail.

Other social phenomena may also be related to the regulatory fit framework described. For example, research on stereotype threat suggests that people's performance in a cognitive task may be impaired if they are a member of a group that is stereotypically thought to be bad at a task and if that stereotype is activated during task performance (e.g. Steele, 1997; Steele & Aronson, 1995). Most research on stereotype threat, however, involves tasks for which people are rewarded for their performance during the task. Thus it is possible that stereotype threat creates a regulatory mismatch, which decreases the involvement of conscious processing used by subjects under threat. Thus it is possible that the effects of stereotype threat may be reversed in tasks with a negative reward structure.

Finally, as cognitive psychologists, we know that there is a wide array of individual differences in task performance that becomes 'noise' in our data. Much of this noise may arise from personality characteristics that affect the chronic regulatory focus of our participants. For example, anxiety may be related to a prevention focus in participants (Higgins, 1987). Furthermore, behavioural inhibition and activation may be related to the motivational states participants bring to studies (Pickering & Gray, 2001). By better understanding the influence of motivational state on the degree of conscious processing in cognitive tasks, we may be better able to control these sources of variability in our experiments. Ultimately, this control will provide us with a better understanding of the interplay of implicit and explicit processes in normal cognitive performance.

Acknowledgments

This research was supported by Air Force Office of Scientific Research grant FA 9550-06-1-0204 and a fellowship in the IC2 institute to ABM.

References

Ashby, F.G. (ed. 1992), *Multidimensional Models of Perception and Cognition* (Hillsdale, NJ: Lawrence Erlbaum Associates).

Ashby, F.G., Alfonso-Reese, L.A., Turken, A.U. & Waldron, E.M. (1998), 'A neuropsychological theory of multiple systems in category learning', *Psychological Review*, **105** (3), pp. 442–81.

Ashby, F.G. & Gott, R.E. (1988), 'Decision rules in the perception and categorization of multidimensional stimuli', *Journal of Experimental Psychology: Learning, Memory, and Cognition*, **14**, pp. 33–53.

Ashby, F.G., Isen, A.M. & Turken, A.U. (1999), 'A neuropsychological theory of positive affect and its influence on cognition', *Psychological Review*, **106** (3), pp. 529–50.

Ashby, F.G. & Maddox, W.T. (2005), 'Human category learning', *Annual Review of Psychology*, **56**, pp. 149–78.

Ashby, F.G. & Waldron, D.M. (1999), 'On the nature of implicit categorization', *Psychonomic Bulletin and Review*, **6** (3), pp. 363–78.

Bechara, A., Damasio, A.R., Damasio, H. & Anderson, S. (1994), 'Insensitivity to future consequences following damage to human prefrontal cortex', *Cognition*, **50**, pp. 7–12.

Beilock, S.L. & Carr, T.H. (2005), 'When high-powered people fail: Working memory and "choking under pressure" in math', *Psychological Science*, **16** (2), pp. 101–5.

Beilock, S.L., Kulp, C.A., Holt, L.E. & Carr, T.H. (2004), 'More on the fragility of performance: Choking under pressure in mathematical problem solving', *Journal of Experimental Psychology: General*, **133** (4), pp. 584–600.

Bowers, K.S., Regehr, G., Balthazard, C.G. & Parker, K. (1990), 'Intuition in the context of discovery', *Cognitive Psychology*, **22**, pp. 72–110.

Briley, D.A. & Wyer, R.S. (2002), 'The effect of group membership salience on the avoidance of negative outcomes: Implications for social and consumer decisions', *Journal of Consumer Research*, **29**, pp. 400–15.

Carver, C.S. & Scheier, M.F. (1998), *On the Self-Regulation of Behavior* (New York: Cambridge University Press).

Crick, F. & Koch, C. (1998), 'Consciousness and Neuroscience', *Cerebral Cortex*, **8**, pp. 97–107.

Cunningham, W.A., Raye, C.L. & Johnson, M.K. (2005), 'Neural correlates of evaluation associated with promotion and prevention regulatory focus', *Cognitive, Affective, and Behavioral Neuroscience*, **5** (2), pp. 202–11.

Dorfman, J., Shames, V.A. & Kihlstrom, J.F. (1996), 'Intuition, incubation, and insight: Implicit cognition in problem solving', in *Implicit Cognition*, ed. G. Underwood (Oxford: Oxford University Press), pp. 257–96.

Gray, R. (2004), 'Attending to the execution of a complex sensorimotor skill: Expertise differences, choking, and slumps', *Journal of Experimental Psychology: Applied*, **10** (1), pp. 42–54.

Higgins, E.T. (1987), 'Self-discrepancy: A theory relating self and affect', *Psychological Review*, **94** (3), pp. 319–40.

Higgins, E.T. (1997), 'Beyond pleasure and pain', *American Psychologist*, **52** (12), pp. 1280–1300.

Higgins, E.T. (2000), 'Making a good decision: Value from fit', *American Psychologist*, **55**, pp. 1217–30.

Higgins, E.T. (2005), 'Value from regulatory fit', *Current Directions in Psychological Science*, **14** (4), pp. 209–13.

Higgins, E.T., Chen Idson, L., Freitas, A.L., Spiegel, S. & Molden, D.C. (2003), 'Transfer of value from fit', *Journal of Personality and Social Psychology*, **84** (6), pp. 1140–53.

Hong, Y.Y. & Chiu, C.Y. (2001), 'Toward a paradigm shift: From cross-cultural differences in social cognition to social-cognitive mediation of cultural differences', *Social Cognition*, **19** (3), pp. 181–96.

Isen, A.M. (2001), 'An influence of positive affect on decision making in complex situations: Theoretical issues with practical implications', *Journal of Consumer Psychology*, **11** (2), pp. 75–85.

Isen, A.M. & Labroo, A.A. (2003), 'Some ways in which positive affect facilitates decision making and judgment', in *Emerging Perspectives on Judgment and Decision Research*, ed. S.L. Schneider and J. Shanteau (New York: Cambridge University Press), pp. 365–93.

Keri, S. (2003), 'The cognitive neuroscience of category learning', *Brain Research Reviews*, **43** (1), pp. 85–109.

Kim, K. & Markman, A.B. (2006), 'Differences in fear of isolation as an explanation of cultural differences: Evidence from memory and reasoning', *Journal of Experimental Social Psychology*, **42**, pp. 350–64.

Loewenstein, G. (1996), 'Out of control: Visceral influences on behavior', *Organizational Behavior and Human Decision Processes*, **65**, pp. 272–92.

Maddox, W.T. & Ashby, F.G. (1993), 'Comparing decision bound and exemplar models of categorization', *Perception and Psychophysics*, **53**, pp. 49–70.

Maddox, W.T. & Ashby, F.G. (2004), 'Dissociating explicit and procedure-learning based systems of perceptual category learning', *Behavioral Processes*, **66** (3), pp. 309–32.

Maddox, W.T., Baldwin, G.C. & Markman, A.B. (2006), 'Regulatory focus effects on cognitive flexibility in rule-based classification learning', *Memory and Cognition*, **34** (7), pp. 1377–97.

Maddox, W.T., Markman, A.B. & Baldwin, G.C. (2006), 'Using classification to understand the motivation-learning interface', *Psychology of Learning and Motivation*, **47**, pp. 213–50..

Markman, A.B., Maddox, W.T. & Baldwin, C.G. (2005), 'The implications of advances in research on motivation for cognitive models', *Journal of Experimental and Theoretical Artificial Intelligence*, **17** (4), pp. 371–84.

Markman, A.B., Maddox, W.T. & Worthy, D.A. (2006), 'Choking and excelling under pressure', *Psychological Science*, **17** (11), pp. 944–8.

Markman, A.B. & Ross, B.H. (2003), 'Category use and category learning', *Psychological Bulletin*, **129** (4), pp. 592–613.

Masters, R.S.W. (1992), 'Knowledge, knerves, and know-how: The role of explicit versus implicit knowledge in the breakdown of a complex motor skill under pressure', *British Journal of Psychology*, **83**, pp. 343–58.

Medin, D.L. & Schaffer, M.M. (1978), 'Context theory of classification', *Psychological Review*, **85** (3), pp. 207–38.

Mednick, S.A. & Mednick, M.T. (1967), *Examiner's Manual: Remote Associates Test* (Boston: Houghton Mifflin).

Nosofsky, R.M. (1986), 'Attention, similarity and the identification-categorization relationship', *Journal of Experimental Psychology: General*, **115** (1), pp. 39–57.

Packard, M.G. & Cahill, L. (2001), 'Affective modulation of multiple memory systems', *Current Opinion in Neurobiology*, **11**, pp. 752–6.

Pickering, A.D. & Gray, J.A. (2001), 'Dopamine, appetitive reinforcement and the neuropsychology of human learning: An individual differences approach', in *Advances in Individual Differences Research*, ed. A. Eliasz and A. Angleitner (Lengerich, Germany: PABST Science Publishers), pp. 113–49.

Posner, M.I. & Keele, S.W. (1970), 'Retention of abstract ideas', *Journal of Experimental Psychology*, **83**, pp. 304–8.

Roediger, H.L. (2003), 'Reconsidering implicit memory', in *Rethinking Implicit Memory*, ed. J.S. Bowers and C.J. Marsolek (New York: Oxford University Press), pp. 3–18.

Shah, J. & Higgins, E.T. (1997), 'Expectancy * value effects: Regulatory focus as determinant of magnitude and direction', *Journal of Personality and Social Psychology*, **73** (3), pp. 447–58.

Sloman, S.A. (1996), 'The empirical case for two systems of reasoning', *Psychological Bulletin*, **119** (1), pp. 3–22.

Steele, C.M. (1997), 'A threat in the air: How stereotypes shape intellectual identity and performance', *American Psychologist*, **52**, pp. 613–29.

Steele, C.M. & Aronson, J. (1995), 'Stereotype threat and the intellectual test performance of African Americans', *Journal of Personality and Social Psychology*, **69** (5), pp. 797–811.

Tohill, J.M. & Holyoak, K.J. (2000), 'The impact of anxiety on analogical reasoning', *Thinking and Reasoning*, **6** (1), pp. 27–40.

Uttal, W.R. (2001), *The New Phrenology* (Cambridge, MA: The MIT Press).

Waldron, E.M. & Ashby, F.G. (2001), 'The effects of concurrent task interference on category learning: Evidence for multiple category learning systems', *Psychonomic Bulletin and Review*, **8** (1), pp. 168–76.

Wickens, T.D. (1982), *Models for Behavior: Stochastic Processes in Psychology* (San Francisco: W.H. Freeman).

Zeithamova, D. & Maddox, W.T. (2006), 'Dual task interference in perceptual category learning', *Memory and Cognition*, **34** (2), pp. 387–98.

Daniel A. Weiskopf

Concept Empiricism and the Vehicles of Thought

Abstract: *Concept empiricists are committed to the claim that the vehicles of thought are re-activated perceptual representations. Evidence for empiricism comes from a range of neuroscientific studies showing that perceptual regions of the brain are employed during cognitive tasks such as categorization and inference. I examine the extant neuroscientific evidence and argue that it falls short of establishing this core empiricist claim. During conceptual tasks, the causal structure of the brain produces widespread activity in both perceptual and non-perceptual systems. I lay out several conditions on what is required for a neural state to be a realizer of the functional role played by concepts, and argue that no subset of this activity can be singled out as the unique neural vehicle of conceptual thought. Finally, I suggest that, while the strongest form of empiricism is probably false, the evidence is consistent with several weaker forms of empiricism.*

1. Introduction

Many empiricist theses fell on hard times in the latter half of the twentieth century. As a semantic thesis, empiricism fell to Quine's critique of verificationist conceptions of meaning. As a thesis about the mind's innate contents and mechanisms, empiricism was a primary target of Chomsky's arguments concerning language learning and the poverty of the stimulus. Finally, empiricism suffered from its traditional connection with purely associationist models of mental processing, which lost ground to computational models implementing rule-based transitions among logically structured representations (at least until the connectionist revival of the late 1980s).

Despite this series of attacks on a variety of empiricist claims, one form of empiricism, namely *concept* empiricism, has been enjoying a resurgence in recent years among philosophers and psychologists (Barsalou, 1999; Goldstone & Barsalou, 1998; Prinz, 2002). Contemporary concept empiricism can be defined as a thesis about the nature of the vehicles of thought. This *perceptual vehicles thesis* states that thoughts are composed of perceptual representations, or copies thereof.[1] Thoughts, in effect, are made up of internally reactivated traces of perceptions. Empiricists marshal philosophical arguments as well as linguistic, psychological and neuroscientific evidence to support the perceptual vehicles thesis. Few, however, have distinguished among various strengths it might come in. We can distinguish these strengths as follows (using 'percepts' to mean 'perceptual representations or copies thereof'):

1. Strong Global Empiricism (SGE): all thoughts are entirely composed of percepts.
2. Weak Global Empiricism (WGE): all thoughts are partially composed of percepts.
3. Strong Local Empiricism (SLE): some thoughts are entirely composed of percepts.
4. Weak Local Empiricism (WLE): some thoughts are partially composed of percepts.

Finally, opposed to all of these empiricisms is the concept rationalist thesis: *no* thoughts are even partially composed of percepts (Fodor, 1975); that is, thought is entirely amodal.[2]

Classical empiricists like Hume and Locke favoured SGE, and their modern descendants such as Prinz and, at times, Barsalou join them in advocating this thesis. Others, e.g. Goldstone & Barsalou, only propose to defend a weaker view: 'our position is that abstract conceptual knowledge is indeed central to human cognition, but that it depends on perceptual representations and processes, both in its

---

[1] Spelled out more thoroughly, the thesis should include both perceptual and *motor* representations, but I will mostly discuss perception here. Also, combinations of copies of perceptual representations should be allowed to be concepts as well. The main argument of the article is unaffected by these omissions.

[2] The weaker grades of empiricism distinguished in (2)–(4) can also be seen as weak forms of rationalism, since they allow that there is more to conceptualized thought than copies of perceptual representations. Moving away from empiricism involves moving closer to rationalism. To keep the terminology simple, though, I will consider these mainly as ways of stating different empiricist claims.

development and in its active use. Completely modality-free concepts are *rarely, if ever*, used, even when representing abstract contents' (p. 146, emphasis mine). This might indicate commitment to WGE or SLE. Some other theorists who are broadly inspired by empiricism are harder to classify (Glenberg & Kaschak, 2002; Glenberg & Robertson, 2000). In this article, I focus on the neuroscientific evidence for what I take to be the boldest and most interesting empiricist claim, namely SGE; it is this that I refer to as 'the perceptual vehicles thesis' from here on.

Empiricists are committed to the idea that the neural correlates of perception coincide, at some level of analysis, with the neural correlates of thought. The first question I will address here, then, is whether neuroanatomical, imaging and single-cell recording studies, as well as other arguments drawing on specifically neurobiological evidence, support SGE. (I set aside consideration of possible purely psychological evidence for SGE in this discussion.) I will argue that once we attend to the way that control of thought and behaviour is causally structured in the brain, we can see that this strong claim is unsupported. A second question I will address is a more general one: what sorts of constraints should be imposed on the search for the neural structures that realize thoughts and other cognitive states? This is an important issue for empiricists and non-empiricists alike. Finally, I will consider whether the evidence offered for SGE might support a weaker, and more plausible, sort of mixed empiricist thesis. I will conclude by assessing the prospects for such weaker forms of empiricism.

2. Discovering Vehicles

Thoughts and concepts, *qua* representational states, can be viewed under at least two aspects: what they represent (what their intentional content is), and what sort of structure does the representing (what the vehicle of that content is). No doubt talk of 'vehicles' and 'content' is metaphorical, but the basic distinction should be clear enough. That Damascus is in Syria, for instance, can be represented by a sentence or a map. The content is the same, the vehicle differs. Similarly in other cases: compare a photograph of the cat asleep on the bed with the sentence 'The cat is asleep on the bed', or compare a linguistic representation of the fact that world oil production is declining this decade with a graph of world oil production. Graphs, maps, photographs, sentences and other representational systems provide different vehicles for representing content.[3] Empiricism says that the vehicles of perception, whatever they are and however they are structured, are sufficient to carry all thinkable thought contents.[4]

The orthodoxy in philosophy of mind holds that mental states (properties, events, processes, etc.) are functionally individuated. Functionalism as a metaphysics of mind can be spelled out in various ways: the commonsense causal functionalism of Lewis and Armstrong, the machine functionalism of Putnam, the teleofunctionalism of Lycan, and so on (see Polger, 2004, for review). These different approaches have in common that they take mental states to be constituted by certain of their causal relations to other mental states, to bodily movements and stimulations, and to the wider environment. This is of a piece with the general reductionist nature of functionalism: mental states are just states that are appropriately situated in the causal network, and this network as a whole can ultimately be characterized just in terms of nonintentional properties and relations.

This functionalist metaphysics leads naturally to a two-stage methodology for discovering the nature of thoughts. In stage one, we spell out the causal role that defines the state type itself — that gives its individuation conditions. Whether this causal role is determined a priori (by conceptual analysis, say), a posteriori, or by some mixture of the two isn't important. In stage two, we look around to see what sorts of things stand in the causal relations specified in stage one; that is, we find the realizers, the things that play the role that individuates the state type.[5] In the case of thoughts and concepts, we need to spell out the causal role that distinguishes conceptualized thought proper, then discover what sort of states realize that role.

---

[3] I have been supposing that these different vehicles *can* represent the same content. Some, e.g. Haugeland (1991), have disagreed with this, saying that different representational genera (he surveys sentences, images and holographic representations) do not in fact carry the same kind of content. Without going as far as Haugeland, we can agree that photographs, for instance, may encode more content than do sentences: a photo of the cat represents her fur as being a certain colour, her head as being tilted at a particular angle, and so on. None of this is represented in the sentence. Still, both the photo and the sentence seem to represent the cat as being asleep on the bed, so there is at least some overlap in content. I think that none of the arguments I will present against empiricism depend on any strong assumptions about the ability of different vehicles to encode the (partially) same content.

[4] It does not, though, claim that all thought *contents* are just perceptual contents. In this respect contemporary empiricism differs from its historical antecedents. See the end of this section for further discussion.

[5] Realizers of one role may themselves be functionally specified as well, of course (Lycan, 1981). Some have argued that all scientific theories, all the way down to basic physics, individuate their properties and kinds functionally — no science tells us about the true intrinsic natures of things (Shoemaker, 1981).

Saying just what constitutes the functional 'essence' of concepts is hardly trivial.[6] Focusing mainly on the criteria used by psychologists yields the claim that concepts are states that are centrally causally implicated in categorization and inference; that is, they are states that function in grouping together objects under a common heading, and in projecting from something's being a member of one class to its having certain further properties. These are clearly fundamental psychological acts. There are other criteria as well: concepts need to be able to combine into larger structures, they need to be publicly shareable, they need to have the right sort of representational content, they need to be learnable, and so on (see Murphy, 2002, for further discussion of the explanatory function of concepts). But the role delimited by categorization and inference is the weightiest factor in the causal profile that defines concepts as a unified object of study. Of course, if the structures that are operative in categorization failed to satisfy other components of the causal role, we would have a problem. We might then need to look for some other states that *could* meet all of the components, or revise the description of the role itself so that it picked out some more narrow class. But here I will assume, to keep the discussion simple, that there is no problem about whether what explains categorization can also explain conceptual combination, intentional content, and so on.

Let us focus, then, on the empiricist argument for the perceptual vehicles thesis. Given the two-stage methodology, the case must be that the neural structures that are most causally significant for explaining the target processes (categorization and inference) elucidated in the concept-role are the very structures that support perceptual representations. An independent way of identifying perceptual representations is to say that they are representations used by sensory systems, defined as a creature's dedicated input systems (Prinz, 2002, p. 115). Given this specification, we can first isolate perceptual representations, then see that the same structures in which these representations are realized are also implicated in the concept role.

So stated, though, empiricism faces a puzzle. If thought vehicles are perceptual vehicles, how are thinking and perceiving distinguished? Why isn't any activation of the perceptual system *de facto* a deployment of concepts? A final condition is needed to draw this crucial

---

[6] One might argue over whether we should begin with the analysis of concepts and then analyse thoughts, or proceed in the other direction. I will assume that the most fundamental fact about concepts in the present context is that they are constituents of thoughts. Given this relationship, it makes no difference whether we begin with the role of concepts or thoughts: either one can be defined in terms of the other.

distinction. To avoid the conclusion that any act of perceiving an object counts as an act of thinking proper, Prinz proposes that 'concepts are spontaneous: they are representations that can come under the *endogenous control* of the organism' (emphasis mine); 'concepts can be freely deployed in thinking, while certain perceptual representations are under environmental control' (Prinz, 2002, p. 197). Perceptual representations become concepts, then, when they are capable of being deployed under endogenous control.

The notion of endogenous control is, unfortunately, not a perfectly clear one. For every particular case in which a representation is activated by an internal cause, we could potentially trace that cause's history back to causes outside the organism as well. Perhaps what is meant is something like this: representations are endogenously controllable when they can be caused by organism-internal states that aren't themselves reliably activated by any particular external stimuli. The endogenous control state itself must be independent of the stimuli presently impinging on the creature. No doubt more could be done to clarify this notion, but since nothing will hang on it, we can set these objections to one side. The general point is that if a representation can *only* be tokened by a perceptual encounter with an object or stimulus, it is a mere percept; if the same representation can be tokened by organism-internal causes, it is a concept. So the criterion of conceptuality is modal: concepts are perceptual representations that *can* be deployed under endogenous control.[7]

3. Convergence Zones and the Locus of Control

Empiricists maintain that the structures activated in categorization that are capable of being deployed endogenously are purely perceptual, i.e. those that are proprietary to some dedicated input system (*or*

---

[7] Concept empiricism is not necessarily committed to the problematic empiricist doctrines mentioned at the beginning of this article. For example, it is not verificationist. Percepts represent perceptual properties, but they may also be used to represent categories that transcend perception. One way to achieve this is by adopting an informational theory of content on which structures represent what they are nomically connected with (for elaboration, see Prinz, 2006). Briefly, on such a theory distal properties whose instances cannot be directly perceived can be represented using perceptual vehicles that correspond with their proximal traces. Whether such a theory of content is ultimately successful is not something I will deal with here; I mention it only to block the immediate charge of verificationism. Neither is concept empiricism committed to associationism. As a claim about representational vehicles, it potentially allows that many kinds of processes may operate in cognition to transform, select, store and combine representations. These need not be limited to Humean or connectionist associations. The perceptual vehicles thesis is intended to be neutral with respect to how concepts get their intentional/representational properties, and with respect to the range of processes that operate on those vehicles.

copies thereof; I ignore this disjunct for the moment, but it will become important later). I'll argue that there are cell assemblies that are plausibly implicated in categorization and that are endogenously deployable that are nevertheless not perceptual representations. If there are, then by the empiricist's reasoning, these must be counted as conceptual. So not all concepts are composed of purely perceptual vehicles, and SGE is false.

Interestingly, some of these assemblies are discussed by Prinz himself: they are so-called *convergence zones* posited by Damasio and colleagues in a number of papers (Damasio, 1989; Damasio & Damasio, 1994; Damasio *et al.*, 2004). Convergence zones are neural ensembles that receive projections from earlier cortical regions (e.g. lower sensory areas), contain feedback projections onto those earlier layers, and feed activity forward into the next highest layers of processing. These zones can also refer back to zones earlier in the processing stream, so that higher-order zones may be reciprocally connected with multiple lower-order zones.[8] The functional role of convergence zones is to orchestrate the reactivation of lower-order activity patterns. A particular zone can become sensitive to the co-occurrence of a particular pattern of activity in the region that feeds it in such a way that that activity pattern can later be reinstated endogenously by activity in the zone itself.

The fact that convergence zones can engineer the re-deployment of perceptual representations of concrete entities and events gives the empiricist some support, since it shows that percepts can be activated off-line during bouts of cognition (e.g. drawing inferences about objects, naming them, recalling their properties, and so on). However, this falls short of showing that only percepts serve as concepts. The problem is that convergence zones *themselves* must be activated in order to orchestrate perceptual re-enactments. Zones may receive downward connections from a variety of areas, including prefrontal cortex, cingulate, basal ganglia, thalamus, and so on. So neuronal ensembles in convergence zones satisfy the endogenous deployability condition.

Do they satisfy the categorization condition, however? It is hard to see why they don't. In any particular episode of categorization, an enormous range of neural structures is implicated. Everything from low-level sensory receptors at the retina and skin through thalamic

---

[8]   Terminological note: I follow neuroscientists' usage in calling a cell assembly higher-order when it receives projections from assemblies that are closer to the sensory periphery, and lower-order when it projects forward to regions that are further from the sensory periphery. That is all that these terms mean in the present context.

relays and associated subcortical structures, sensory cortices and various prefrontal regions receive activation; and this list doesn't include the output side involved in generating behavioural responses. Included in this vast pattern of activation are convergence zones: if a person is trying to recognize a perceived object, zones are activated that aid in retrieving its name and associated properties. If an object is being perceived for the first time, zones are receiving inputs that train them on the particular pattern of co-occurring perceptual properties. If no object is presented, but an inference must be made about a class of objects, zones are again re-activated as part of the process of knowledge access. So in many paradigmatic categorization tasks, convergence zones are implicated, insofar as they are central to retrieving the representations of perceptual features of objects.

Convergence zones, in fact, seem to make a unique contribution towards representing conceptual contents. Individual representations of perceptual features are realized in modality-specific sensory cortices. When some set of those features are active, we can say that the system is representing certain properties of a perceived or remembered object. However, complete concepts and thoughts are composed of more than just co-activated features. To see this, consider the set of features RED, ROUND, BLUE, SQUARE. This set is indeterminate between representing a red round object and a blue square object and representing a blue round object and a red square one. The mere co-occurrence of those features doesn't decide which concepts are bound together as representing the same objects; this is the familiar 'binding problem' as it is discussed in the neuroscience literature.

Convergence zones are responsible for re-activating perceptual features, but moreover it has also been claimed that they represent 'the combinatorial arrangements (binding codes) which describe their pertinent linkages in entities and events (their spatial and temporal coincidences)' (Damasio, 1989, p. 39). So it is the activity in the relevant convergence zone that determines which of the two possible pairs of bindings of adjectival and nominal concepts is the correct one in the example given above. This semantic function is essential, since it makes the difference between a mere loose bag of concepts that are co-tokened and an articulated representation with predicative and propositional structure. On this interpretation, convergence zones are essential to representing the most abstract, amodal aspects of thought contents, namely their logical skeleton.[9]

---

[9] I ought to stress that this interpretation is highly conjectural. I'm not endorsing it wholeheartedly here, just raising it to illustrate a possible role that convergence zones might fill.

Given that they satisfy the causal-role conditions on being concepts as well as perceptual representations do, convergence zones have an equal right to be seen as (part of) vehicles of thought. This possibility threatens Strong Global Empiricism. If all thoughts have some amodal component, the strongest claim that can be established is Weak Global Empiricism. In discussing this objection, Prinz says:

> Convergence zones may qualify as amodal, but they contain sensory records, and they are not the actual vehicles of thought. Convergence zones merely serve to initiate and orchestrate cognitive activity in modality-specific areas. In opposition to the rationalist [amodal representation] view, the convergence-zone theory assumes that thought is couched in modality-specific codes. (Prinz, 2002, p. 137)

First, this seems to overstate the commitments of the theory as Damasio *et al.* express it. It isn't a necessary part of believing in convergence zones that one believe the perceptual vehicle thesis. A slimmer commitment will do, namely the thesis that perceptual representations are causally necessary for carrying out certain kinds of categorization and inference involving some categories. It might be useful to re-activate perceptual records of one's encounters with dogs in deciding what shape a German shepherd's ears are, or records of frog encounters in deciding whether they have lips. This shows that re-enacted perception is useful, and perhaps necessary, in many contexts. Convergence zones may be instrumental in making this re-enaction happen. But it's a further step to thinking that the vehicles of thought are *just* the re-enacted perceptions.

Second, in the present context it is question-begging to assert that convergence zones aren't vehicles of thought. As we've seen, the higher level non-perceptual states that cause the re-enactions have an equal right to be seen as vehicles along with the perceptual states themselves. This might seem to serve empiricists a qualified victory: *some* thoughts are made of percepts. But in the very same episodes of occurrent thought there are non-perceptual representations active as well. The most radical concept rationalists might be unhappy with this conclusion. Even so, the strongest version of the perceptual vehicles thesis seems similarly unsupported.

The empiricist has another possible reply at this point. He might maintain that convergence zones aren't representational at all. Rather, they are *mechanisms* for generating representations. This is hinted at in the claim that they 'orchestrate' re-activation of perceptual states. Barsalou, too, suggests that '[a]lthough mechanisms outside sensory-motor systems enter into conceptual knowledge, perceptual symbols always remain grounded in these systems. Complete transductions never occur whereby amodal representations that lie in associative areas totally replace modal representations' (Barsalou, 1999, p. 583). While this claim is cautiously hedged, it suggests a reply similar to Prinz's: *mechanisms* outside the senses enter into concepts.[10] Empiricists might, then, propose a strong distinction between (i) representational states and (ii) non-representational mechanisms that token and transform those states. In its most general form, the *mechanism strategy* (as I will call it) involves arguing that any putatively non-perceptual representational activity can be re-interpreted as the activity of a mechanism.

This strategy faces several problems, however. First, it isn't clear that the strong distinction mentioned above can be sustained, because some mechanisms might *also* be representations. Consider a mechanism that implements a transition from symbols shaped like 'P→Q' and 'P' to symbols shaped like 'Q'; that is, a mechanism that implements a transition corresponding to the application of *modus ponens* (MP). One might argue that a system containing this mechanism, in virtue of containing it, *implicitly represents* the rule of MP. Cummins (1989) argues that computational systems frequently include such implicit representations. Generally, systems may implicitly cognize a rule by having a mechanism the operation of which can be semantically interpreted as corresponding to the application of the rule. In virtue of having a mechanism by which complex symbols can be transformed in the right sort of way, the system grasps the rule of MP. Implicit representation shows one way in which mechanisms might also be themselves representational. Since some mechanisms (e.g. the one that transforms symbols in accord with MP) implicitly represent, calling convergence zones mechanisms doesn't automatically show that they aren't also representations.

Further, cognitive and neural mechanisms are complex structures that may themselves contain various sorts of *explicit* representations (for analysis of the notion of a mechanism, see Machamer, Darden & Craver, 2000). Mechanisms contain parts that operate together in a spatiotemporally organized way to subserve a certain function. These parts themselves may be explicitly representational. For example, there might be an amodal representation DOG tokened in a higher-order convergence zone that functions to re-activate perceptual traces

---

[10] The quoted passage is, in fact, somewhat more hedged than this, since it seems to admit the possibility that there *are* amodal symbols somewhere in the mind/brain. Prinz at times seems to want to avoid even this conclusion. For more on this issue, see the discussion of multimodal cells in the next section.

of dogs in lower-order sensory regions. These amodal representations might be part of mechanisms for the directed retrieval of perceptual information in the service of carrying out particular cognitive tasks that are best addressed by using this information. So, as this simple example illustrates, the mere claim that convergence zones are mechanisms doesn't by itself establish their non-representational credentials (I will develop this objection further in Section 6).

Moreover, it isn't clear that the mechanism strategy is consistent with some empiricists' preferred informational theory of content (on informational semantics, see Dretske, 1981; Fodor, 1990).[11] On informational psychosemantics, roughly speaking, a state's content is the condition that it nomically covaries with. In the case of percepts, this is the state that nomically causes them; in the case of motor representations, it is the state that they nomically cause. Convergence zones, as understood on the mechanism strategy, are analogous to motor representations: they function to reliably bring about a certain (neural, not behavioural) effect state, namely the re-enactment of lower-order perceptual representations. If this relationship is nomic, it seems that on an informational account it would be difficult to resist the conclusion that they represent. Just what their content is isn't entirely clear; perhaps they represent the perceptual representations that they function to produce, or perhaps they represent the properties that those percepts represent.[12] In any event, whatever one says about the precise nature of their content is less important than the fact that they can plausibly be seen as non-perceptual representations.

One might try to block the conclusion that convergence zones are amodal representations by appealing to a more stringent notion of representation. It might be that nomic covariation is insufficient for representation. Perhaps having the right sort of function is also required. Representations might need to play the role of 'standing in' for what they represent when those things themselves are absent. In that case, if

---

[11] Prinz is most explicit in adopting informational semantics. But it is worth noting that informational approaches are consistent with what many neuroscientists seem to believe about neural representation. The standard empirical method for assigning content to a cell assembly is to locate the stimulus conditions that cause it to fire above its normal baseline. These conditions can be regarded as the properties that the cell is 'locked onto', in the jargon of informational semantics. Receptive and projective field mapping are, then, ways of empirically discovering neural content on the assumption that this content is fundamentally informational.

[12] Note that not everything that represents what a perceptual representation does needs to itself be a perceptual representation. So even if convergence zones could represent perceptual properties, they wouldn't therefore be perceptual states. Perceptual states are, for the empiricist, defined as being part of perceptual systems. But there is no apparent reason why the content of those states can't be duplicated elsewhere in the brain.

convergence zones always co-occur with lower-level perceptual states, they cannot *represent* those states (or those states' content). This criterion of representation, though, may be too stringent. It runs the risk of ruling out motor representations, for example, which by design play an active role in producing the movements that they represent. The challenge in making good on this anti-representationalist manoeuvre, then, is to find a condition on representation that rules in motor representations but rules out convergence zones. This is, at least, a significant challenge.

For a variety of reasons, then, the mechanism strategy seems unpromising. There is a strong case for seeing convergence zones as non-perceptual representations that play a central role in categorization processes.

4. Modality-Responsiveness and Perceptual Representation

At this point we can see that more than purely perceptual representations seem to be implicated in the overall categorization process. But empiricists cite other evidence to support the perceptual vehicles thesis. They might argue, for example, that there are no genuinely amodal cells anywhere in the brain: all neurons are plausibly associated either with perceptual processing or with interfaces among perceptual systems. While amodal cells might be taken to be the hallmark of non-perceptual representation and processing, empiricists can argue that any evidence for purportedly amodal cells could be reinterpreted as being evidence for bimodal or multimodal cells instead. Since bimodal or multimodal cells can be seen as being perceptual representations, their existence doesn't threaten empiricism.

Discussion of modality-specific neurons arises in the context of a potential objection to empiricism. Newborn children are able to map stimuli perceived in one sense modality onto stimuli perceived in another. So, for instance, at one month of age they can map objects felt with their tongues (such as distinctively shaped pacifiers) onto seen objects (pictures of those pacifiers) (Meltzoff & Borton, 1979). One candidate explanation of this ability is that there are cells in regions such as the superior colliculus that function to map stimuli from one sense modality to another. An anti-empiricist might contend that these are genuinely amodal cells that plainly function in categorizing stimuli (deciding that *what is felt* is the same as *what is seen*, for instance). If there are amodal cells that have this function, then one might conclude that there are genuine amodal neural representations at work in cognition.

It is crucial to guard against a conflation between *a cell's being modality-responsive* and *its being a component of a perceptual representation*. Being modality-responsive is a matter of whether a stimulus of a certain type causes a neuron to activate, or causes it to activate preferentially. Prinz characterizes the senses as 'dedicated input systems', meaning that they (1) function to receive inputs from outside the brain, (2) are distinguished on the basis of the different physical magnitudes that they respond to, and (3) are housed in separate neural pathways, as identified by neuroanatomical and functional considerations (Prinz, 2002, pp. 115–17). So while modality-responsiveness is necessary for being a perceptual representation, it isn't sufficient. Even if it turns out that there are widespread unimodal cells in the brain, more is needed to show that these are components of perceptual representations. Specifically, one needs to show that these cells are part of separate, internally distinguished neural systems that have the function of processing physical input magnitudes.

Prinz's response to the challenge from amodal cells seems to overlook this caveat, though. He suggests two possibilities: the empiricist could either argue that apparently amodal cells are really modality specific, or argue that they are multimodal. But showing that these cells are genuinely specific in their response pattern to stimuli from a certain class of magnitudes doesn't show them to be perceptual representations unless it's also established that they are part of a distinctive neural system that has the right sort of input function. Distinguished response patterns are only one component of perceptual representation.

The multimodal cell response needs further consideration. Here the proposal is that multimodal cells have a foot in more than one sensory system and function to map information from one system onto another. In the case of intermodal transfer it might be reasonable to think that a relatively simple interface might do to link distinct sensory systems. But it is questionable whether every body of multimodal cells is implementing such a (relatively) simple mapping. So even if some multimodal cells can be treated as boundaries or interfaces between sensory systems, not all of them plausibly can.

These larger populations of multimodal cells may comprise distinct, *non-perceptual* processing systems. Given the size of multimodal cell populations, in fact, it seems quite likely that there are non-perceptual processing systems in the brain. Large portions of the prefrontal cortex are dedicated to multimodal processing, including dorsolateral, superior and inferior regions, pars triangularis and pars orbitalis (Kaufer & Lewis, 1999). It is implausible that these are simply serving as interfaces between sensory systems. The greater the size and complexity of the multimodal region that mediates between sensory systems, the less it appears to be a simple interface or boundary and the more it appears to be a distinct, non-sensory system dedicated to carrying out a separate cognitive task. So the multimodal cell response does not generalize: not every multimodal cell is just part of an interface.

This last claim can be strengthened by considering recent evidence that multimodal cells are widely distributed in the brain, even in so-called primary sensory regions (this evidence is reviewed extensively in Ghazanfar & Schroeder, 2006). These multimodal cells are frequently specialized to fire in the presence of congruent multisensory stimuli. For instance, certain cells in the primary auditory cortex of monkeys fire preferentially when a face and a voice are present together, and the so-called fusiform face area (located in a traditional 'visual' cortical region) has been found to activate to familiar voices as well as familiar faces.

These findings also challenge the notion that 'each type of [perceptual] symbol becomes established in its respective brain area. Visual symbols become established in visual areas, auditory symbols in auditory areas, proprioceptive symbols in motor areas, and so forth' (Barsalou, 1999). One prominent conception of what makes something a perceptual system (as noted, a conception endorsed by Prinz) is its responsiveness to a unique physical magnitude. But not every representational tokening in a visual region may count as a 'visual symbol' if some visual cells have their response properties modulated by non-visual stimuli as well. None of this is to say that an empiricist might not be able to construct a definition of a sensory system, and hence of perceptual representations, that is compatible with widespread distribution of cells that respond to different classes of physical magnitudes. But if traditional unimodal sensory regions in fact contain a large percentage of cells that respond to bimodal or multimodal stimulation — hence, that respond to many different kinds of physical magnitudes — the notion of a pure or dedicated sensory system on which empiricism depends may have to be revised.

To summarize, then, there are three separate roles that multimodal cell populations might be playing: (1) they might be interfaces between sensory systems; (2) they might be non-sensory processing systems; or (3) they might be parts of sensory systems that are directly modulated by activity in other sensory systems. Insofar as roles (2) and (3) predominate, multimodal cells cannot easily be interpreted in a way that is compatible with empiricism.

5. Copies and the Collapse of Empiricism

Earlier I noted that the perceptual vehicles thesis is disjunctive: concepts are either percepts or *copies* thereof. The notion of a copy now needs closer scrutiny. I've argued that at several crucial functional regions in the brain there are cell assemblies active in concept-central tasks that aren't employing perceptual representations. The grounds for thinking that these representations are non-perceptual is that they are not the proprietary currency of any of the senses, where these are understood as dedicated input systems in the brain. Empiricists might still be able to accept this and argue instead that cells in convergence zones or regions that are identified with working memory such as prefrontal cortex can be regarded as manipulating copies of perceptual representations. The notion of a copy, when scrutinized, turns out to undermine the substance of the contemporary empiricist thesis.

Copying can be construed in several ways. In classical empiricism, copies of impressions — ideas — necessarily preserved their phenomenological qualities modulo a lesser degree of 'vividness'. Crudely, a copy was a state that appeared in consciousness as a 'washed-out' perception. In contemporary empiricism, though, phenomenological properties aren't necessarily preserved in copies; indeed, phenomenology is not even necessary for something's being a perceptual representation, since a lot of perceptual processing is non-conscious. Copying is, broadly, a causal process that produces new representations from old ones. This suggests that copies obey an etiological condition: a copy has its causal source in the representation that is its original. A chance resemblance in two structures isn't enough for one to be a copy of the other.

In addition to etiology, there is a common content condition: For one representation to be a copy of another, it is necessary that it share content with its original. If copying doesn't preserve content, it isn't distinguished from inference and other processes of information transformation. But shared content isn't sufficient for something to be a copy. This is because the same content can be re-encoded into different formats — different kinds of vehicles. Consider an analogy. A low-fidelity hand-drawn sketch made from an ornately decorated treasure map might be a copy of that map even if it omits much of the detail in the original map. It can be a copy even if it is a different size, and if it replaces, say, a picture of a treasure chest with an 'X' to mark the location of the loot. But a detailed verbal description of the location of the buried treasure is not a copy of it. The description might preserve the map's content, but that isn't enough for it to count as a

copy. Some degree of vehicular similarity is needed as well. In particular, we need at least to have the same vehicle *type* in both the original
and the copy. Both original and copy need to be maps, and maps that
contain the same content. Small details in the way that content is
marked on each map may not count as differences in either content or
vehicle (unless they have some significance in the representational
scheme or in the way the vehicle is processed, in which case they are
clearly relevant to determining the similarity of an original and its
putative copies).

Prinz seems to endorse this conclusion. He suggests that a necessary condition for something's being a copy is that it preserve such
properties of the vehicle's format: 'Imagine, for example, that a visual
percept is a pattern of neural activity in a topographic map corresponding to the visual field. A stored copy of that percept might be a
similar pattern in a topographic map stored elsewhere in the brain'
(Prinz, 2002, p. 108; emphasis mine). Let's assume, then, that it is necessary and sufficient for something's being a copy of a percept that:

1. it has its causal source in the original percept;
2. it has the same content as the original; and
3. it is similar enough in its vehicular properties to the original
   perception.

The question for the empiricist now becomes how widespread these
copies are in the brain.

At least some brain areas that process sensory information do so
in a different way than do primary sensory cortices. The superior
colliculus, for instance, receives visual, tactile and auditory sensory
inputs and is implicated in directing eye movements towards targets
that can be localized using all of these sensory cues. It might seem that
the colliculus contains perceptual copies, since it is roughly organized
as a series of maps of different sensory spaces laid on top of one
another. In the case of vision this map is similar to others found in primary visual cortex. But on closer inspection things aren't so simple.
The auditory map in the colliculus, for example, seems to represent
the origin of sound sources in space around the organism. Primary
auditory cortex, though, *doesn't* contain a spatial map of sound
sources. Rather, it encodes a tonotopic map in which sound frequencies are mapped onto groups of neurons (low to high frequencies are
mapped caudally to rostrally; see Middlebrooks, 2000). The primary
auditory map represents frequencies, not locations of sounds. Since
the auditory map in the superior colliculus is not only *structured* differently from the map in primary auditory cortex but also represents

different *content* than that map, it cannot be a *copy* of an auditory representation but must be seen as a distinct structure for using auditory information in a task-specific way (probably integrating multisensory information for guidance of eye movements). It would not be entirely surprising if later representations of perceptual information employed specialized formats more suitable to the particular task they are involved in carrying out.

Another region that might be thought to contain copies of perceptual representations is prefrontal cortex (PFC), particularly the dorsolateral or anterior pole of PFC. It is not known exactly how to characterize the activity of PFC, but it has been implicated in retrieval from episodic memory, intentional direction of attention, planning, and setting and maintaining goals beyond the immediate context (see Ramnani & Owen, 2004, for review). PFC also receives reciprocal connections from many sensory cortices. Importantly, PFC neurons seem to represent perceptual information differently than do the sensory areas that feed them. For example, Freedman *et al.* (2001) trained monkeys to discriminate cats from dogs based on computer-generated images. A range of 'cat' and 'dog' images was created by morphing the focal cat and dog images together in varying percentages. Recording from cells in the monkeys' ventrolateral PFC revealed that some cells fired selectively for all dog stimuli, some for all cat stimuli. Moreover, when a monkey trained on this task was retrained on three new perceptual categories, these cells changed their response properties to fire selectively for the members of the newly relevant category.

This suggests that cells in some PFC regions may be adaptive, changing their representational properties with the task demands (Duncan, 2001). While there may be distributed representations of the perceptual properties of cats and dogs in various sensory cortices, it is less clear that there are specific cell populations that co-vary with particular categories of dogs and cats as such. These would be akin to the fabled 'grandmother' cells that encode memories of particular individuals (e.g. Grandma) and categories. Perhaps one role of PFC is to assemble these transient 'grandmother'-like structures on-line. Regardless of whether this speculation is correct, the point of interest is just that PFC may contain neural vehicles that differ from those deployed in sensory systems. Hence it cannot just contain copies of perceptual vehicles, even if it contains re-representations of categories that are also encoded perceptually.

Finally, evidence that neurons in PFC represent information differently than do perceptual systems comes from Rao, Rainer & Miller (1997). It is widely known that in visual processing, information about an object's identity is processed separately from information about its spatial location. An alternative way to characterize this split is as being between information that is used for the spatial control of behaviour with respect to an object and information used to categorize an object (Milner & Goodale, 1995). However it is characterized, the former sort of information is processed in the dorsal stream of the visual system and the latter in the ventral stream.[13] Separate representations and mechanisms operate on each kind of information. However, populations of neurons in the dorsolateral PFC are responsive to both information about an object's spatial location *and* information about its category membership. These cells seem to integrate information from both visual processing streams. But this means that they cannot simply be *copies* of earlier perceptual representations, since the visual system represents this information separately. Neither are they easily seen as simple interfaces between two visual streams, since these cells are located in a highly multimodal region that engages in elaborate processing and retrieval of information for top-down control of behaviour.

Ultimately, the copy proposal poses a dilemma for empiricists. Either copies are required to have a high degree of vehicular fidelity or they aren't.[14] If they aren't, then, potentially any content-identical state can be a copy of a percept. But this undermines the central empiricist idea that thinking involves re-activating and re-using the very representations that are employed in perceiving objects and events. One might as well believe in an amodal language of thought on this conception of a copy. Further, it is far from clear what relevance the neuroscientific and psychological data about the use of perceptual representations could have, if copies need not themselves have similar structure or function as those percepts. Presumably the support that these studies give to empiricism is in showing that properly perceptual representations are recruited in a wide array of conceptual tasks. Moreover, if the vehicular similarity clause is dropped, empiricists would then be vulnerable to a charge they sometimes make against amodal theorists, namely that their theory can account for potentially

---

[13] There may also be several separate types of information processed within the dorsal and ventral streams. These distinctions are coarse, but sufficient for the present discussion.

[14] Of course, the notion of 'fidelity' here is a graded one, since it relies on the notion of *similarity* in neural vehicles. The issue is complicated by the fact that vehicles can be similar in some respects but different in others. A spatial map of visual space in one region of the brain may not behave the same as a map of the same space in another region of the brain, owing for example to differences in the local connectivity patterns within each region. When to count any two maps as being similar enough to one another to support the same representations is a difficult issue to decide.

any observations, and hence becomes drained of distinctive testable consequences. Perceptual representations can be independently identified, given a definition of what counts as a perceptual system. Copies of perceptual representations that differ in their vehicular properties, though, cannot.

On the other hand, if copies are required to be highly similar in vehicular properties to perceptual representations, then it's an open question how widely they are distributed throughout the brain. Many regions outside the bounds of perceptual systems manipulate and process perceptual *information*. But, as the examples presented here suggest, they may do so using differently structured representational vehicles. So the distribution of copies may not be as extensive as empiricists require to establish the perceptual vehicles thesis. To establish the full version of the copy proposal, empiricists need to provide convincing evidence that the vehicular properties of neural populations in perceptual regions are duplicated elsewhere in the brain. To date, this evidence is lacking.

6. Refining Neural Correlates

I have raised a number of arguments against the perceptual vehicles thesis. The common structure of the arguments that I have been offering is, essentially, the following: in explaining the central functions of the conceptual system, we will need to appeal to many neural activation patterns beyond those in the perceptual systems; these neural activation patterns are not themselves perceptual representations or copies thereof; hence SGE cannot be correct, since it presumes that all of the representations involved in these central functions are perceptual.

Note that the form of argument given here doesn't show that we won't also, at least sometimes, need to explain people's reasoning and behaviour by appeal to perceptual representations. (Perhaps we'll always need to appeal to the deployment of some perceptual representation or other; I am agnostic on this issue.) An empiricist, then, might reply to these arguments by saying that neural activity in non-perceptual systems shouldn't be counted as activity that partially realizes thoughts. That is, an empiricist might try to *carve off* part of the ongoing pattern of activity in the brain — namely, the part involving only perceptual representations — and argue that, while other brain regions might be causally involved in deploying these percepts, they aren't constitutive of thoughts themselves. On this strategy, what is needed is some way to draw a distinction between neural states that are (merely) *causally involved* in the production of a thought, and states that *constitute* a thought.

In principle this distinction might seem easy enough to draw. Isn't it obvious, after all, that there is a clear boundary around the occurrence of a particular thought here and now and everything else that is going on in my mind, body and environment right now, including that thought's causes and effects? Mustn't there be such a boundary if there is a fact of the matter about what particular thoughts I am entertaining, both at a time and diachronically? Perhaps some intuitions say so. In practice, however, locating the boundaries around these thoughts as they are realized in the brain is considerably harder.

This task bears a powerful resemblance to the task of locating the so-called neural correlate(s) of consciousness (NCC). The logical structure of this task has recently attracted a fair amount of attention (Block, 2005; Chalmers, 2000; Noë & Thompson, 2004). Looking at the structure of this related debate can help to shed light on our present topic, which we might call the search for the *neural correlate of conceptual thought* (NCCT).

The job of finding an NCC, for some particular conscious phenomenal state type, involves locating a neural state the activation of which co-varies appropriately with the occurrence of the phenomenal type. Chalmers (2000) gives a general definition of an NCC as follows: 'An NCC is a minimal neural system N such that there is a mapping from states of N to states of consciousness, where a given state of N is sufficient, under conditions C, for the corresponding state of consciousness' (p. 31). So, for instance, if we are talking about the state of consciously experiencing a red patch in a region of visual space, consciously perceiving a horizontal line, or some other visual state that has a phenomenological component, the neural correlate of that state is nomically sufficient for the occurrence of that experience under the appropriate conditions.

Saying what makes a set of conditions appropriate is difficult. Chalmers notes that normal conditions are plausibly taken to require an intact (unlesioned, developmentally ordinary) brain, although it may undergo unusual stimuli (either external or internal, e.g. presentation of unusual stimuli via normal perceptual channels, microelectrode stimulation, or transcranial magnetic coil stimulation) during experimental procedures. Since brain lesions can induce widespread changes in the architecture and function of normal brains, he cautions against taking the conditions C to include them.[15]

Moreover, and significantly given our present concerns, a neural correlate must be a *minimal* state, that is, the smallest region the activation of which is sufficient to produce the phenomenal state in question. This is to rule out taking the entire brain of a creature to be some state's neural correlate. Clearly some activation pattern in the whole brain would suffice for the occurrence of a particular conscious state, but that would not be very informative about what features of the brain in particular were responsible for producing consciousness.

A final condition on this minimal neural state is that according to Chalmers it must be a *content match* for the conscious state of which it is a correlate. The neurons that are activated must represent the same content that is revealed in consciousness. For instance, if a neuron fires preferentially to a horizontal line in its receptive field, then it may provisionally be tagged as a representation of a horizontal line in such-and-such a location, and can potentially count as a correlate for the conscious experience of seeing such a line.

An empiricist might try to exploit the twin conditions of minimality and content matching in order to winnow down the NCCT. Here is one way this argument might go:

1. Content matching requires that the NCCT, no less than the NCC, carries the same content as does the thought of which it is a correlate.
2. While there is widespread neural activity during conceptualized thought, *only* the activity in perceptual regions carries the same intentional/representational content as the thought being realized.
3. By minimality, the NCCT should be identified with the smallest neural region that satisfies content matching.
4. Hence, only the activity in perceptual regions counts as the NCCT.

---

[15] For this reason, as well as considerations of space, I have omitted discussion of the role that evidence from category-specific deficits might play in establishing empiricism. Generally, the findings involve showing that lesions to perceptual regions produces selective deficits in identifying and reasoning about entire classes of objects (e.g. living things or artifacts). However, it is far from clear whether there is any consistent correlation between lesioning a region and production of a certain deficit; in addition, there is little standardization of the tests that demonstrate these deficits, so different researchers characterize them in different ways. For a review of the literature and discussion of models that might explain category-specific deficits, see Caramazza & Mahon (2003) and Humphreys & Forde (2001).

The argument is a valid one. Premises (1) and (3) are simply state-ments of the conditions on neural correlates adapted from Chalmers' discussion of NCCs, which aren't controversial in the present context. The key empirical premise in the argument is (2). We should consider, then, what arguments can be given to support it.

First, note that the definition of a neural correlate requires that the activity be sufficient for occurrence of a thought.[16] But if we are con-sidering just the intrinsic activity of a perceptual system at a time, this just raises the very problem for empiricism that was mentioned in Sec-tion 2, namely the problem of distinguishing thought from perception. There I followed empiricists in distinguishing concepts from percepts on the basis of whether they could be brought under endogenous con-trol. As noted, though, this is a modal criterion. It can't tell us whether a particular pattern of activity in visual cortex is a *perception* of a dog or an internally re-activated perceptual state being deployed as a *thought* about dogs. The pattern itself doesn't determine which of these possible cognitive states is occurring. If that activity *could* have been generated endogenously, then those representations count as both conceptual and perceptual. But this won't tell us whether the organism is *now* using them to think or to perceive. Putting the point somewhat differently, the endogenous control principle can distin-guish concepts from percepts, but not thinking from perceiving.

We might try extending the endogenous control principle here to distinguish occurrent thoughts from occurrent perceptions. *Actual* causal etiology might distinguish thinking from perceiving. Perhaps occurrent thoughts are those perceptual states that are actually caused endogenously, and perceptions are states that are caused by external stimuli. This won't quite work as a sufficient condition, though, since hallucinations are internally caused *perceptual* states. There is no dagger before me when I hallucinate one; the dagger appearance is caused by some state of my disordered brain. Moreover, it's not clear that this proposal works as a necessary condition, either, since not all thoughts must actually be endogenously caused. Perceptual beliefs are occasioned by perceptions, which in turn are actually caused by the environment, but there is nevertheless a difference between occurrent

---

[16] In their critique of the notion of an NCC, Noë and Thompson (2004) argue that insisting on sufficiency presupposes an *internalist* notion of content, since on externalist notions of content, including informational semantics, factors outside the neural state itself help to fix what it represents. So the mere occurrence of that state itself, in abstraction from its sur-roundings, need not constitute the tokening of a contentful representation. An analogous critique might be raised in the present case, but the argument that I am presently making applies even if Noë and Thompson's problem could be solved.

perceptual belief and perceiving. So actual etiology seems unable to draw this distinction.

This problem about distinguishing thinking from perceiving is relevant to empiricists who want to exploit minimality in order to locate the NCCT in perceptual regions, since activity in those regions might be sufficient for *either* perceiving or thinking. But perhaps this disjunction doesn't matter to the issue of whether those regions are NCCTs, as long as the activity in these perceptual regions is a content match for the thought that the creature is entertaining. The fact that we don't have a clear criterion for distinguishing perceptual system activation that is thinking from that which is perceiving might be a non-issue as long as the underlying neural state in each case is the *only available* content match for the thoughts that we are trying to correlate with the underlying brain states. Rather than pursue the problem of distinguishing thought and perception further, then, I will turn to the issue of the uniqueness of content matching.

Unfortunately for the empiricist, we have already seen, in the earlier discussion of convergence zones (see Section 3), that content-bearing states are potentially widely distributed throughout the brain. This means that there are many alternative candidates for the NCCT. Higher-order convergence zones provide one instance, regions in prefrontal cortex provide another (these may not be exclusive categories). Both of these regions potentially carry representational content; indeed, as the Freedman *et al.* study showed, cell assemblies in prefrontal cortex can adapt their response properties to different categories depending on the task demands.[17] Suppose, then, that we have simultaneous (or nearly so) activity in both a higher-order region such as a prefrontal cell assembly and a lower-order perceptual region, say some part of visual cortex. Perhaps the lower-order activity is under the active causal control of the higher-order state, thus satisfying the endogenous deployment condition. Are there *any* grounds for decisively singling out the perceptual activation as the minimal bearer of

---

[17] Although I should note that this depends on convergence zones being representations of the appropriate intentional content. If they either are not representations or are representations only of the lower-order neural states themselves, then this line of argument fails. But as I argued earlier, we *have* reason to think that they are representations. Reason to think that they represent what lower-level perceptual states represent might come from other cases in which representational content is 'borrowed'. For instance, a child may learn an elephant concept by encountering not elephants themselves but words and pictures of elephants. The concept learned borrows its content from these representations. Perhaps the same thing happens with convergence zones: they represent what the perceptual representations do, rather than the vehicles themselves. If this is true, then they are candidates for the NCCT.

intentional content in this case as opposed to the higher-order state that is causally directing it?

I suggest that we don't have such grounds. It seems equally possible that the intentional content of thought is represented in the activated higher-order regions as in the lower-order perceptual regions. To see how this might be possible, consider one model I sketched earlier in discussing what I called the mechanism strategy. On this model of neural processing, there is an amodal representation of a certain category, say DOG, in some extra-perceptual area. This representation is deployed as part of a process of making some inferences about dogs, e.g. deciding whether dogs have spleens. The functional role of this representation might be to guide further mental processing in deciding this question by coming to judge either DOGS HAVE SPLEENS or DOGS DON'T HAVE SPLEENS. Suppose now that as part of the mental processing that goes into answering this question one activates some mental images of dogs — perhaps culled from a television programme on veterinary medicine or a textbook of dog anatomy, for example. These images might be realized neurally as patterns of activity in some part of visual cortex, and these patterns might represent dogs, their spleens, and so on. By manipulating these images — say, comparing the visual representation from the veterinary programme with a stored visual representation of a human spleen — one might be able to make the appropriate inference. If there is an appropriate visual match, then one comes to judge that dogs do in fact have spleens.

I'd like to stress that I'm not offering this as a detailed and realistic model of how categorization judgments are processed in the brain, although something like it might not be too far from the truth. Often we seem to use visual images to solve problems, and using such images involves re-activating parts of perceptual areas (Kosslyn, 1994). Some evidence for a structuring of control and retrieval systems in the brain akin to the one proposed here comes from Rowe *et al.*, who found that activity in dorsolateral PFC (Brodmann area 46) is associated with retrieval of items from memory to guide behavioural responses (Rowe *et al.*, 2000). For a perspective on the role of PFC similar to the one sketched here, see Miller, Freedman & Wallis (2002). If this simple model is correct, we have *two* candidate regions that might serve as the NCCT: the perceptual regions themselves and the higher non-perceptual cortical regions that are orchestrating the activity in perception. On this interpretation of what is happening in this categorization task, the intentional contents DOG, SPLEEN, etc., are represented in both modality-specific and amodal neural regions. If this is the case, we cannot privilege *either* region as the unique neural vehicle of thought, given the constraints of minimality and content matching.[18]

Generally, the empiricist's strategy of locating content-matching neural states solely in perceptual regions faces problems because categorization and inference are typically processes that involve activating goal representations, searching through memory and comparing category representations, and other directed cognitive activities. Representations in perceptual areas are usually tokened in the course of processing incoming perceptual stimuli. On the sort of model sketched above, though, they are activated in a top-down fashion to assist in these sorts of conceptual processes. That means that there are very likely a set of distinct control states and processes, wherever they may be located in the brain, that are orchestrating this complex activity in perceptual cortices. In order for the appropriate perceptual representations to be retrieved from memory and compared, they need to be content matching with respect to the higher-order representations that activate them. A control system for using perceptual memory in categorization is only effective if higher-order tokenings of DOG lead to retrieval of percepts that also represent dogs. So considering the plausible design features of these mechanisms of categorization and inference, it doesn't seem unreasonable to suppose that they might *also* contain candidate content matching states. If this is the case, then premise (2) of the empiricist's argument concerning the NCCT can't be sustained.

7. Conclusions

I've argued that the Strong Global version of the perceptual vehicles thesis isn't supported by the neuroscientific evidence. The anti-empiricist case has four main components. First, representations beyond percepts are causally implicated in implementing the causal role distinctive of concepts. Second, evidence of widespread modality-specific cells is either a red herring or threatens to undermine the neat definition of the senses that empiricism requires. Third, falling back on the notion of a 'copy' threatens to either deflate or falsify the

---

[18] At least, we cannot do so based only on the criteria so far laid out to distinguish occurrent thoughts from other psychological states and processes. Remember that the dialectical context here is that of assessing the *empiricist's* account of what sorts of states realize our thoughts. Non-empiricists, e.g. concept rationalists, might want to propose functional role criteria that rule decisively in favour of the non-perceptual vehicles. Perhaps some plausible constraints on concepts entail that perceptual vehicles are unsuitable candidates for realizing the concept role. But we are not attempting here to prejudge the question of whether empiricism or rationalism is the correct account of concepts.

thesis. Fourth, appealing to conditions on what makes some neural state a correlate of conceptual thought won't determinately single out activity in perceptual regions as the vehicles of thought. Nothing we now know of allows us to rule out minimal NCCTs that include both perceptual and non-perceptual regions, and considerations on the design of categorization mechanisms hint that this is in fact a plausible arrangement.

So despite this criticism of SGE, I haven't been arguing decisively for concept rationalism here. In effect, SGE attempts to localize occurrent thoughts in our sensory systems by pinpointing activity in those regions of the brain as the unique filler of the causal role played by concepts. However, occurrent perceptual representations are causally intertwined with activity in numerous non-perceptual regions. This is even more the case when perceptual representations are being activated *as* concepts, under the organism's own control. Undeniably, perceptual representations and processes are tapped as resources in a surprisingly large range of tasks. Some of these are even tasks that we have no *prima facie* reason to think will implicate perception. But this isn't enough to show that thinking just is playing with percepts.

What, then, is the status of empiricist claims that rest on neuroscientific foundations? Ruling out SGE leaves Weak Global Empiricism and Strong and Weak Local Empiricism as open possibilities. The argument of Section 6, however, seems to threaten *any* Strong version of empiricism, since it calls into question our ability to single out perceptual representations as the fillers of the concept role. Given the redundant and distributed way in which intentional content can potentially be represented in the brain, it might be that uniquely perceptual correlates of thought are difficult to find. If this is correct, then the most promising remaining options are Weak Global and Local Empiricism. On both views, at least some thoughts are partially perceptual and partially amodal. This sort of position, somewhere between empiricism and rationalism, is less radical but a better fit for the evidence. Developing specific, testable models that conform to these positions is a task for further research.

Acknowledgements

Thanks to Martin Hahn, Edouard Machery, Pete Mandik, Chase Wrenn, two anonymous referees for this journal, and the editor of this special issue, Rocco Gennaro, for their helpful comments on this paper and earlier versions thereof.

References

Barsalou, L.W. (1999), 'Perceptual symbol systems', *Behavioral and Brain Sciences*, **22**, pp. 577–609.

Block, N. (2005), 'Two neural correlates of consciousness', *Trends in Cognitive Science*, **9**, pp. 46–52.

Caramazza, A. & Mahon, B.Z. (2003), 'The organization of conceptual knowledge: The evidence from category-specific semantic deficits', *Trends in Cognitive Science*, **7**, pp. 354–61.

Chalmers, D.J. (2000), 'What is a neural correlate of consciousness?', in *Neural Correlates of Consciousness: Empirical and Conceptual Questions*, ed. T. Metzinger (Cambridge, MA: MIT Press).

Cummins, R. (1989), 'Inexplicit information', in *The Representation of Knowledge and Belief*, ed. M. Brand & R. Harnish (Tuscon, AZ: University of Arizona Press).

Damasio, A.R. (1989), 'Time-locked multiregional retroactivation: A systems-level proposal for the neural substrates of recall and recognition', *Cognition*, **33**, pp. 25–62.

Damasio, A.R. & Damasio, H. (1994), 'Cortical systems for retrieval of concrete knowledge: The convergence zone framework', in *Large-Scale Neuronal Theories of the Brain*, ed. C. Koch (Cambridge, MA: MIT Press).

Damasio, H., Tranel, D., Grabowski, T., Adolphs, R. & Damasio, A. (2004), 'Neural systems behind word and concept retrieval', *Cognition*, **92**, pp. 179–229.

Dretske, F.I. (1981), *Knowledge and the Flow of Information* (Cambridge, MA: MIT Press).

Duncan, J. (2001), 'An adaptive coding model of neural function in prefrontal cortex', *Nature Reviews Neuroscience*, **2**, pp. 820–9.

Fodor, J. (1975), *The Language of Thought* (Cambridge, MA: Harvard University Press).

Fodor, J. (1990), 'A theory of content II', in *A Theory of Content and Other Essays* (Cambridge, MA: MIT Press).

Freedman, D.J., Riesenhuber, M., Poggio, T. & Miller, E.K. (2001), 'Categorical representation of visual stimuli in the primate prefrontal cortex', *Science*, **291**, pp. 312–16.

Ghazanfar, A.A. & Schroeder, C.E. (2006), 'Is neocortex essentially multisensory?', *Trends in Cognitive Science*, **10**, pp. 278–85.

Glenberg, A.M. & Kaschak, M.P. (2002), 'Grounding language in action', *Psychonomic Bulletin & Review*, **9**, pp. 558–65.

Glenberg, A.M. & Robertson, D.A. (2000), 'Symbol grounding and meaning: A comparison of high-dimensional and embodied theories of meaning', *Journal of Memory and Language*, **43**, pp. 379–401.

Goldstone, R. & Barsalou, L.W. (1998), 'Reuniting perception and conception', *Cognition*, **65**, pp. 231–62.

Haugeland, J. (1991), 'Representational genera', in *Philosophy and Connectionist Theory*, ed. W. Ramsey, S. Stich & D. Rumelhart (Hillsdale, NJ: Lawrence Erlbaum).

Humphreys, G.W. & Forde, E.M. (2001), 'Hierarchies, similarity, and interactivity in object recognition: "Category-specific" neuropsychological deficits', *Behavioral and Brain Sciences*, **24**, pp. 453–509.

Kaufer, D.I. & Lewis, D.A. (1999), 'Frontal lobe anatomy and cortical connectivity', in *The Human Frontal Lobes: Functions and Disorders*, ed. B.L. Miller & J.L. Cummings (New York: Guilford Press).

Kosslyn, S.M. (1994), *Image and Brain: The Resolution of the Imagery Debate* (Cambridge, MA: MIT Press).

Lycan, W. (1981), 'Form, function, and feel', *Journal of Philosophy*, **78**, pp. 24–50.

Machamer, P.K., Darden, L. & Craver, C.F. (2000), 'Thinking about mechanisms', *Philosophy of Science*, **67**, pp. 1–25.

Meltzoff, A.N. & Borton, R.W. (1979), 'Intermodal matching by human neonates', *Nature*, **282**, pp. 403–10.

Middlebrooks, J.C. (2000), 'Cortical representations of auditory space', in *The New Cognitive Neurosciences*, ed. M.S. Gazzaniga (2nd edn., Cambridge, MA: MIT Press).

Miller, E.K., Freedman, D.J. & Wallis, J.D. (2002), 'The prefrontal cortex: Categories, concepts, and cognition', *Philosophical Transactions of the Royal Society of London B*, **357**, pp. 1123–36.

Milner, A.D. & Goodale, M.A. (1995), *The Visual Brain in Action* (Oxford: Oxford University Press).

Murphy, G. (2002), *The Big Book of Concepts* (Cambridge, MA: MIT Press).

Noë, A. & Thompson, E. (2004), 'Are there neural correlates of consciousness?', *Journal of Consciousness Studies*, **11**, pp. 3–28.

Polger, T. (2004), *Natural Minds* (Cambridge, MA: MIT Press).

Prinz, J. (2002), *Furnishing the Mind* (Cambridge, MA: MIT Press).

Prinz, J. (2006), 'Beyond appearances: The content of sensation and perception', in *Perceptual Experience*, ed. T.S. Gendler & J. Hawthorne (Oxford: Oxford University Press).

Ramnani, N. & Owen, A.M. (2004), 'Anterior prefrontal cortex: Insights into function from anatomy and neuroimaging', *Nature Reviews Neuroscience*, **5**, pp. 184–94.

Rao, S.C., Rainer, G. & Miller, E.K. (1997), 'Integration of what and where in the primate prefrontal cortex', *Science*, **276**, pp. 821–4.

Rowe, J.B., Toni, I., Josephs, O., Frackowiak, R.S.J. & Passingham, R.E. (2000), 'The prefrontal cortex: Response selection or maintenance within working memory?', *Science*, **288**, pp. 1656–60.

Shoemaker, S. (1981), 'Some varieties of functionalism', *Philosophical Topics*, **12**, pp. 83–118.

Jesse Prinz

Mental Pointing
Phenomenal Knowledge Without Concepts

It is one thing to have phenomenal states and another thing to think about phenomenal states. Thinking about phenomenal states gives us knowledge that we have them and knowledge of what they are like. But how do we think about phenomenal states? These days, the most popular answer is that we use phenomenal concepts. Phenomenal concepts are presumed to be concepts that represent phenomenal states in a special, intrinsically phenomenal, way. The special nature of phenomenal concepts is said to be important for defending materialism against epistemic arguments for dualism. In this paper I present an account of phenomenal knowledge that does not depend on phenomenal concepts. In fact, I argue that we have no phenomenal concepts. Instead my account appeals to mental pointing, a process that I explain in terms of phenomenal demonstratives. Phenomenal demonstratives are sometimes referred to as concepts in the literature, but I suggest that this is a mistake. I also present a theory of phenomenal demonstratives that equates them with attentional control structures in working memory. In a concluding section I describe how this theory can be used to defuse the knowledge argument for dualism. That is only a subsidiary goal, and my response to the knowledge argument echoes others in the literature. I think the project of developing a substantive, empirically informed theory of phenomenal knowledge has interest independent of debates about mental ontology. That is my central focus. Thinking about phenomenal knowledge can shed light on the relationship between consciousness, attention and memory. This paper has a philosophical agenda and an empirical agenda. Those who reject my philosophical claims about the nonexistence of phenomenal concepts, the conditions required for phenomenal knowledge, and the truth of physicalism, could accept some of my empirical claims about the neurofunctional correlates of consciousness and the resources available for accessing phenomenal states. Of course, I think the empirical claims support my philosophical conclusions.

1. The AIR Theory of Consciousness

1.1. Outline of the theory

Any account of how we think about our phenomenal states must depend on the nature of those states. Therefore, this discussion cannot get off the ground without a theory of consciousness. I cannot defend such a theory here, but I will summarize a theory that I have defended elsewhere (Prinz, 2000; 2001; 2005; forthcoming). The account of phenomenal knowledge will draw on ideas from this theory, but is compatible with other approaches to consciousness as well.

The theory I endorse has two components. First, there is an account of the contents of consciousness. I believe that all consciousness is perceptual, which is to say that consciousness attends only representations in sensory systems (Prinz, 2007). I also believe that consciousness arises only at an intermediate stage of perceptual processing (Jackendoff, 1987). Sensory systems are organized hierarchically, and there is a progression from representations of very local features of a stimulus all the way up to highly abstracted categorical representations that capture features of stimuli that are comparatively invariant across perspectives. In between are representations that are coherent rather than local and vantage point specific rather than invariant. Following Jackendoff, I locate consciousness here. Activity in the neural correlates of intermediate-level areas correlates with conscious experience, and cells in these areas have contents that agree with experience. Low-level representations are more fragmented than experience, and high-level representations are too abstract. Consider the cells that are used to recognize something as a face. The cells are typically invariant across a range of viewing angles, which is to say the same cell fires if the face is seen straight on or nearly in profile. In sharp contrast, a phenomenal experience of a face is orientation-specific. I do not want to deny that high-level representations can have conscious effects. For example, they often result in conscious verbal imagery ('there's a chair'), conscious action tendencies (the preparation to sit) and shifts in attention. The last of these will be important in the discussion below.

The intermediate-level hypothesis is a theory of the contents of consciousness. But we also need a theory of how these contents become conscious. Mere activation of intermediate-level perceptual states is not sufficient for consciousness. In subliminal perception, there is activation throughout the perceptual hierarchy without any corresponding experience (e.g. Moutoussis and Zeki, 2002). Therefore consciousness requires not mere intermediate-level activation, but activation of a particular kind. But what kind? The second part of my account extends Jackendoff's theory by addressing this question. I am persuaded that consciousness arises when and only when we are paying attention. Consider research on inattentional blindness. In these studies, subjects are given a task that demands considerable attention, such as comparing the length of two similar lines or counting how many times moving objects collide, and while they are engaged, an unexpected stimulus is presented in plain view (Mack and Rock, 1998; Most et al., 2005). Many subjects fail to notice the unexpected stimulus under these conditions, even though the stimulus would be readily perceived under conditions that were less attentionally demanding. Or consider the attentional blink (Vogel and Luck, 2002). In these studies subjects are presented with a sequence of stimuli and are asked to look for two target stimuli in the sequence; if the second target appears shortly after the first, many subjects fail to perceive it, because the first target has temporarily consumed their attention. Or consider visual neglect. In this disorder, brain injuries in structures that control attention result in blindness for part of the visual field. All these phenomena suggest that attention is necessary for consciousness. Putting this conclusion together with the conjecture about the content of consciousness, we are left with the following theory: phenomenal states are attended intermediate-level representations, or AIRs.

To avoid circularity, the AIR theory must incorporate an account of attention that is not defined in terms of consciousness. Ultimately, that theory might be specified in precise neurocomputational terms. Short of that goal, we can give an analysis of attention in psychological terms and then relate the psychology to gross neuroanatomy. On the view I favour, attention is a process that allows information to flow from perceptual systems to systems involved in working memory. Working memory is actually an umbrella term for a number of different capacities: the capacity to retain information, to transform perceptual states imaginatively, to select behavioural responses and to carry out various executive responses, such as object tracking, comparison and verbal reporting. In a popular phrase, working memory allows for maintenance and manipulation. When we attend, aspects of what we perceive become available thereby to be maintained for brief periods and manipulated. If this is what attention does and consciousness requires attention, then consciousness arises when perceptual states send signals to working memory. Anatomically, attention is associated with structures in parietal cortex, and working memory is associated with lateral frontal cortex. Intermediate-level visual perception is located in temporal cortex. So visual consciousness, on this view, involves a circuit that includes temporal, parietal and frontal cortices. Other senses may involve other structures, but the basic principles will be the same: consciousness arises when perception plus attention allows working memory access.

1.2. Encoding or availability?

This formulation of the theory raises a question. The phrase 'working memory access' is ambiguous. It can refer to the process by which information in perceptual systems becomes accessible or it can refer to the processes by which working memory systems actually access perceptual states. Metaphorically, we can talk of broadcasting or receiving. Presumably these processes are distinct. Attention leads to specific changes in how perceptual states are processed and those changes allow perceptual states to send information forward to working memory systems, which then receive, or 'encode', the states. So the question is, does consciousness arise when perceptual systems broadcast or only when working memory systems receive the broadcast? I want to suggest three lines of evidence for thinking broadcasting is sufficient.

First, consider change blindness. When presented with a change-blindness display, subjects actively scan every corner of the image in an effort to detect the change. Presumably, this process involves the allocation of attention and whatever we attend to becomes available to working memory. A person staring at a change-blindness display could report on any feature that she happens to be staring at. But there is reason to think that the features that are available to working memory are not actually getting recorded in working memory, because, if they were, the changes would be easier to detect. This interpretation gets some support from neuroimaging. In a change blindness task, Beck *et al.* (2001) found greater activation in working memory areas when the change was detected as compared to when a change went undetected. This is not to say that there is no working memory activation when no change is detected. Working memory seems to automatically store the gist of an image, even when details are lost. Dramatic changes affecting the significance of the display (such as the gender of a person we are looking at) are typically noticed (Simons and Levin, 1997). Moreover, we can, by act of control, focus on any given detail of a display and retain it from one moment to the next, but this takes effort, and we don't know antecedently what feature to focus on. When trying to find a change, we might arbitrarily focus on one feature after another, until we hit on the one that changed. Once we find it, the change is easy to detect. But, while searching for the change, the majority of details in a display are not retained, even though they can be plainly seen. This suggests a difference between two kinds of processes: attention without retention and attention with retention. That distinction can be explained by presuming that attention makes each part of the image available to working memory, as we scan it, but working memory receives only select portions of that signal. We scan strategically for bits that we think might be likely to change, and then when, by arbitrary chance, our eyes cross such a bit, we maintain a representation of it in memory.

The second reason for thinking that there can be consciousness without encoding in working memory comes from studies in which stimuli are presented very briefly. If a stimulus is very briefly displayed (e.g. 16 milliseconds) and followed by a mask, it will not be seen at all. Subjects will have no idea that something was presented. If there are some trials in a study in which a stimulus is presented for 16 milliseconds, and others in which a blank screen is presented, subjects will be at chance in guessing whether a stimulus was presented, even though 16 milliseconds is long enough for priming to take place (e.g. Dehaene *et al.*, 1998). But now suppose the stimulus is presented for a longer duration, say 50 milliseconds. Then, depending on the stimulus, subjects may know that *something* was flashed but they won't know what it was. In other words, as we approach the threshold for conscious recognition in priming studies, subjects report a phenomenal experience, but they cannot describe it. Importantly, it's not merely that subjects fail to identify the stimulus; they don't even retain information about it's shape (if they did, recognition would be possible). This is comparable to the experience of participating in the widely discussed experiments of Sperling (1960). Sperling found that, when a grid of letters is presented for 50 milliseconds without a mask, subjects can report the numbers in one row, but not the others. Indeed subjects can be cued to recall *any* row. The other numbers are experienced but not identified. Sperling's study was important because it proved the existence of iconic memory: a very brief period in which a perceptual

stimulus is retained after offset. Iconic memory is different from working memory: it is really a perceptual after-effect, caused presumably
by the slow delay rate of visual states. It does not require encoding or
permit retrieval. So we should not infer from Sperling's conclusion
about iconic memory that consciousness involves encoding in working memory. Indeed, I interpret these results as evidence for the opposite conclusion. I would say that all the numbers are *accessible* to
working memory, but only some are *accessed* by working memory.
The Sperling case and near-threshold priming provide an interesting
contrast to inattentional blindness and very fast priming. In the latter
two cases, subjects have no awareness of the stimulus; they have no
idea that something was displayed. In the Sperling case and the near-
threshold case, subjects experience something, but they do not retain
its specific properties. This suggests a three-way distinction between
being encoded in working memory (the cued numbers in a Sperling
display), merely being broadcast to working memory, and not being
broadcast at all.

   The third line of evidence against the necessity of working memory
encoding may be the most important of all. There is good reason to
think that working memory *cannot* encode perceptual states at the
same level of resolution at which they are consciously experienced.
We experience the world in incredible detail. Subtly different colours,
for example, can be distinguished. Yet such fine details are lost when
we try to retain memories of what we have just perceived over temporal intervals. Imagine being presented with a blue colour patch and
then having to select that very same blue five seconds later from an
array of three similar shades. You won't be able to do it. Accuracy is
nearly perfect for simultaneous side-by-side colour matching, but
highly inaccurate with a delay (e.g. Pérez-Carpinell *et al.*, 1998). This
suggests that working memory stores colours (and other visual features) in a code that abstracts away from their precise details. In other
words, it looks as if working memory uses something more like
high-level visual representations. Indeed, there is evidence from cognitive neuroscience that working memory actually uses high-level
perceptual representations rather than it's own proprietary codes. On
this view, brain structures associated with working memory in lateral
frontal cortex work in concert with structures in inferotemporal cortex
during visual working memory tasks; frontal structures maintain representations in temporal structures (Postle, 2006). If this is right, then
working memory encoding is a matter of maintaining activity in the
higher levels of the sensory pathways. I already argued that high-level
perceptual representations fall outside experience; they are more abstract

that anything we experience phenomenologically. This implies that consciousness cannot depend on encodings in working memory, because such encodings are far less detailed than the contents of experiences. It also follows that perceptual memories, both short-term and long-term, are stored in a code that lies outside consciousness. Of course, a perceptual memory can become conscious through the construction of a mental image. On my view, that happens when high-level representations are used to generate intermediate-level representations through efferent connections in the perceptual hierarchy. This story explains why mental images are often vague or imprecise. In imagery, we generate intermediate-level perceptual states from high-level records that have abstracted away crucial details. When we try to fill in missing details, we are forced to guess what they were. As a result, images can be inaccurate, unstable or sketchy.

Together the foregoing considerations support the contention that consciousness does not require encoding in working memory. I conclude that consciousness involves broadcasting to working memory rather than reception by working memory. The last consideration about the grain of representation raises a bit of a puzzle. If working memory cannot encode the details of experience, then what sense does it make to say that experience involves broadcasting to working memory. How and why would the visual system broadcast information that cannot be received? Isn't this like sending TV broadcasts into outer space? This puzzle threatens to undermine the theory of consciousness that I have been defending — a theory that says consciousness arises when intermediate-level visual states are broadcast to working memory.

I think the answer to this puzzle requires that we move away from the broadcasting metaphor and think about the relationship between consciousness and working memory in a slightly different way. The intermediate level of perceptual processing presents the world as a collection of features and objects, presented in space from a particular point of view. Working memory selects from this array, but to understand the selection process we need to distinguish two stages, each of which might be understood by a different metaphor. First of all, attention functions like a spotlight, illuminating some proper subset of the perceived features, objects and locations. These are the things that are consciously experienced. Then, working memory systems select from this subset. We can compare that selection process to an artist's schematic sketch of the objects on display. The sketch is not a faithful copy, but merely a rough approximation of items in the spotlight. The sketch is also selective, leaving out many things, and transient: the artist will discard most sketches immediately, placing only a few into long-term storage. Like any metaphor, this one is far from perfect, but it improves over broadcasting in two crucial respects. First, it emphasizes a two-stage selection process: the spotlight and the sketch. Second, it emphasizes the loss of fidelity at the second stage.

2. Phenomenal Knowledge

2.1. Having, categorizing, noticing and pointing

The preceding discussion of consciousness will be helpful in addressing the main topic under investigation here: phenomenal knowledge. I use this term to designate knowledge of our conscious states as such. I equate consciousness with phenomenality (see Block, 2002). To be conscious is to feel like something, or to have 'phenomenal qualities'. Phenomenal knowledge is knowing what a state feels like. It is usually assumed that we have such knowledge. It seems obvious to many that if we know anything at all, we know what our conscious states are like. I want to problematize this assumption. I will not deny that we have phenomenal knowledge, but I will try to suggest that phenomenal knowledge is, in some respects, extremely limited.

Before offering an account of phenomenal knowledge, it is useful to distinguish several different relationships we can have with a phenomenal state. First of all, we can experience the state. Grammatically, this phrase is somewhat misleading. When we experience external things, such as earthquakes or sunsets, there is a clear distinction between the object of experience and the experience itself. But this distinction collapses when we experience our phenomenal states. When we experience a phenomenal state, there are not two things in play — the state and our experience of it — but rather one thing: the state being experienced. Experiencing a phenomenal state is simply being in that state. On the theory of consciousness that I endorse, an experienced state is just a perceptual state that is being processed in a way that makes it available to working memory. Experiencing a phenomenal state can be thought of as a relation, because there is an organism who has the experience, but it is not a representational or intentional relation: the organism is not representing the state.

Note that this last claim marks a sharp contrast between the view I defend and higher-order thought theories (HOT). I prefer the AIR theory to the HOT approach because I think it is supported by the evidence that I have summarized, and because I think higher-order thought theories erroneously assume that we have representations as finely detailed as the features available to us in consciousness. If we had such representations of everything we can experience, as the HOT approach requires, then I don't see why we wouldn't be able to recall precise colours after brief delays. I also don't see why the nervous system would include a redundant system of representation. Obviously, it would take much more space to develop these objections in a compelling way. I mention these points of concern to indicate my own reasons for preferring AIRs to HOTs, and to underscore the difference between these approaches. This difference — the lack of meta-representation in the AIR theory — will be important in what follows.

My claim about metarepresentation is that we cannot represent our phenomenal states using representations that have the same precise detail. In making this claim, I do not want to deny that we can represent our phenomenal states. We can, and often do, categorize our experiences. Categorization is the second relation to phenomenal states that I want to consider. If I am looking at the sky on a clear day, and having an experience of blue, I can place that experience under the category blue.

Categorization typically involves the deployment of concepts. As I will use the term, concepts are mental representations that have two important properties. First, concepts can be activated by the organism that possesses them, rather than being activated only by an external stimulus (Prinz, 2002). In Kantian jargon, concepts are capable of being used spontaneously, not just receptively. Second, concepts must be capable of being used to re-identify the things that they represent (Millikan, 2000). We must be able to re-deploy a concept on different occasions to keep track of things. It follows that concepts must be representations that we can store in memory. A representation that was not stored could not be re-tokened or actively used, outside stimulus control, by an organism. Notice that this requirement does not entail that concepts be amodal symbols. Perceptual states can be stored in memory and re-deployed by an organism. Stored perceptual states can be concepts (Prinz, 2002). I think that ordinary colour concepts are stored records of visual states. But, for reasons I have given, the only perceptual states that we store are high-level perceptual representations. The concept of blue is a high-level perceptual representation that could be activated by a range of spectral properties — the range we call 'blues'. We can store records and recognize relatively specific shades of blue as well (e.g. the blue used in the paintings of Yves Klein), but there are limits on this. High-level colour representations are invariant across small changes in hue and value. Retention and recognition of very precise shades may be impossible (unless, of course, we measure the spectral properties of a sample that we are observing and store a verbal record of its precise scientific description).

In cases where we cannot categorize our phenomenal states, I think we can still notice them. Noticing is less demanding then categorizing, because we can notice things that we do not have the capacity to recall or re-identify. I think noticing is best analysed in terms of working-memory encoding. Something gets noticed if and when it gets encoded in working memory.

I want to distinguish noticing from another relationship that we can have with our phenomenal states. It seems that while we are having a phenomenal state, we can mentally point to it. When having an experience we can say, 'that's spicy' or 'that's blue' or 'that's what a D-minor sounds like'. In each of these cases, we are applying a concept (SPICY, BLUE, D-MINOR). These concepts may be stored high-level perceptual representations. The concept, spicy, for example, may be a high-level gustatory or, more likely, nocireceptive representation that has been stored on previous encounters with spicy food. But what is expressed by the word 'that' when we say 'that's spicy' or 'that's blue'? It seems that we are somehow able to point inwardly to an experience. The thought expressed by the sentence, 'that's blue' seems to have two components, one corresponding to the word 'blue' and the other corresponding to the word 'that'.

Unfortunately, not much is known empirically about what goes on when people point to their experiences in thought. There seem to be two possibilities. One possibility is that inner pointing does not involve anything above and beyond having an experience. On this view, when I say 'that's blue', the non-linguistic thought that this expresses contains no representations other than an experience of blue (an AIR) and a high-level perceptual representation (the concept BLUE). If so, the word 'that' doesn't really express any mental representation. It is just a way of verbally labelling the experience itself. Another possibility is that the word 'that' expresses an actual pointer in the mind. On this view, there are states that refer to phenomenal states by means of a relationship that is analogous to pointing. Some philosophers think about these internal states as demonstratives, but I will suggest in a moment that if mental pointers exist they differ from ordinary linguistic demonstratives in an important respect.

I am not aware of any decisive empirical evidence that can distinguish between the hypothesis that we point using inner pointers and the hypothesis that pointing to a mental state is a merely verbal act — an act of saying 'that' as we have an experience. There are, however, three related lines of phenomenological evidence that lead me to favour the view that there are internal pointers. First, phenomenologically, there seems to be a difference between mentally pointing and having an experience accompanied by the word 'that'. Try to say 'that' while having an experience, and then try to mentally point, and see if you find a difference. Some people will undoubtedly be baffled by the instruction to mentally point. The exercise will not work for them. I find the idea of mentally pointing somewhat intuitive and it seems to be different from merely uttering the word 'that' while having an experience. Second, it seems to me that I can point in the absence of silent speech. For example, it seems to me I can have thoughts that I would express by saying 'now, that's delicious!' without actually saying that's delicious to myself. Third, it seems to me that when I do silently utter the word 'that' during an experience it's very clear to me which item of my experience I am ostending. While looking at a complex visual scene, I can shift the apparent reference of the linguistic demonstrative without changing my direction of gaze. Phenomenological arguments are tricky because not everyone reports the same phenomenology, but these considerations are collectively convincing to me.

If mental pointers are real, we need an account of what they are. The metaphor of mental pointing is a reasonable starting place, but we need to move from metaphor to mechanism. Let's consider the case of looking at a complex scene. It seems to be that there are two ways in which we can mentally point to an item in a scene. First. we can identify a particular region of space in which the item is located. Second, we can apply a perceptual concept. Perceptual concepts, I suggested, are stored records of high-level representations. If you are looking at a table setting, you might focus on the left and see what's there or you might look for the salad fork and focus on it, by using a high-level salad fork template. Notice that I used the word 'focus' in both cases. The phenomena I have just described is known in psychology as top-down selective attention. It is well established that top-down attention can be driven by object-representations or by spatial locations (e.g. Hayden and Gallant, 2005). I think mental pointing is achieved by top-down attention.

I have already argued that consciousness requires attention. To avoid confusion, I want to make it clear that not all attention is top down. When task demands do not require a strategic visual exploration of the world around us, attention may be applied quite diffusely, or we may scan, in a more or less bottom-up way from object to object in our surround. Attention can be captured by things we see, and we can attend in a way that does not single out any specific object or region of space (consider the command 'pay attention!'). Top-down selective attention is a distinctive phenomenon. Attention is, on my view, just a process by which perceptual information becomes available to working memory, but that process can be controlled by a variety of different mechanisms. Top-down selective attention is attention that occurs under the control of object representations or spatial maps. I think this process captures the phenomenology of mental pointing very well. For example, when I silently utter the word 'that' while looking at a scene, it seems to apply to whatever object I have brought into focus by top-down control. When this happens, I think the object to which we are attending comes into sharper view, or higher resolution. There is evidence that when we attend, receptive fields in the visual system expand so that more cells than usual respond to the attended object (Olshausen *et al.*, 1993). The attended object may also receive more attention then the surrounding space. Attention is not an all or nothing affair. I think it can come in degrees, and hence consciousness too, which depends on attention in grades. When we use top-down attention to single out an object, it becomes more conscious than the surround.

This account suggests a three-way distinction between kinds of conscious episodes. In Section 1, I distinguished cases in which a perceived stimulus gets encoded in working memory from cases in which it is merely available to working memory. Using the terminology introduced in this section, I label that distinction by the contrast between noticing something and merely experiencing it. I have also introduced a distinction between objects that are within the spotlight of attention and those to which we attend by an act of top-down control. We can label these by referring to experiencing and noticing on the one hand, and mentally pointing on the other. All these three conditions are states of consciousness and, in all three, consciousness arises via the same mechanism: AIRs. The differences have to do with what gets encoded outside consciousness, in working memory, and what unconscious mechanism-control attention. These unconscious differences can affect the degree and allocation of focal attention, as well as what information gets maintained or manipulated.

Let us assume that this account of mental pointing is correct. It is instructive to compare mental pointing to linguistic demonstratives, such as 'this' and 'that'. In his highly influential analysis, Kaplan (1989) argues that a demonstrative is a term that refers rigidly to something that is made salient in a context. The demonstrative itself has no descriptive content, so it cannot determine which object has been designated. But demonstratives are used in conjunction with other representational resources, which Kaplan calls 'demonstrations' to reference. If you say 'that' while pointing, for example, the direction of your finger serves as the demonstration. Or one might refer to 'that man' in a room full of women, and the word 'man' will serve to make the man salient in that context, and the word 'that' will refer to him. Kaplan uses the schema 'dthat[]' to represent the structure of a demonstrative use of the word that, where the brackets get filled in by a demonstration. Mental pointers can be regarded as phenomenal demonstratives. They refer to the conscious perceptual states that are made salient by a mental demonstration. If the analysis I've offered is right, a mental demonstration is a high-level perceptual representation of a representation of a region in space. A phenomenal demonstrative has the structure 'pthat[]' where the brackets are filled in by a mental demonstration. If I mentally point to a salad fork, my phenomenal demonstrative refers to my conscious experience of the fork by using a schematic, high-level representation of a fork to draw attention to that part of the visual scene.

On this story, there are parallels between the way mental pointers work and the way linguistic demonstratives work. But there are also differences. In language, demonstratives are words. I don't think it's helpful to think of phenomenal demonstratives as mental words — symbols in a language of thought — much less as images (e.g. an image of a pointing finger). It's better to think of them as control structures. By this, I simply mean that they are things that have causal control over things. Phenomenal demonstratives use representations of objects in space to direct focal attention on a perceived scene. They are individuated by their causal powers.

In summary, there are at least three ways we can be related to our phenomenal states. We can experience them (or have them), we can categorize them, or we can point to them. In the next subsection, I will argue that these relations allow for phenomenal knowledge only in a very limited sense.

2.2. Knowing what it's like

Having distinguished experiencing, categorizing and pointing to phenomenal states, we can now ask which if any of these constitutes phenomenal knowledge. Recall that phenomenal knowledge is knowledge of what our phenomenal states are like. I will argue that the notion of phenomenal knowledge is actually more problematic than is sometimes appreciated.

Let's begin with experience. Does experience of a phenomenal state constitute knowledge of what that state is like? I don't think so. This may sound surprising, or even heretical. After all, it's trivially true that there is something it is like to have an experience, and it is often said that experiences give us direct knowledge of what phenomenal qualities are like. Indeed, traditional epistemologies, such as sense data theory, have been taken to imply that phenomenal qualities are the only thing we really know directly. I think that it's a mistake to describe experience as a kind of phenomenal knowledge. Experiences are like something, but they do not qualify as *knowledge* of what it's like. Knowing is a transitive relation. It is a relation we bear to something. When we talk about knowing something, we imply that there is both an object of our knowledge and an epistemic relation to that object. Now consider a phenomenal state. What is the object and what is the epistemic relation? What is it that we know when we have a phenomenal state? It is arguable that phenomenal experiences give us knowledge of what they represent. If I am experiencing a particular colour, my experience may be said to give me knowledge of that colour. But this is knowledge that I can have in the absence of consciousness. An unconscious colour representation gives me (unconscious) knowledge of that colour. Patently, this is not knowledge of what it's like to have an experience. So the question is, does a phenomenal state yield knowledge of *itself* in addition to knowledge of what it represents? Here, I want to suggest a negative answer. I don't think there is any *direct* entailment from having a phenomenal state to knowing what that state is like. In general, knowing some object *o* seems to require representing *o*. On the theory of consciousness I favour, unlike higher-order representation theories, one can have a conscious experience without representing it. If knowledge requires representation of the object of knowledge, then having an experience does not entail knowing what it's like.

Another possibility is that knowing what an experience is like is a matter of categorizing the experience. Suppose you've eaten a guava fruit, and you can recognize one by taste. It is tempting to suppose that knowledge of what guava fruit is like consists in your ability to recognize one when you taste it. On this view, knowing what it's like is a matter of acquiring a concept that allows you to re-identify the things you've perceived before. On closer examination, however, such conceptual capacities are neither necessary nor sufficient for phenomenal knowledge (knowing what it's like). Suppose you have never eaten guava before, but now, at this moment, have a first taste of guava in the form of a sauce on the fish you ordered. You can't identify the flavour you are tasting, and you might not recognize it if you tasted it again, but it might be true of you that you know what guava is like, nevertheless. As you taste it and focus on the flavour, you can say things such as 'this sauce is delicious' and when you do so, you are referring to the flavour of guava. You base your appraisal of the sauce on your current knowledge of what it's like. Because you would not recognize the flavour again, it would be wrong to say you have a concept of the flavour, but it would certainly be appropriate to say that you know, then and there, what it's like. This shows that concepts used to categorize phenomenal states are not necessary for phenomenal knowledge.

Nor are they sufficient. It is noteworthy that when we apply concepts to our experiences, the concepts typically refer to features of the world. The flavour of guava is, arguably, a feature of the fruit itself, not a feature of our minds. Such concepts don't satisfy the criterion for conveying phenomenal knowledge, because they are not representations of phenomenal states. Of course, there can be concepts that refer to phenomenal states; consider the concept expressed by the phrase 'the phenomenal character of guava'. Is this concept sufficient for conferring phenomenal knowledge? Perhaps not. If the AIR theory is right, phenomenal states get their character from their perceptual qualities. Two states are phenomenally alike if and only if they represent the same perceptual features in the same sense modality. If that is right, then a concept referring to the phenomenal character of guava can be possessed and tokened in the absence of phenomenal experience. Such a concept is just a mental representation that can be used to distinguish the gustatory and olfactory state that we have when tasting guava from other gustatory and olfactory states. There is no obvious reason why such a concept cannot be applied unconsciously. That suggests that application of such concepts is not sufficient for phenomenal knowledge.

For these reasons, I do not think that the concepts we use in perceptual classification are the best candidates for explaining phenomenal knowledge. That leaves us with one more candidate: mental pointing. Predictably, I think that mental pointing is the key. Mental pointing can confer knowledge of what something is like. As I have suggested, merely having an experience does not qualify as knowledge of the experience, because knowledge is a transitive relation. When we mentally point, there is a mental control structure that uses representations of objects or spatial locations that focuses in on some aspect of experience. I said this control structure works in ways that parallel linguistic demonstratives. I would argue that, like linguistic demonstratives, phenomenal demonstratives qualify as representations. They represent the phenomenal qualities to which they point. If I am right, then phenomenal demonstratives can confer phenomenal knowledge even though mere experience cannot. When we merely experience our phenomenal states, we do not represent them. When we mentally point, experiences are represented; pointing is transitive. This distinction has some intuitive plausibility to me. My intuition (for what it's worth) is that we would not credit a person who merely experienced something with knowledge of what that experience is like, but, when that person focuses on the experience in a top-down way, we do credit her with knowledge of what it's like. If you share this intuition, it is another reason for thinking that phenomenal demonstratives can constitute phenomenal knowledge even if experience itself does not.

The present proposal overcomes the objections that I raised to the suggestion that we attain phenomenal knowledge when we categorize our phenomenal states. I said above that the concepts used in phenomenal categorization can also be applied unconsciously, and this raises doubts about whether they are sufficient for phenomenal knowledge. I also said that they are not necessary, because we can attain phenomenal knowledge without storing concepts of the phenomenal qualities we come to know. Phenomenal demonstratives, in contrast, cannot occur without consciousness. Mental pointing serves to direct attention, and attention gives rise to consciousness. Mental pointing can also be achieved without using concepts of the qualities that we represent. For one thing, we can point using spatial representations. We can also point using object representations that are much more abstract than the quality to which we point. We can focus in on *that taste* without forming a concept that would allow us to reidentify the taste we are now experiencing.

Suppose that this is a correct analysis of phenomenal knowledge. One striking implication is that phenomenal knowledge is much more limited than we might have imagined. By that I mean the vehicles by which we come to know our phenomenal states are much coarser in detail than that which they represent. Phenomenal demonstratives do not refer by fully describing what they represent. They refer by directing attention. They have two components: a control structure and a demonstration. The control structure presumably has no descriptive content. It is not a description of any particular phenomenal state. The same control structure is used to point to different phenomenal states. Taken on it's own, these control structures do not represent anything. Demonstrations have richer representational content, but they do not represent what our phenomenal states represent. Some demonstrations simply represent regions in space. Others represent objects (or features), but they are high-level representations that are comparatively abstract. When combined, the control structure and representation serve as a representation of whatever precise phenomenal quality they end up focusing on, but they do so in virtue of the causal impact they have on the allocation of attention.

It follows from this that two token-identical phenomenal demonstratives could have different content. Consider a case when we focus attention on the upper-rightmost region of visible space. The content of such a focusing will depend on what happens to be located in that region at a particular time. Thus, the vehicles of phenomenal knowledge cannot be used to 'read-off' what experience is like. Like a pointing finger, mental pointers represent; but if we were to examine a pointer itself we wouldn't learn much about what it represents. Paradoxically, we come to know what it's like via representations that aren't like anything — representations that do not re-present what it's like.

One might think that this analysis of phenomenal demonstratives is problematic for the following reason. Imagine looking at two colour patches and thinking, demonstratively, that one is different from that one. If phenomenal demonstratives do not describe what they designate, then it is not immediately clear how such thoughts would be possible. Wouldn't the mental pointings be the same and hence indistinguishable? I think this puzzle has a simple solution, but the solution reveals an interesting fact of phenomenal knowledge. I suggested that phenomenal demonstratives are, on any occasion, partially constituted by high-level perceptual representations or representations of space. These components can distinguish two pointings. If the colour patches are in different locations, then the mental pointers can contain different spatial representations, and if the colours differ in some dimension that we can conceptualize (e.g. if they belong to colour categories that we can store in memory and distinguish), the pointers can use different high-level perceptual representations. But suppose that the two colours are located in the same space (i.e. they are interspersed at a frequency that has finer spatial resolution than attention), *and* suppose they belong to categories that we cannot conceptually distinguish. If both of these conditions are met, then I would say we cannot have a demonstrative thought of the form that one differs from that one. Of course we can point to both and form a thought about that mix of colours, but we cannot conceive of the colours in the mix separately. This is an empirical consequence of the theory that I have been defending and it could be tested empirically. I'd like to think it's a virtue of a theory of phenomenal knowledge that it makes testable predictions about what kinds of thoughts are possible or impossible. My point here is that the range of atomic thoughts we can have using phenomenal demonstratives is narrower than the range of states we can experience.

2.3. There are no phenomenal concepts

Before drawing philosophical conclusions from this account, I want to point out that it differs from an approach that is gaining popularity in the literature. A number of authors believe that we attain phenomenal knowledge via phenomenal concepts (e.g. Loar, 1990; Perry, 2001; Papineau, 2002). Loar characterizes a phenomenal concept as a special kind of recognitional concept that is dependent on a phenomenal state that it classifies. Perry treats phenomenal concepts as concepts that pick out phenomenal states indexically, rather than by merely describing them. Papineau suggests that phenomenal concepts are quotational: they contain the phenomenal states to which they refer. As I understand these proposals, they can be captured by a common definition: a phenomenal concept is a concept that both represents phenomenal qualities and cannot be possessed without having those phenomenal qualities. I think no such concepts exist.

Notice first that the concepts we use to categorize our experiences are not phenomenal concepts. This follows directly from my argument that these concepts can be possessed without consciousness. It also follows from the fact that these concepts are too coarse-grained. They do not represent the precise qualities that are available to us in experience. These concepts represent comparatively abstract distal features of the environment.

The natural move at this point would be to say that phenomenal demonstratives are phenomenal concepts. A number of defenders of phenomenal concepts have offered demonstrative accounts. They equate phenomenal concepts with phenomenal demonstratives. I think this proposal is indefensible. It is widely agreed among concepts researchers that concepts are mental entities that can be generated by an organism to re-identify things. To qualify as a concept, a mental representation must be capable of being stored. I think that phenomenal demonstratives cannot be stored in the way that matters. Phenomenal demonstratives work by focusing on an aspect of current experience. I have argued that records of experiences cannot be stored, because experience resides at a level of representation that cannot be encoded in memory. Now one might think that one could store a phenomenal demonstrative. For example, one might think that one can store a record of the phenomenal demonstrative we use to focus on a particular region of space. Perhaps each day we spend an hour focusing on the upper left, and we store a record of the command to stare in that direction. Does this stored demonstrative qualify as a phenomenal concept? I claim that it doesn't. The stored command does not represent a phenomenal quality. It only represents a phenomenal quality on those specific occasions when it is put into use and, on each occasion, it may represent a different quality. So phenomenal demonstratives cannot be stored in a content-preserving way. They cannot qualify as concepts of phenomenal qualities.

Of course, there is one way to store a precise record of what we experience: we can store precise descriptions of phenomenal states in a topic-neutral language. For example, I can store the concept 'the blue that I would experience when looking at a such-and-such colour chip under such-and-such viewing conditions' or 'the taste I would experience when I'm in such-and-such brain state'. Such descriptive representations may be able to represent specific phenomenal qualities if fully spelled out, but they are not phenomenal concepts because they can be possessed without ever having had the particular experience that they represent.

Before closing this section, let me mention one quick objection. I have been claiming that there are no phenomenal concepts, and my basic argument for that claim is that concepts are stored representations, and we don't store records of phenomenal states. Against this, one might argue that there are obvious examples of stored phenomenal qualities. We can recall what various colours, tastes and sounds are like, and we can form conscious mental images of these. Doesn't this show that there are phenomenal concepts?

Earlier I suggested that conscious imagery is mediated by stored high-level perceptual representations. If so, the existence of imagistic recall does not show that we have phenomenal concepts. High-level perceptual representations are not phenomenal concepts. They do not represent phenomenal states (they represent objects), and they can exist without phenomenal qualities. These representations can be used to generate intermediate-level perceptual states through efferent pathways. The states that are generated in this way are mental images, and when we attend to those images they are consciously experienced. But notice that the experience of images is not mediated by phenomenal concepts. Notice too, as remarked above, that high-level perceptual representations abstract away from many features of perception and, as a result, the intermediate-level representations that they generate in imagery are correspondingly inexact. It is difficult to imagine a specific shade of blue, for example. What we get in imagery is an unstable, ephemeral and pale counterpart of the kind of blues we experience in perception. If you imagine blue and then try to match your image precisely to a colour chip, you will find it difficult or impossible. The range of blues we can point to in experience outstrips those we can imagine. In sum, the stored records used to generate images do not qualify as phenomenal concepts, and in any case they also cannot be used to fully explain phenomenal knowledge.

I conclude that we have no phenomenal concepts. I see no way to store a representation that represents a specific phenomenal quality in a way that depends on the experience of that quality. This conclusion depends on the specific definition of concepts that I am using, but that definition is not unusual. Concepts researchers widely and routinely assume that concepts are stored records that can be used to re-identify their referents. I would encourage consciousness researchers to drop the term 'phenomenal concept' on the grounds that is gives a misleading impression of the way we represent our phenomenal states.

3. The Knowledge Argument

3.1. What Mary learns

Recent interest in phenomenal concepts has been driven by the hope that phenomenal concepts can help to undermine the 'knowledge argument' for dualism (Loar, 1990; Hill, 1997; Perry, 2001; Papineau, 2002). The most influential version of the knowledge argument has been put forward by Frank Jackson (1982). He uses epistemic premises to support the conclusion that some of the facts about phenomenal experience are not physical. Like all other physicalists, I think the argument is fallacious but, because I reject phenomenal concepts, I don't think that they can be used to expose the fallacy. That said, my explanation of the fallacy, which calls on phenomenal demonstratives, closely parallels what others have said under the rubric of phenomenal concepts. So my treatment here will be brief.

Jackson's most widely discussed version of the knowledge argument hinges on a thought experiment about a brilliant neuroscientist named Mary, who has been trapped inside a black and white room. Mary learns everything about what goes on in the brain when people see colours and, as a result, she can be said to know every physical fact about colour experience. But when she is finally exposed to colours for the first time, she learns something new. She learns, for instance, what the colour that people call 'blue' is like. This, Jackson maintains, is a fact she didn't know before. Thus, some facts about colour experience are not included in the sum of all physical facts. Some facts are non-physical. This, we are invited to infer, means that physicalism is false.

The standard version of the phenomenal concepts reply goes like this. Mary does not learn a new fact; she learns a new way of representing facts she already knew. That new way of representing old facts arises because she acquires a new concept. Initially, Mary just has neural concepts, learned from her textbooks on neuroscience, to describe phenomenal states. But when she sees colours for the first time, she acquires phenomenal concepts, according to the standard story. These concepts represent the same brain states as her neural concepts, but they do so in a phenomenal way.

At first, this appeal to phenomenal concepts may not appear especially helpful. Usually, when two concepts co-refer they refer via different properties. For example, 'triangle' and 'trilateral' refer to the same polygons by reference to their interior angles and sides, respectively. If phenomenal concepts were co-extensive with neural concepts, the very fact that these concepts differ would suggest that they would still imply that they refer via different properties, and that would suggest that phenomenal concepts refer via properties that are not physical. This is one reason why phenomenal demonstratives are so appealing. Demonstratives do not refer by fully describing their contents; they refer by being in the right relation to their contents. So postulating phenomenal demonstrative does not lead to proliferation of properties. Moreover, phenomenal demonstratives work by pointing to occurrent phenomenal states, which means that one cannot have a phenomenal demonstrative without having the state to which it refers. This explains why Mary needs to experience colours to know what they are like.

I find this account congenial. My main quibble is that I don't think that phenomenal demonstratives are concepts. Mary can learn what it's like without acquiring any concepts; she can think to herself that red is like that (while mentally pointing), without being able to recognize, recall or imagine red on a future occasion. This distinguishes my proposal from Loar's seminal recognitional concepts account. Perry (2001) also claims that Mary acquires a recognitional concept, but my account is, perhaps, closer to his, because he emphasizes the role of attention in mental pointing. In denying that Mary can necessarily recognize red, I am also implicitly departing from Lewis's (1990) and Nemirow's (1990) suggestion that what Mary acquires is a new ability (compare Tye's, forthcoming, response). I do think that there is a kernel of truth to the ability proposal, however. As remarked above, I think phenomenal demonstratives are control structures. The deployment of a phenomenal demonstrative involves a kind of procedural knowledge. But rather than saying that Mary learns how to recall and recognize colours, I'd say that she acquires the ability to focally attend to them. My view is not a radical departure from the others in the literature; it builds on the lessons of each. But the subtle differences invite a shift away from the focus on concepts and onto the topic of attention as investigation (both philosophical and empirical) of phenomenal knowledge moves forward.

It's worth noting here that Mary would not necessarily learn what colours are like if she were merely able to perceive them. Colours can be perceived unconsciously. For example, if you are briefly presented with a red flash and a green flash, you will experience neither red nor green, but yellow. Suppose Mary's first encounters with colour took this form. She would know what yellow is like, but not red and green. The story that I have been telling explains this. Attention takes time. When red and green are flashed briefly, one cannot attend to them. By the time attention allows information to flow forward to working memory, the aftereffects of the red and green stimuli have blended together, and we experience the result as yellow. Nevertheless, the red and green are perceived. We know this because images embedded in briefly flashed colours cause stimulus specific brain responses, even though the figures are not perceived (Moutoussis and Zeki, 2002). This underscores the suggestion that phenomenal knowledge is not constituted by perceptual states, but rather requires attention to such states.

The phenomenal demonstratives story can be used to refute the core assumption underlying the knowledge argument. The assumption, often discussed under the rubric of '*a priori* physicalism' says: if phenomenal states were physical, knowledge of what they are like could be deduced from knowledge encoded in physical vocabulary (Chalmers and Jackson, 2001). I argued above that phenomenal knowledge is very limited. We know what our experiences are like via demonstratives that refer by their causal relations to what they represent, not by describing them (cf. Loar, 1990). One can make a deductive inference about the applicability of a concept only if that concept decomposes into descriptive features, and one could infer what phenomenal qualities are like only if our knowledge of what they are like were encoded in concepts that decompose into features that are functional or physical. Phenomenal knowledge is not encoded in that way and therefore cannot be deduced from physical descriptions of the brain. Above I also distinguished knowing what an experience is like and having that experience. Having an experience is not knowledge of the experience. It should be obvious that knowledge of the brain is not sufficient for having an experience, any more than knowledge of how wings work is sufficient for having wings.

That said, I do think that knowledge of the brain might be useful for inferring *something* about phenomenal states. Such knowledge could be used to deduce facts about which qualities are similar to each other and which features of the world cause our qualitative experiences. These deductions might allow us to determine what concepts people have for classifying phenomenal states. It might not suffice for *acquiring* such concepts, but it would at least allow us to generate plausible lists of what those concepts are. Mary might deduce the categorical boundaries of colours, just as we can deduce perceptual similarity spaces from creatures with sensory systems that differ from our own. The concepts used to categorize phenomenal states encode information about similarities between experiences, as well as information about distal features, and such information can be discovered by observing brain mechanisms and behaviour. But, I have argued that these concepts are not themselves phenomenal. They do not constitute a form of phenomenal knowledge, and they are not necessary or sufficient for knowing what phenomenal states are like. The fact that Mary can deduce these things without knowing what it's like to have phenomenal states suggest that phenomenal knowledge is not merely knowledge of what our phenomenal states represent. Thus, I think the knowledge argument is a good argument against some forms of representationalism about consciousnesses; in particular, it counts against the view that the phenomenal character of an experience is nothing beyond what that experience represents.

In sum, I have endorsed the view that phenomenal demonstratives can explain what's wrong with the knowledge argument. Mary does not learn any new facts when she learns what it's like. Instead, she enters into an epistemic situation in which she can mentally point to a perceptual state caused by seeing something that is coloured. Mentally pointing gives her knowledge of what colours are like. She didn't have this knowledge before and she couldn't have it, if she couldn't focus attention on her perceptual states.

3.2. Three brief objections

Some objections have been raised against the suggestion that what Mary learns can be explained by appeal to phenomenal demonstratives.

In this final section, I will briefly discuss three objections. More detailed discussion can be found in the literature.

One objection is discussed by Nina-Rümelin (2002), though she recognizes that it can be answered. Demonstratives require reference-fixing demonstrations. If I merely say 'that' without a demonstration, my demonstrative will not refer. I must say something like 'that table' or 'that' while pointing, to make some object salient. There is a worry that, in order for phenomenal demonstratives to refer, they would need reference fixes that are phenomenal in nature. How, one might wonder, can you point to a phenomenal state except by demonstrating its phenomenal character? If pointing to phenomenal states requires the use of phenomenal reference fixers, the phenomenal demonstrative account would be no better than the simplest version of the phenomenal concepts account. It would introduce phenomenal properties as modes of presentation for phenomenal states.

My account of phenomenal demonstratives addresses this concern. I have proposed that the demonstrations used by phenomenal demonstratives are not themselves phenomenal. They are high-level perceptual representations or representations of locations in perceptual space. These representations are unconscious on my view, and they merely serve to direct attention. So my account does not introduce a regress of reference-fixing phenomenal properties.

A second objection owes to Chalmers (2002). He distinguishes phenomenal demonstratives from 'pure phenomenal concepts', concepts that refer directly to specific phenomenal qualities. Demonstratives, according to Kaplan, have both content (what they refer to) and character (the rule by which they refer). As a result, two token-identical phenomenal demonstratives could refer to different things in different worlds — a point I made above. Chalmers postulates that pure phenomenal concepts do not admit of a character/content distinction. Moreover, he says, we can have informative thoughts of the kind we might express by 'that is such-and-such' where 'that' expresses a phenomenal demonstrative and 'such-and-such' expresses a pure phenomenal concept. This suggests that these two kinds of representations are different and, Chalmers claims, Mary's new knowledge should be characterized in terms of the acquisition of a pure phenomenal concept, not a phenomenal demonstrative.

I flatly reject Chalmers' claim that there are pure phenomenal concepts. I have argued that such concepts do not exist. We certainly have phenomenal states (I am a phenomenal realist), but it's quite another thing to assume we have concepts that refer to these states, much less concepts that refer in the direct way that Chalmers has in mind (in his terms, concepts with the same primary and secondary intensions). I see no reason to believe that such concepts exist. In arguing for such concepts, Chalmers alleges that there is an informative identity expressed by 'that is such-and-such'. I don't share his intuition. I frankly have no idea what thought this would be. I can certainly form the thought that I would express by 'that is the colour people call "blue" ', but I cannot imagine an informative thought expressed by 'that is blue' where 'blue' names a concept that is neither functional nor physical nor deferential. Suppose I know nothing about brain or colour vocabulary. Now I have a colour experience. I can imagine thinking about the experience by attending to it. But, when I hold this colour in mind, the only *identity* claim I could come up with would be the trivial one expressed by 'that is that'. I would have only one way of thinking about this colour: namely pointing to it in my mind. To show that there are phenomenal concepts in addition to phenomenal demonstratives, Chalmers would have to show that one could think about phenomenal qualities as such without being able to point to them, and conversely. I just don't see any reason to accept this conjecture.

There are other objections in the literature that are intended to undermine any attempt to explain Mary's knowledge by appeal to new ways of representing old facts. For example, Chalmers (2006) has recently devised a new general-purpose argument against phenomenal concepts, which could be adapted to argue against the non-conceptual phenomenal demonstrative proposal that I have defended. Roughly, he says that if a theory of phenomenal concepts that can be stated in physical terms (hence consistent with physicalism) is such that we could conceive of the theory being realized by an unfeeling zombie, then the theory cannot explain what is special about Mary's epistemic situation. Whatever she learns, it's different from what her zombie counterpart would learn. This argument can be used to challenge the view that Mary's knowledge is given to her by phenomenal demonstratives. I have defined these as mental pointers that give us access to perceptual states by directing top-down attention. Mary's zombie counterpart could have top-down attention. Zombie Mary would, upon first seeing colours, be able to focus in on a visual state caused by a coloured object. This would be new knowledge, knowledge that she might describe as what it's like to see colours, but it would be different from the knowledge that Mary learns.

In a compelling response to this objection, Carruthers and Veillet (this volume) argue that, were zombies possible, zombie Mary would indeed be in the same epistemic situation as Mary. Zombie would learn just as much as Mary does, and for exactly the same reason. They say that the object of knowledge would be different in the two cases. Mary would have knowledge of a phenomenal state and zombie Mary would not, but that does not mean they are in different epistemic situations towards those objects of knowledge, and therefore the materialist account of what Mary learns can explain her epistemic predicament.

I think that Carruthers and Veillet give the right response to Chalmers. Mary and zombie Mary would be in the same epistemic situation, in the relevant sense. They would both come to know something new, because they would be able to form demonstrative thoughts by mentally pointing to their perceptual representations of colours. Chalmers thinks it is obvious that their epistemic situations are different. I think this intuition derives from the fact that Mary clearly learns something different from zombie Mary. Mary learns that red is like *that*, where 'that' refers to a phenomenal state. But this difference is irrelevant here. An account of phenomenal demonstratives is not supposed to explain phenomenology. It is supposed to explain why phenomenal knowledge cannot be inferred from physical descriptions. It handles this explanatory burden well. Both physicalists and dualists typically agree that phenomenal knowledge uses representations that one could not use if one did not have the states in question. Phenomenal demonstratives prove that this is consistent with physicalism. Demonstratives are representations that work by pointing, and mental analogues of demonstratives cannot apply without being in the mental states to which they point. This is a simple and principled point about representation, and it's enough to prove that some kinds of knowledge, namely demonstrative knowledge, cannot be deduced from physical descriptions. Moreover, there is good reason to think that our knowledge of phenomenal states is demonstrative. So, we have reason to think, antecedently, that phenomenal knowledge is not deducible.

Given the availability of such promising physicalist replies to the knowledge argument, I think we might do well to stop worrying about zombies for a while and dedicate more energy to trying to identify the actual mechanisms underlying phenomenal states and phenomenal knowledge.

4. Conclusions

Let me conclude by listing the main claims that I have made in this discussion. I began by saying that conscious states are AIRs, attended intermediate-level representations. I also claimed that attention works by making information available to working memory, but I noted that the information does not need to be encoded in working memory to have a conscious experience. I then distinguished three relations with experiences: we can have them, classify them or point to parts of them. The last of these, mental pointing, is achieved by means of phenomenal demonstratives, which I analysed in terms of top-down attention. I argued that phenomenal demonstratives are the source of phenomenal knowledge, but they represent our phenomenal states without fully describing them. I do not think that phenomenal demonstratives are concepts, and I claimed we have no phenomenal concepts, i.e. concepts that both represent phenomenal states and require that we have the phenomenal states that they represent. Finally, I endorsed the view that phenomenal demonstratives can block the dualist conclusion of the knowledge argument.[1]

References

Beck, D.M., Rees, G., Frith, C.D. and Lavie, N. (2001), 'Neural correlates of change detection and change blindness', *Nature Neuroscience*, **4**, pp. 645–50.

Block, N. (2002), 'The harder problem of consciousness', *Journal of Philosophy*, **XCIX**, pp. 391–425.

Chalmers, D. (2002), 'Content and epistemology of phenomenal belief', in *Consciousness: New Philosophical Essays*, ed. Q. Smith and A. Jokic (Oxford: Oxford University Press).

Chalmers, D. (2006), 'Phenomenal concepts and the explanatory gap', in *Phenomenal Concepts and Phenomenal Knowledge: New Essays on Consciousness and Physicalism*, ed. T. Alter and S. Walter (Oxford: Oxford University Press).

Chalmers, D. and Jackson, F. (2001), 'Conceptual analysis and reductive explanation', *Philosophical Review*, **110**, pp. 315–60.

Dehaene, S., Naccache, L., Le Clec, H.G., Koechlin, E., Mueller, M., Dehaene-Lambertz, G., van de Moortele, P.F. and LeBihan, D. (1998), 'Imaging unconscious semantic priming', *Nature*, **395**, pp. 597–600.

Hayden, B.Y. and Gallant, J.L. (2005), 'Time course of attention reveals different mechanisms for spatial and feature-based attention in area V4', *Neuron*, **47**, pp. 637–43.

Hill, C.S. (1997), 'Imaginability, conceivability, possibility, and the mind-body problem', *Philosophical Studies*, **87**, pp. 61–85.

Jackendoff, R. (1987), *Consciousness and the Computational Mind* (Cambridge, MA: MIT Press).

Jackson, F. (1982), 'Epiphenomenal qualia', *Philosophical Quarterly*, **32**, pp. 127–36.

Kaplan, D. (1989), 'Demonstratives', in *Themes From Kaplan*, ed. J. Almog, J. Perry and H. Wettstein (New York: Oxford University Press), pp. 481–564.

Lewis, D. (1990), 'What experience teaches', in *Mind and Cognition*, ed. W. Lycan (Oxford: Basil Blackwell).

Loar, B. (1990), 'Phenomenal states', *Philosophical Perspectives*, **4**, pp. 81–108.

[1] I am immensely indebted to Rocco Gennaro and two anonymous referees, who provided extensive comments. This paper would have been far worse without their help.

Mack, A. and Rock, I. (1998), *Inattentional Blindness* (Cambridge, MA: MIT Press).

Millikan, R. (2000), *On Clear and Confused Ideas* (Cambridge: Cambridge University Press).

Most, S.B., Scholl, B.J., Clifford, E. and Simons, D.J. (2005), 'What you see is what you set: Sustained inattentional blindness and the capture of awareness', *Psychological Review*, **112**, pp. 217–42.

Moutoussis, K. and Zeki, S. (2002), 'The relationship between cortical activation and perception investigated with invisible stimuli', *Proceedings of the National Academy of Sciences*, **99**, pp. 9527–32.

Nemirow, L. (1990), 'Physicalism and the cognitive role of acquaintance', in *Mind and Cognition*, ed. W. Lycan (Oxford: Blackwell).

Nina-Rümelin, M. (2002), 'Qualia: The knowledge argument', *Stanford Encyclopedia of Philosophy*, http://plato.stanford.edu/entries/qualia-knowledge/

Olshausen, B.A., Anderson, C.H. and Van Essen, D.C. (1993), 'A neurobiological model of visual attention and invariant pattern recognition based on DynamicR of information', *Journal of Neuroscience*, **13**, pp. 4700–19.

Papineau, D. (2002), *Thinking about Consciousness* (New York: Oxford University Press).

Pérez-Carpinell, J., Baldovi, R., de Fez, M.D. and Castro, J. (1998), 'Color memory matching: Time effect and other factors', *Color Research and Application*, **23**, pp. 234–47.

Perry, J. (2001), *Knowledge, Possibility, and Consciousness* (Cambridge, MA: MIT Press).

Postle, B.R. (2006), 'Working memory as an emergent property of the mind and brain', *Neuroscience*, **139**, pp. 23–8.

Prinz, J.J. (2000), 'A neurofunctional theory of visual consciousness', *Consciousness and Cognition*, **9**, pp. 243–59.

Prinz, J.J. (2001), 'Functionalism, dualism and the neural correlates of consciousness', in *Philosophy and the Neurosciences: A Reader*, ed. W. Bechtel, P. Mandik, J. Mundale and R. Stufflebeam (Oxford: Blackwell).

Prinz, J.J. (2002), *Furnishing the Mind: Concepts and Their Perceptual Basis* (Cambridge, MA: MIT Press).

Prinz, J.J. (2005), 'A neurofunctional theory of consciousness', in *Cognition and the Brain: Philosophy and Neuroscience Movement*, ed. A. Brook and K. Akins (Cambridge: Cambridge University Press), pp. 381–96.

Prinz, J.J. (2007), 'All consciousness is perceptual', in *Fundamental Debates in Philosophy of Mind*, ed. J. Cohen and B. McLaughlin (Oxford: Blackwell).

Prinz, J.J. (forthcoming), *The Conscious Brain* (New York: Oxford University Press).

Simons, D.J. and Levin, D.T. (1997), 'Change blindness', *Trends in Cognitive Science*, **1**, pp. 261–7.

Sperling, G. (1960), 'The information available in brief visual presentations', *Psychological Monographs*, **74**, pp. 1–29.

Tye, M. (forthcoming), 'Knowing what it is like: The ability hypothesis and the knowledge argument', *Protosociology: Collection of Essays for David Lewis*.

Vogel, E.K. and Luck, S.J. (2002), 'Delayed working memory consolidation during the attentional blink', *Psychonomic Bulletin & Review*, **9**, pp. 739–43.

Peter Carruthers
and Bénédicte Veillet[1]

The Phenomenal Concept Strategy

A powerful reply to a range of familiar anti-physicalist arguments has recently been developed. According to this reply, our possession of *phenomenal concepts* can explain the facts that the anti-physicalist claims can only be explained by a non-reductive account of phenomenal consciousness. Chalmers (2006) argues that the phenomenal concept strategy is doomed to fail. This article presents the phenomenal concept strategy, Chalmers' argument against it, and a defence of the strategy against his argument.

1. Introduction

Being in pain feels a certain way. Looking at a red rose, smelling it, feeling the thorns on its stem: these experiences all feel a certain way as well. We will call these feels 'phenomenal feels' and we will say that anyone who has such phenomenal feels is phenomenally conscious. Philosophers have presented and defended a range of arguments and thought-experiments designed to show that phenomenal feels cannot be reduced to anything purely physical. There is the famous Mary who is born and kept in a black-and-white room and grows up to become the world's leading expert on colour vision, but is said to learn *new* facts about colour when she experiences colours for the first time (Jackson, 1986). There are zombies and colour inverts

---

[1] The ordering of the authors' names is alphabetical. We would like to thank David Chalmers, Rocco Gennaro, Georges Rey, and an anonymous referee for the *Journal of Consciousness Studies* for their helpful comments on earlier drafts of this paper.

(Chalmers, 1996): creatures who are physically, functionally and intentionally identical to us but who lack phenomenal feels altogether; or creatures physically, functionally and intentionally identical to us who, when *we* have *this* experience (a red experience, say) have *that* experience (a green experience). Then, of course, there is the *explanatory gap* (Levine, 1983; Chalmers, 1996): it seems that no matter how much information we are given about conscious experience in physical, functional or intentional terms, that information won't really explain why our experiences should feel to us the way that they do.

Physicalists in the last decade or so have fleshed out a seemingly powerful reply to these arguments and thought-experiments, by invoking *phenomenal concepts*. According to physicalist proponents of this strategy (which we will call 'the phenomenal concept strategy', following Stoljar, 2005, and Chalmers, 2006), we possess a special set of concepts for referring to our own experiences. What is said to be distinctive of such concepts is that they are *conceptually isolated* from any other concepts that we possess, lacking any a priori connections with non-phenomenal concepts of any type (and in particular, lacking such connections with any physical, functional or intentional concepts). Given that phenomenal concepts are isolated, the physicalist argues, then it won't be the least bit surprising that we can conceive of zombies and inverts, or that there should be gaps in explanation. This is because no matter how much information one is given in physical, functional or intentional terms, it will always be possible for us intelligibly to think, 'Still, all that might be true, and still *this* [phenomenal feel] might be absent or different'. There is no need, then, to jump to the anti-physicalist conclusion. All of the arguments referred to above are perfectly compatible with physicalist accounts of phenomenal feelings.

Chalmers (2006) argues that the phenomenal strategy is doomed to fail, however. Either appeals to phenomenal concepts open up a new explanatory gap, one with which the physicalist can't deal, or phenomenal concepts simply can't do the work that the physicalist intends them to do. This paper will first spell out the phenomenal concept strategy in more detail. It will then present Chalmers' sweeping argument against it, before offering our replies.

2. The Phenomenal Concept Strategy

Defenders of the phenomenal concept strategy all agree that phenomenal concepts are special in a way that permits a reply to anti-physicalist arguments. But different physicalists have different ways of characterizing *what*, exactly, is special about phenomenal concepts. We will briefly review some influential accounts.

2.1 Phenomenal concepts

According to Loar (1990), Carruthers (2000) and Tye (2000), phenomenal concepts are recognitional concepts of experience. A recognitional concept, unlike a theoretical concept, is applied directly on the basis of perceptual or quasi-perceptual acquaintance with its instances. Consider, for instance, the concept RED, which is often construed as a prototypical recognitional concept. It seems plausible that we apply the concept RED directly upon perceiving red things. Like the concept RED, phenomenal concepts are recognitional concepts. But they are concepts *of experience*, which means that we apply them directly on the basis of acquaintance with experiences, as when I say that *this* is my blue-cup experience. Phenomenal concepts aren't *merely* recognitional, however. For if they were, then they would be no different from a number of other recognitional concepts like RED. They are, to use Carruthers' terminology, *purely* recognitional. A concept is purely recognitional if it is both applied directly to instances *and* if it is conceptually isolated from other concepts. The concept RED, in contrast, is connected to concepts like SURFACE; and our judgments of RED are modified by our beliefs about normal lighting, normal perceiver conditions, and so forth.

Perry (2001) and O'Dea (2002), in contrast, argue that phenomenal concepts are a form of *indexical*. They are concepts that pick out brain states under an indexical mode of presentation, in something like the way that the concept *I* picks out its referent (me) under an indexical mode of presentation. The concept THIS, in '*This* is my blue-cup experience', is such an indexical concept. Indexical concepts are sometimes believed to be isolated from non-indexical concepts. According to some (Perry, 1979), knowing every non-indexical fact about the world won't be enough for one to deduce what time it is *now*. Similarly, then, knowing every non-phenomenal fact about the world won't enable me to deduce any phenomenal facts about it.

Papineau (2002) suggests instead that phenomenal concepts are quotational concepts. They are concepts that somehow *contain* the states to which they refer. Just as words can be embedded within quotation marks, as in 'blue cup', so Papineau argues that actual phenomenal states (either perceptual states, or images of perceptual states) will be embedded within phenomenal concepts. When I say, '*This* is a blue cup experience', the relevant phenomenal concept THIS in fact has the following sort of form: THIS: _____, where the blank is filled by an actual phenomenal state. Again it will follow from such an account that one cannot deduce which quotational concepts apply to something just from knowledge of which non-phenomenal concepts apply to it.

2.2 The strategy

A number of other accounts of phenomenal concepts have been offered (Nagel, 1974; Sturgeon, 1994; Hill, 1997; Rey, 1998; Levine, 2001). But we should now see where all such proposals are leading. Phenomenal concepts, on each of these views, are conceptually isolated; and this conceptual isolation is all that is needed to reply to the anti-physicalist arguments described above. Mary, in her black and white room, may know all one can know about colour and colour vision; but that won't help her to deduce what seeing red feels like. To know what seeing red feels like requires deploying a phenomenal concept. It is just such a concept that she learns upon leaving her room. Why couldn't she learn that concept before? Wasn't her extensive knowledge of colour vision enough to enable her to learn that phenomenal concept? No. Since it is conceptually isolated, no physical (or functional, or representational) knowledge about colour vision would have enabled her to learn the relevant phenomenal concept. So when she leaves her room, she does acquire the capacity to think some new thoughts (these are thoughts involving phenomenal concepts). Hence she also learns some new facts (in the sense of acquiring some new true thoughts). But for all that the argument shows, these new thoughts might just concern the very same physical facts that she already knew, only differently represented (now represented by means of phenomenal concepts).

Given the existence of phenomenal concepts, moreover, we should expect zombies and colour inverts to be conceivable. Indeed, since such people are supposed to be duplicates of ours, when we describe their physical make-up we deploy all of the same physical (and functional, and representational) concepts that we would apply in describing ourselves. Since phenomenal concepts are conceptually isolated, however, applying all these physical concepts to our duplicates doesn't entail anything about which phenomenal concepts, if any, will apply to them. Hence I can conceive that my duplicate would lack *this* experience, and *this* one, and every other. Alternatively, I can conceive that instead of having *this* experience, my duplicate would have *that* one.

Finally, on this view it is no wonder that there is an explanatory gap. To give an explanation of phenomenal feels in physical (or functional, or representational) terms is to deploy only physical, or functional, or representational concepts in the course of the explanation. To think or speak about phenomenal feelings (which is what we hope to explain) is to deploy phenomenal concepts. It is experiences like *these* that we hope to give an account of. The explanation cannot feel satisfactory, therefore, since the concepts used in the physical explanation don't entail any applications of the phenomenal concepts in terms of which the explanandum is characterized.

It should now be clear how the phenomenal concept strategy is intended to work. The physicalist will agree with his opponent that there *is* an explanatory gap, and that zombies and inverts *are* conceivable. Physicalists deny the next step in the anti-physicalist argument, however. The best explanation for the conceivability of zombies and for the existence of the explanatory gap is not the one the anti-physicalist believes it to be. There is an alternative explanation of these facts, namely that they arise from our possessing and using conceptually isolated phenomenal concepts. Anti-physicalist arguments hence fail to secure their conclusion.

Note that the phenomenal concept strategy takes for granted that the notion of intentional content doesn't presuppose or implicate phenomenal consciousness. One can only usefully think that some of the puzzling facts about phenomenal consciousness (the conceivability of zombies, the explanatory gap, and so on) are explicable by appeal to the character of our phenomenal concepts, if one also thinks that concepts, and intentional contents more generally, don't give rise to just the same puzzles. This assumption is by no means uncontroversial, of course, but in our view it is warranted by, among other things, the extensive use that is made of intentional concepts in cognitive science, in ways that make no appeal to phenomenal consciousness. Since Chalmers' argument doesn't depend upon challenging this assumption, it can be taken as common ground between us for present purposes.

2.3 *Phenomenal concepts: first versus third person accounts*

It is important to note that there are, according to proponents of the phenomenal concept strategy, two quite different ways in which phenomenal concepts can be thought about and characterized.[2] One is from the

---

[2]   These two ways correspond roughly to the distinction that Chalmers (2006) draws between *phenomenal* concepts and what he calls *quasi-phenomenal* or (mostly) *schmenomenal*

first-person perspective of the users of those concepts, or in terms that otherwise presuppose such a perspective. Thus I might say to myself, 'A phenomenal concept is a concept like the one that I hereby deploy when thinking about *this* experience', for example. Or I might say that a phenomenal concept is a concept that is applied in a recognitional way to phenomenal states, and then go on to characterize the latter first-personally, by thinking that they are states like *this* or *that* or *that*.

The other way of characterizing phenomenal concepts is third-personal, and might take any of the forms sketched above. Thus one might say that phenomenal concepts are conceptually isolated recognitional concepts that are deployed in the presence of perceptual states with certain sorts of intentional content, for example. Note that such a description isn't meant to be a *definition*, for that would conflict with the claim that phenomenal concepts are conceptually isolated. (Precisely what it means to be conceptually isolated is to possess no conceptual connections to other concepts, including functional and/or intentional concepts like 'concept', 'perceptual state', and so on.) Rather, such accounts are substantive, empirical, claims about the characteristic functional and intentional roles of the concepts in question. Those who adopt the phenomenal concept strategy argue that if some such claim is true, then the anti-physicalist's arguments from zombies, from inverts, and from the explanatory gap, can all be undermined.

It is imperative that the distinction between first-person and third-person descriptions of phenomenal concepts shouldn't be conflated with the (alleged) distinction between the *wide* and *narrow* intentional contents that such concepts might possess. (This is important, *inter alia*, because many philosophers deny that narrow contents are even so much as coherent.) Such a confusion might arise quite naturally, because a widely-individuated phenomenal concept (individuated in such a way as to embrace the phenomenal state that is its referent) must be one that a zombie duplicate will lack, just as we will claim that a first-personal description fails to fit any of the zombie's concepts. Likewise, a narrowly-individuated phenomenal concept (individuated in abstraction from the phenomenal state that is its referent) would be one that a zombie duplicate must possess, just as we will claim that a third-personally described phenomenal concept is one that the zombie must have. So in this respect the two distinctions march in parallel.

concepts. (The latter are the sorts of concepts that a zombie might employ in the presence of its own perceptual states.)

Our distinction, however, carries no commitments concerning the nature of intentional content or its individuation conditions. Although the third-person description of a phenomenal concept is couched in terms of a (conceptually isolated) form of functional role, it carries no commitment to the truth of any kind of conceptual role semantics, or to the sorts of narrow intentional contents that such a semantics might be thought to warrant. Even a convinced information-semanticist like Fodor (1990) can agree that although phenomenal concepts are individuated in terms of the information that they carry (say), it is still *true* that they have a conceptually isolated role. This truth is all that is necessary for the phenomenal concept strategy to succeed. To put the same point slightly differently: we don't need to claim that my zombie twin and I deploy the *same* (narrowly individuated) concept in order for our points to go through. It just has to be the case that the zombie deploys a concept that is like mine in the relevant functional-role respects. For it turns out that it is this (conceptually isolated) role that is sufficient to explain the conceivability of zombies, the appearance of an explanatory gap, and so forth.

3. Chalmers Against the Phenomenal Concept Strategy

Chalmers (2006) argues that no appeal to phenomenal concepts of any of the sorts sketched above can constitute an adequate defence of physicalism. This is because phenomenal concepts can't *both* effectively defuse the anti-physicalist arguments *and* be physically explicable themselves. Here is the argument as he sees it:

(1) Either we can conceive that Chalmers' zombie duplicate (call him 'Zombie Chalmers') lacks phenomenal concepts, or we can't conceive that he lacks such concepts.

(2) If we *can* conceive of Zombie Chalmers lacking phenomenal concepts, then a new explanatory gap is formed and phenomenal concepts turn out to be physically inexplicable.

(3) If we *can't* conceive of Zombie Chalmers lacking phenomenal concepts, then phenomenal concepts can't explain the explanatory gap.

(4) It follows that either phenomenal concepts aren't physically explicable or they don't explain the explanatory gap.

The argument seems powerful. Premise (1) looks like a necessary truth. Premise (2) looks to be true. For anything that Chalmers has that Zombie Chalmers can be imagined to lack (given that the latter is physically, functionally and intentionally identical to Chalmers) will be physically inexplicable. Premise (3) also seems true, for if Zombie Chalmers can't be conceived to lack phenomenal concepts, then that must mean that those concepts are physically or functionally explicable; but we have already agreed that physical and functional facts can't explain phenomenal consciousness; in which case phenomenal concepts won't be able to do the work required of them, either. Moreover, the argument as a whole appears valid.

On further reflection, however, the argument as it stands can be seen to be problematic. For in order for (1) to be a necessary truth, the phrase 'phenomenal concepts' will have to be taken univocally. But then when we see that term at work in the two premises that follow, it seems that it must be taken in a different way in each. The usage in Premise (2) seems to require the first-personal understanding of phenomenal concepts distinguished in Section 2.3. (If Zombie Chalmers is conceived to lack phenomenal states, then he must equally be conceived to lack a concept of the sort that I hereby deploy when thinking about *this* conscious state.) The usage in Premise (3), in contrast, seems to require a third-personal understanding. (Since Zombie Chalmers shares all of Chalmers' physical, functional and intentional properties, then the former must also possess conceptually isolated recognitional concepts, say, which he deploys in the presence of his perceptual states.) Hence the argument, as it stands, commits a fallacy of equivocation.

It would certainly make life easy for physicalists if Chalmers' argument could be defeated so easily! But in fact it can be reformulated to avoid the difficulty, by framing a version of Premise (1) that no longer purports to be a necessary truth. Thus:

(1*) Phenomenal concepts can either be characterized in a first-person way, or they can be characterized in third-person terms.

(2a) If phenomenal concepts are characterized in first-person terms, then we can conceive of Zombie Chalmers lacking such concepts.

(2b) If we can conceive of Zombie Chalmers lacking phenomenal concepts, then a new explanatory gap is formed and phenomenal concepts turn out to be physically inexplicable.

(3a) If phenomenal concepts are characterized in third-person terms, then we can't conceive of Zombie Chalmers lacking such concepts.

(3b) If we can't conceive of Zombie Chalmers lacking phenomenal concepts, then phenomenal concepts can't explain the explanatory gap.

(4)   It follows that neither way of characterizing phenomenal concepts can help with the problem of phenomenal consciousness — either they introduce a new explanatory problem, or they can't do the explanatory work required.

This argument commits no fallacy that we can see, and all of its premises present at least the appearance of truth. So is the phenomenal concept strategy defeated? We believe not. For we think that there are sufficient grounds for denying the truth of Premise (3b). This will form the focus of the remainder of the article.[3]

4. Can Phenomenal Concepts Explain our Epistemic Situation?

Chalmers' defence of the claim made in Premise (3b) is quite complex, turning crucially on his discussion of what he calls 'epistemic situations'. Throughout the discussion of this conditional, however, it should be borne in mind that phenomenal concepts are to be understood in third-person terms, as conceptually isolated concepts being deployed in the presence of certain perceptual states.

Let us recall the original explanatory gap problem, the conceivability of zombies, and the argument from Mary's new knowledge. Let us, in addition, consider claims such as, 'I am phenomenally conscious'. These problems (and others like them) and this claim (and others like it) form what Chalmers calls our *epistemic situation* when it comes to phenomenal consciousness. Proponents of the phenomenal concept strategy believe that our possession of phenomenal concepts can explain our epistemic situation. We have already seen how the physicalist will argue that phenomenal concepts explain why there is a gap in explanation, why zombies and inverts are conceivable, and what Mary learns. When I say, 'I am phenomenally conscious', it may be that I am in fact saying something like: 'I have experiences like *these*', where THESE is a phenomenal concept. We are now in a position to schematize Chalmers' argument for Premise (3b) as follows:

(i)   If zombies do indeed possess phenomenal concepts (which must be the case if Zombie Chalmers can't conceivably lack phenomenal concepts, characterized in the third-person way), but don't share our epistemic situation, then *our* having phenomenal concepts can hardly explain *our* epistemic situation.

---

[3]   For present purposes we propose to concede the truth of Premises (2a) and (2b). We would actually want to argue against (2b) that there is no *new* explanatory gap formed; but this isn't really relevant to our main goal: defending the phenomenal concept strategy.

(ii)   Zombies don't share our epistemic situation.

(iii)   It follows that the possession of phenomenal concepts can't explain our epistemic situation (given a third-person characterization of phenomenal concepts).

According to the first premise of this argument, if Chalmers and Zombie Chalmers don't share the same epistemic situation, then phenomenal concepts can't explain our epistemic situation. Chalmers provides an argument for this claim which parallels, again, the original arguments from zombies and the explanatory gap. The original arguments can be summarized like this: if you can imagine two physical duplicates, one phenomenally conscious and the other not, then phenomenal consciousness can't be explained in physical terms. Now we can say this: if we can imagine two duplicates both possessing phenomenal concepts, one in our epistemic situation and the other not, then our epistemic situation isn't explicable in terms of phenomenal concepts. We will grant Chalmers the truth of this premise.

Premise (ii) asserts that Chalmers and his zombie twin don't share the same epistemic situation. This is more questionable. According to Chalmers (2006, p. 11), for two duplicates to share the same epistemic situation is for their corresponding beliefs to have the same truth-values and the same epistemic status 'as justified or unjustified, and as substantive or insubstantive'. Corresponding beliefs, Chalmers goes on to say, need not have the same contents. Oscar and Twin Oscar, he argues, share the same epistemic situation.[4] Oscar's belief that water [H_2O] is refreshing and Twin Oscar's corresponding belief that twater [XYZ] is refreshing will both be true, even if the two beliefs don't have the same content. Chalmers argues that he and his zombie twin, unlike Oscar and Twin Oscar, do *not* share the same epistemic situation. Chalmers' belief that he is phenomenally conscious is true, whereas Zombie Chalmers' belief that he is phenomenally conscious is false. Or think back to Mary, and imagine her possessing a zombie twin. Mary gains new introspectible knowledge when she is finally freed from her room, whereas Twin Mary doesn't gain all of the same knowledge. So they don't seem to share the same epistemic situation.

---

[4]   For those unfamiliar with the famous Twin Earth thought-experiment (Putnam, 1975), Twin Oscar is a microphysical duplicate of Earthling Oscar who lives on Twin Earth, a planet just like Earth except that the identical-looking stuff in the lakes, rivers, and so on, isn't H_2O but XYZ. The latter is a substance that can only be distinguished from H_2O by means of sophisticated laboratory tests. (Of course Twin Oscar cannot be a *complete* duplicate of Oscar, since his body contains XYZ whereas Oscar's contains H_2O. But by hypothesis this is supposed to make not the smallest difference to their cellular, neurological, or cognitive processes.)

Chalmers concludes that our zombie twins cannot share our epistemic situation.

We now propose to argue that Premise (ii) is false, however, and that zombies do share our epistemic situation (in one good sense of the notion of 'epistemic situation' — we will return to this point in Section 5).

Chalmers compares zombie duplicates to Oscar and Twin Oscar. Oscar, on Earth, is entertaining a thought that he would express with the words, 'Water is refreshing'. Our intuition is that Oscar is referring to H_2O. When Twin Oscar thinks a thought that he, too, would express with the words, 'Water is refreshing', our intuition is that he is referring to XYZ, and not to H_2O. Oscar and Twin Oscar both possess concepts that they deploy under the same circumstances (when they are thirsty), which are associated with certain kinds of perceptual states (seeing a colourless liquid), and so forth. But, according to the externalist, those corresponding concepts will have different contents. The content of Oscar's concept is tied to H_2O, whereas the content of Twin Oscar's concept is tied to XYZ. Chalmers seems ready to accept the externalist conclusion. He argues that Oscar and Twin Oscar have corresponding beliefs with the same truth-values but different *contents*. When they say, 'This is water', both are right, although they are talking about different things: Oscar is talking about water (H_2O), his twin is talking about twater (XYZ) (Chalmers, 2006, p. 11). Yet despite this, they share the same epistemic situation.

What prevents us from saying the same thing about Chalmers and his zombie twin? Chalmers and Zombie Chalmers both have concepts that they deploy in similar circumstances in the presence of certain perceptual states, that are conceptually isolated, and so on. An externalist (of the sort that Chalmers seems to be throughout his paper) could very well say that the contents of Chalmers' phenomenal concepts differ from the contents of his zombie twin's phenomenal concepts. The content of one of Chalmers' phenomenal concepts will turn out to involve a phenomenal state, whereas the content of his twin's corresponding phenomenal concept can't possibly involve such a state.[5] According to Chalmers it seems plausible that the content of a zombie's phenomenal concepts would be *schmenomenal* states. (These would be states that have the same physical, functional and intentional

---

[5]   This isn't to say that phenomenal concepts are *characterized* in terms of those phenomenal states, as they are on a first-person interpretation. Again, throughout this section of the paper phenomenal concepts are characterized as conceptually isolated concepts deployed in the right sorts of circumstances. But (and this is our point) there is no reason to think that our phenomenal concepts have the same content as our zombie twins' corresponding concepts.

properties as Chalmers' states, but that aren't phenomenally conscious; see Chalmers, 2006, p. 19.) The physicalist would then argue that Chalmers' and Zombie Chalmers' corresponding beliefs have the same truth-values and are justified in similar ways, but they are quite importantly *about* different things. So Chalmers and Zombie Chalmers can share the same epistemic situation after all, just as do Oscar and his twin.

Chalmers argues that defending this kind of reply, 'requires either deflating the phenomenal knowledge of conscious beings, or . . . inflating the corresponding knowledge of zombies' (Chalmers, 2006, p. 20). He goes on to argue that either strategy has counterintuitive consequences. No one thinks that Zombie Mary learns just *as much as* Mary (an implication of the inflationary move). No one thinks that Mary learns just *as little as* Zombie Mary does (an implication of the deflationary move). When we think of zombies, we aren't conceiving of creatures possessing something epistemically just as good as consciousness. We are conceiving of deprived creatures with impoverished knowledge of themselves.

But Chalmers is surely confused here. Arguing that zombies' phenomenal concepts have different contents enables us to say the following about Mary and her zombie twin: they both gain the same *amount* of knowledge but (and this is crucial) it is the same amount of knowledge *about different things*. Mary's knowledge is knowledge *of phenomenal states*, Zombie Mary's knowledge is knowledge *of schmenomenal states*, just as Oscar's knowledge is *of water* (H_2O) and his twin's is knowledge *of twater* (XYZ). Physicalists needn't deflate the knowledge gained by Mary or inflate the knowledge gained by Zombie Mary in order for the phenomenal concept strategy to work. All we need to point out is that the *objects* of their knowledge are very different.

Physicalists can now deal with a variety of third-person claims quite effectively. Consider, for instance, the discussion that Chalmers imagines between a zombie eliminativist and a zombie realist. The eliminativist argues that there is no such thing as phenomenal consciousness and the realist maintains that there is such a thing. Here is what Chalmers says about them:

> When such a debate is held in the actual world, the . . . materialist and the property dualist agree that the zombie realist is right, and the zombie eliminativist is wrong. But it is plausible that in a zombie scenario, the zombie realist would be wrong, and the zombie eliminativist would be right. (Chalmers, 2006, p. 12.)

But in the zombie scenario, it is just as plausible that the zombies would simply not be talking about *phenomenal* consciousness. Their debate is about the existence of *schmenomenal* consciousness. Again, both the realist and his zombie twin may very well be right; their beliefs may very well both be true.

We can say the same type of thing when it comes to the explanatory gap, or the conceivability of zombies. Zombies are thinking about schmenomenal consciousness using their phenomenal concepts, which are conceptually isolated from their other concepts. They will conclude from their reflections that there is a gap in explanation between *schmenomenal* consciousness and their physical world. They will also conclude that it is conceivable for someone to be physically, functionally and intentionally identical to them and yet lack *this* (where the concept THIS that they deploy picks out a schmenomenal state). And so forth.

This difference-in-content move now allows us to deal with a variety of first-person claims as well. Zombie Mary, after she leaves her room, may well come to believe something that she would express by saying, '*This* is an experience of blue'. What will make this belief true isn't her actually having a *phenomenal* experience of blue, but rather her having a *schmenomenal* experience — whatever that turns out to be. So both her beliefs and Mary's beliefs could plausibly have the same truth-values. Similarly when Chalmers says, 'I am phenomenally conscious', and his zombie twin utters the same string of words, both are in fact saying something different. To assume that they are saying the same thing (that they are both talking about *phenomenal* consciousness) is to assume that the contents of their states and concepts will be the same. But if there is no reason to assume this about Oscar and Twin Oscar, then there is no reason to assume this about Chalmers and his zombie twin. Zombie Chalmers is really saying that he is *schmenomenally* conscious, and we have every reason to think that he is right in thinking that, just as Chalmers is right is thinking he (Chalmers) is *phenomenally* conscious.

Chalmers, to block this line of reply, may now resort to our intuitions about zombies. We have claimed that they will turn out to have something epistemically just as good as phenomenal consciousness, namely schmenomenal consciousness. But doesn't that feel wrong? When we are conceiving of zombies, aren't we conceiving of beings with nothing at all that is epistemically like consciousness?

Well, on our view zombies are still zombies in that they are *not* phenomenally conscious. Their perceptual states don't have phenomenal feels. In this respect it *is* all dark inside. Yet they have something playing a certain role in their psychology — a role analogous to the role that phenomenal consciousness plays in ours. They have something *epistemically* just as good as consciousness, but they don't have anything that is *phenomenally* as good. It seems that this is what matters here. The schmenomenal states they undergo do not *feel* like anything. Even though their schmenomenal beliefs are *true* when our corresponding phenomenal beliefs are, their beliefs are, sadly enough, not *about* the same good stuff as our corresponding beliefs — they are not about the *feel* of experiences. Zombies are still, it seems, in quite a dreadful situation. So our intuitions about zombies are preserved.

5. Of Zombies and Zombie Zombies

We have shown that there are good reasons to resist Chalmers' claim that zombies fail to share our epistemic situation. If he can't make this case, then he can't argue successfully for Premise (3b). So it *isn't* true that if zombies conceivably possess phenomenal concepts, then phenomenal concepts can't do the work that physicalists want them to do. Or at least, we have been given no reason to believe that this is so. There is, however, a further line of reply open to Chalmers, which we consider in the present section.

5.1 On epistemic situations

We think that Chalmers will object that in conceiving of an 'epistemic situation' in such a way that both Chalmers and Zombie Chalmers share the same epistemic situation, the facts crucial to our actual epistemic situation have been omitted. For when I make the judgment that I might express by saying, '*This* is a blue-cup experience', I don't *just* deploy a conceptually isolated concept in the presence of an intentional state representing the presence of a blue cup. In addition, I deploy such a concept on the basis of my awareness of *this* type of mental state. By hypothesis, Zombie Chalmers doesn't have awareness of any such state. While Chalmers and Zombie Chalmers have much in common — in particular, they make similar judgments in similar circumstances (all of which can be true) and the epistemic liaisons of those judgments (when characterized in third-person terms) are all precisely parallel to one another — there are also crucial differences. For Chalmers' judgments are grounded in the presence of mental states like *these* and *those* and *this* and *that* (where the indexicals here express phenomenal concepts), whereas Zombie Chalmers' judgments are not. This seems like it might be an important — indeed, vital — part of Chalmers' epistemic situation. In which case the crucial premise in the argument outlined in Section 4 is true: zombies don't share our epistemic situation.

Another way of expressing the point just made would be this: Chalmers may deny that the distinction between a *property* and its *mode of presentation* finds any application in connection with phenomenal consciousness. Since H_2O and XYZ are presented to Oscar and Twin Oscar in the same way, we can say of them that (1) they possess concepts that play similar roles in their mental lives, and (2) they apply those concepts on the basis of the same mode of presentation. Only when these two conditions are met can we say that the twins share the same epistemic situation. Phenomenal properties, in contrast, provide their own modes of presentation: their modes of presentation are essential to them (Kripke, 1972). It follows that a phenomenal property and another distinct (schmenomenal) property *cannot* be presented to Chalmers and his zombie twin in the same way. So the pair of them possess, at most, (1): concepts that play similar roles in their mental lives. Since they can't possibly apply those concepts on the basis of the same modes of presentation, they cannot share the same epistemic situation, just as Chalmers maintains. Seen in this light, Chalmers ought to concede that it was a tactical error (or at best misleading) for him to have introduced Oscar and Twin Oscar into the discussion.

Recall, however, the distinction drawn in Section 2.3 between first-person and third-person characterizations of phenomenal concepts — a distinction similar to one Chalmers himself makes between phenomenal and schmenomenal concepts. We claimed there (again roughly as Chalmers himself does) that we could think of phenomenal concepts as applied *either* in response to phenomenal states (first-person characterization) *or* in response to perceptual states with certain sorts of intentional content (for example). According to the second horn of Chalmers' argument that we have been considering since the outset of Section 4, moreover, phenomenal concepts are to be characterized in *third-person terms*. So both Chalmers and Zombie Chalmers should be said to employ concepts whose applications are prompted by the presence of certain distinctive sorts of intentional / functional state, where those concepts are conceptually isolated from others. In which case, to introduce the feel of the state into our description of the mode of presentation of Chalmers' concepts is to switch illegitimately to a first-person characterization of those concepts. If we do restrict ourselves to a third-personal account of the concepts involved, in contrast, then the comparison with Oscar and Twin Oscar is entirely appropriate: in both cases we have pairs of people whose concepts have similar modes of presentation and play the same conceptual roles, but where those concepts happen to pick out different things.

We have alleged that the response that we made on Chalmers' behalf would re-introduce (illegitimately) first-personal phenomenal concepts into the defence of Premise (3). Chalmers might reply, however, that this allegation is unfounded. For it isn't the characterization of phenomenal concepts that is in question here. What is at issue isn't what we mean by 'phenomenal concept'. Rather, what is in question is the presence, or absence, of the states picked out by such concepts, when those concepts are used by their possessors. It is the presence of *this state* (the state, not the concept of the state here deployed) that is partly distinctive of Chalmers' epistemic situation, and which marks its difference from Zombie Chalmers' epistemic situation.

But now a problem of a different sort emerges. If Chalmers' epistemic situation is partly characterized in terms of the presence of *this state* (a phenomenal state), which we can imagine Zombie Chalmers to lack, then this amounts to saying that it is an important part of Chalmers' epistemic situation that he has phenomenally conscious mental states, whereas Zombie Chalmers doesn't. Doesn't that now beg the question? For this is something that is supposed to be granted on all hands. Defenders of the phenomenal concept strategy, too, allow that we can conceive of someone who is physically, functionally and intentionally identical to Chalmers (that is, Zombie Chalmers), but who lacks any of the phenomenally conscious mental states that Chalmers enjoys; and we claim to be capable of *explaining* how such a thing can be conceivable in a way that doesn't presuppose the existence of anything beyond the physical, the functional and/or the intentional.

Asserting that this strategy cannot work because phenomenal states themselves are part of what is distinctive of Chalmers' epistemic situation, and pointing out that the strategy can't explain *them*, is to insist that the phenomenal concept strategy should explain phenomenal consciousness. But that was never at issue. The phenomenal concept strategy is a strategy for explaining the conceivability of zombies, the explanatory gap, and so forth, not for explaining phenomenal consciousness *per se*. To put the point somewhat differently, the phrase 'our epistemic situation' is supposed to be a handy label for the various phenomena that the phenomenal concept strategy is intended to explain (the conceivability of zombies etc.). But since that strategy was never intended as a reductive explanation of phenomenal consciousness as such, 'our epistemic situation' should *not* be understood in such a way as to encompass phenomenal feelings.[6]

The true dialectical situation is as follows, we believe. Insofar as they argue legitimately, Chalmers and other anti-physicalists are asserting that the *best explanation* of the conceivability of zombies, the conceivability of experiential inversions, the explanatory gap, and so on, is that our experiences possess distinctive properties (call them 'qualia') that cannot be reductively explained in physical, functional or intentional terms. Chalmers might concede that we do possess phenomenal concepts, characterized in something like the way that the proponent of the phenomenal concept strategy characterizes them (conceptual isolation and so forth). But he denies that an appeal to these concepts alone can explain what needs to be explained (the possibility of zombies, the explanatory gap, and so forth). His opponent, in contrast, asserts that we don't need to appeal to any special properties of phenomenally conscious experience to do the work: the entire explanatory burden can be taken up by appeal to the phenomenal concepts in terms of which we think about those experiences.

5.2 Zombie-Zombie Chalmers

In order to move this debate forwards, we need to introduce a further character into the story: Zombie-Zombie Chalmers. Recall that Zombie Chalmers has been allowed to possess phenomenal concepts, characterized in a third-person way. For example, he has concepts that are applied purely recognitionally on the basis of his perceptual and imagistic states, and which are conceptually isolated from all of his other concepts (whether physical, functional or intentional). Possessing such concepts, Zombie Chalmers will be able to conceive of a zombie version of himself (Zombie-Zombie Chalmers). If on a given

---

[6] It is important to note, too, that a physicalist who deploys the phenomenal concept strategy is *not* here arguing *for* physicalism. Stoljar (2005) goes wrong on just this point, for he claims that the physicalist's reply to conceivability arguments comes in two stages, the first of which is that the conceptual isolation of phenomenal concepts/truths entails that the conditional, (1) *If P, then P**, is a posteriori necessary (where P is a summary of all physical truths, and P^* is a summary of all phenomenal truths). But physicalists who adopt the phenomenal concept strategy aren't attempting to show the truth of this entailment. Making the case that (1) is a necessary truth would, it is true, be making the case for physicalism. But the phenomenal concept strategy is only intended to be defensive. The physicalist is only arguing that the conceivability arguments don't show that physicalism is *false*, despite what their proponents claim: there is another explanation for why we can conceive of these things, an explanation that appeals to phenomenal concepts. So Stoljar misses the fact that the phenomenal concept strategy is essentially a defensive strategy. It is a strategy that physicalists employ to show that the key anti-physicalist arguments fail. It isn't meant to make a positive case for the truth of physicalism, or for the necessary a posteriori truth of (1).

occasion he uses the word 'this' to express one of his phenomenal concepts, then he will be able to entertain thoughts that he might articulate by saying, 'There might exist someone who is physically, functionally and intentionally identical with myself, but who nevertheless lacks anything resembling *this* type of state'. Since his phenomenal concept is conceptually isolated, there will be no hidden contradiction in this thought that he would be capable of detecting a priori.

Likewise if Zombie Chalmers uses the word 'this' to express a phenomenal concept that applies to one of his percepts of colour. (For these purposes, Zombie Chalmers' perceptions of colour need to be characterized purely functionally and intentionally, of course. They are perceptual states with a fine-grained intentional content representing properties of surfaces that impact the latter's reflection of light, perhaps.) Then he, too, will fall subject to the Mary thought-experiment. He will be inclined to think, 'Mary brought up in her black and white room couldn't know what it is like to undergo *this* type of perceptual state, no matter how much she knows about the physical, functional and intentional properties of colour vision'; and he will be inclined to think this precisely because the concept that he expresses by 'this' is a conceptually isolated one.

By the same token, Zombie Chalmers will think that there is an explanatory gap between all physical, functional and intentional facts, on the one hand, and his own mental states (characterized using phenomenal concepts), on the other. Because those concepts are conceptually isolated ones, he will be able to think, 'No matter how much you tell me about the physical, functional and intentional facts involved in perception, it will still be possible that all of what you tell me should be true, while states of *this* sort are absent or inverted'. So he, too, will be inclined to think that there is something mysterious about his perceptual (and imagistic and emotional) states, which puts them outside the reach of physicalist explanation.

It is plain that it is Zombie Chalmers' possession of phenomenal concepts that explains why he should find the existence of Zombie-Zombie Chalmers conceivable. Likewise it is his possession of such concepts that explains the conceivability to him of perceptual inversions, that explains why he thinks Mary would learn something new, and that explains why he would think that there is an explanatory gap between the character of his own mental states and all physical, functional and intentional facts. Plainly, since Zombie Chalmers is being conceived to lack any phenomenally conscious states, it cannot be the presence of such states in him that explains the conceivability of Zombie-Zombie Chalmers, and the rest.

Zombie Chalmers, when presented with the phenomenal concept strategy for explaining the conceivability of Zombie-Zombie Chalmers and so forth, might even be inclined to insist that this strategy can't explain what is distinctive of his own epistemic situation. He will allow that Zombie-Zombie Chalmers would make parallel judgments to himself, of course, and would act in exactly similar ways and on similar grounds. But he will be inclined to insist that something crucial is left out by the phenomenal concept strategy. What is left out is that he (Zombie Chalmers) bases his judgments on the presence of states like *this* and *this* and *that*, whereas, by hypothesis, Zombie-Zombie Chalmers is being conceived to lack such states.

Now we can bring it all back home. For in connection with everything that Chalmers thinks, and for every possibility that Chalmers can conceive, and for every argument that Chalmers can offer, Zombie Chalmers can offer a parallel one. Of course, from our perspective, conceiving all of this along with Chalmers, we are conceiving that they are thinking about different things: Chalmers is thinking about phenomenal states, whereas Zombie Chalmers is thinking about schmenomenal states. But this difference plays no role in explaining what each is capable of thinking. On the contrary, it is their mutual possession of phenomenal concepts (characterized in the third-person way) that does that. Since it can't be the fact that Zombie Chalmers possesses phenomenal states that explains his capacity to conceive of Zombie-Zombie Chalmers and the rest (for by hypothesis he possesses no such states), we shouldn't allow that Chalmers' possession of phenomenal states plays any role in explaining how he can conceive of Zombie Chalmers, either.

This 'zombie-zombie argument', as one might call it, seems to us to decisively shift the burden of proof in this area onto the anti-physicalist.[7] Since an appeal to phenomenal concepts (characterized in a third-person way as conceptually isolated and so on) can explain everything that Zombie Chalmers is inclined to think and say (and in particular since it can explain the conceivability to Zombie Chalmers of Zombie-Zombie Chalmers), and since everything that Zombie Chalmers is inclined to think and say, Chalmers is also inclined to think and say and vice versa (controlling for what will seem from Chalmers' perspective to be differences of content), the most reasonable conclusion to draw is that it is Chalmers' possession

---

[7] Remember, though, that the argument isn't supposed to be an argument in support of physicalism. It is rather a defensive argument intended to undermine a set of arguments *against* physicalism (the arguments from zombies, explanatory gaps, and so forth).

of phenomenal concepts, too, that explains the conceivability of zombies, the explanatory gap, and so forth.

5.3 Replies to objections

Chalmers will surely reply as follows: the zombie-zombie argument presupposes that when Zombie Chalmers claims, 'I am phenomenally conscious', he says something *true*, and yet (Chalmers will insist) it is much more plausible that this claim is false. Surely, in the zombie world, there is no phenomenal consciousness, and so Zombie Chalmers' claim, in that world, that he is phenomenally conscious must be false.[8]

This can't possibly be a good reply to the argument of the present article, however. Certainly it can't be if it assumes that Zombie Chalmers' concept PHENOMENAL CONSCIOUSNESS refers to phenomenal consciousness. For as we have shown in Section 4, Zombie Chalmers' phenomenal concepts plausibly refer to his perceptual states (characterized purely functionally and intentionally). Actually, it isn't in the least plausible that a zombie's phenomenal concepts (characterized third-personally) should be referring to the zombie's (non-existent) phenomenal states (which would make what he says wrong). This would be like saying that Twin Oscar's twater concept actually refers to H_2O, in which case he is wrong every time he says, 'This water tastes good'. But clearly that is just absurd. No theory of concepts does (or should) yield such a counterintuitive claim. Zombie Chalmers is correct when he says that he is conscious, because he isn't saying that he has phenomenal states as *we* understand them. He is correct because he means that he has schmenomenal states, and he has them.

As we have argued, all of Zombie Chalmers' beliefs turn out to have the same truth-values as Chalmers' corresponding ones. As a realist about phenomenal consciousness, Chalmers here on Earth will say, 'There are phenomenal states', and he will be right. His zombie twin will utter the same words but will mean that there are schmenomenal (i.e. physical, functional and/or intentional) states, and he, too, will be right. Likewise, if someone here on Earth denies that there are phenomenal states and turns out to be wrong, his zombie twin will likewise turn out to be wrong in the zombie world, since he will be denying, there, that there are schmenomenal (e.g. functional and/or intentional) states.

---

[8]   Chalmers (2006) makes a very similar reply to an argument by Balog (1999) that parallels ours (but deployed in the service of a different conclusion: Balog is interested in denying that there is a link between conceivability and possibility).

In fact, it seems that such pairs of corresponding beliefs will turn out *not* to have the same truth value only if dualism is true. If dualism is true and Chalmers says, 'Phenomenal states aren't physical', then he will be right; but his zombie twin uttering the same words will mean that schmenomenal (e.g. functional and/or intentional) states aren't physical, and he will be wrong; for by hypothesis his schmenomenal states *are* physical. Since Chalmers' overall goal is to argue for dualism and against physicalism, he begs the question when he assumes that his zombie twin's corresponding beliefs don't have the same truth-values as his own.[9]

Chalmers is very likely to adopt a rather different tactic, however: he will argue that the zombie's phenomenal statements are false, not because they refer to phenomenal states that he doesn't have, but because they fail to refer altogether. The right analogy isn't between Earth and Twin Earth but rather between Earth and Dry Earth. Dry Oscar's claims about water (e.g. that it is refreshing) are false because he is subject to some sort of grand illusion: there is no such thing as water in his environment. If this is the right analogy then we would have to grant Chalmers that the epistemic situation of zombies isn't, as a matter of fact, the same as ours. But we have two responses to make to this argument. One is to deny that this *is* the right analogy. The other is to say that even if it is, we can still run a version of the zombie-zombie argument. Let us elaborate.

How *could* Zombie Chalmers' phenomenal concepts fail to refer? For these are concepts that, in their third-person characterization, are applied in a recognitional way in the presence of content-bearing mental states of a distinctive sort (perceptual and imagistic states). How could these concepts fail to refer to the very states that prompt their application? One option would be to claim that there is something *else* built into their content. For example, as Chalmers once suggested (1996, p. 204), they might include the commitment that they should *not* refer to any physical or functional property. But this would be inconsistent with the claim that phenomenal concepts are conceptually isolated. Concepts that are so isolated must lack any commitments of this sort.

Another option would be to claim that the presence of phenomenal consciousness is a *constitutive* aspect of the *content* of a phenomenal concept. In which case Zombie Chalmers' 'thoughts' involving

---

[9]   Our own argument, in contrast, isn't question-begging. For as we pointed out in Section 5.1, the phenomenal concept strategy is only intended as a defence of physicalism against anti-physicalist arguments, not as an independent argument in support of physicalism, nor as a purported reductive explanation of phenomenal consciousness itself.

phenomenal concepts will be either false or truth-valueless because employing a contentless concept. (Such a position is developed at length in Chalmers, 2003.) But this option is entirely question-begging in the present context. Chalmers (2003) develops his account of the content of phenomenal concepts within the framework of his own anti-physicalist position, assuming that there are irreducible qualia and such like. But that position is supposed to be established on the basis of arguments from the conceivability of zombies and so forth, and hence cannot be taken for granted in the evaluation of those arguments. Moreover, the horn of Chalmers' dilemma that we have been addressing for most of this paper (Section 4 onwards) presupposes a third-person characterization of phenomenal concepts. Given such a characterization, there is no reason whatever to think that the thoughts of Zombie Chalmers, employing such a concept, should be empty.

Even if we allow that Zombie Chalmers' phenomenal concepts might fail to refer, however, we can still run a version of the zombie-zombie argument. For we surely need to explain the inferences that the zombie makes, and the reasons why he thinks (granted, mistakenly) that he can conceive of a zombie version of himself. The fact that the zombie's beliefs are false (because containing an empty term) doesn't mean we are under no obligation to explain his reasoning and his behaviour. We can explain why it is that little John wants to be nice by appealing, in part, to his (false) belief that Santa will only give him presents if he is nice. Although his concept SANTA fails to refer, it still plays a role in his reasoning and behaviour. What, then, explains the zombie's reasoning and behaviour? Clearly, the presence of phenomenal feels can't explain that reasoning. Just as in the case in which we assume that the zombie's phenomenal concepts refer to physical states, so in the case in which his concepts are empty, his reasoning can't be explained by an appeal to phenomenal *states*. The only thing that can truly explain the relevant bits of reasoning is the fact that Zombie Chalmers has a concept (in the original case, referring to a physical property, now being allowed to be empty) which is conceptually isolated from all physical, functional and intentional concepts.

What emerges, then, is that the zombie-zombie argument can still work even if we allow that Chalmers and Zombie Chalmers don't share the same epistemic situation (because all of the latter's beliefs involving phenomenal concepts are false by virtue of failing to refer). Since it is the conceptual isolation of Zombie Chalmers' (empty) phenomenal concepts that explains the conceivability to him of Zombie-Zombie Chalmers and so forth, parity of reasoning suggests that in

Chalmers' case, too, it is the conceptual isolation of his phenomenal concepts and *not* the presence of phenomenal consciousness itself which explains the various problematic thought experiments. We want to emphasize, however, that we are actually very unwilling to allow that the corresponding beliefs of Chalmers and Zombie Chalmers should differ in truth value. We think that it is *much* more plausible that Zombie Chalmers' phenomenal concepts should refer successfully to his schmenomenal states.

6. Conclusion

It is worth noting in closing that there is both a weaker and a stronger conclusion that might be drawn from our defence of the phenomenal concept strategy. The weaker conclusion is that the arguments from zombies, from the explanatory gap and so forth, to the mysterious and/or non-physical nature of phenomenal consciousness is decisively blocked. For everyone can agree that our phenomenal concepts fit some or other variant of the third-person descriptions canvassed in Section 2. Everyone can agree that it is possible for us to form concepts of experience that are purely recognitional, or that 'quote' percepts or images, or whatever. What they will disagree about is whether our phenomenal concepts are *exhausted by* such factors. Anti-physicalists will insist that something has been left out, namely that those concepts pick out non-relational, non-intentional properties of experience like *these*. So if the zombie and explanatory gap thought experiments can be fully explained in terms of our possession of phenomenal concepts, then there is no longer any *argument* from those thought experiments to the existence of qualia, the mysteriousness of consciousness, property dualism, and so forth. Such claims might still be correct, but the arguments for them have collapsed.

The stronger conclusion that might be drawn from our discussion is this. Once we see that all the puzzling factors can be explained in terms of our deployment of phenomenal concepts; and perhaps especially once we see in those terms that even the conceived-of zombies will be able to conceive of zombie versions of themselves, then the most plausible conclusion to draw overall is that there is nothing *more* to our phenomenal concepts than is described in the third-person description. (Remember, however, that the third-person description is *not* supposed to be any sort of analysis or partial definition of our phenomenal concepts.) So the most reasonable conclusion is that a phenomenal state just *is* a perceptual state with a certain distinctive sort of intentional content (non-conceptual, perhaps) that occurs in such a way as to ground the application of phenomenal concepts. Hence we can conclude that phenomenal consciousness can be fully reductively explained (somehow — of course there are a number of mutually inconsistent competing accounts here)[10] in physical, functional and/or intentional terms.

We have provided a number of reasons for thinking that Chalmers' argument against the phenomenal concept strategy is unsuccessful. On the contrary, that strategy still stands as providing a powerful response to a wide range of anti-physicalist thought-experiments, enabling us to draw the anti-physicalist sting from the latter.

References

Balog, K. (1999), 'Conceivability, possibility, and the mind-body problem', *Philosophical Review*, **108**, pp. 497–528.

Burge, T. (1986), 'Individualism and psychology', *Philosophical Review*, **95**, pp. 3–45.

Carruthers, P. (2000), *Phenomenal Consciousness* (Cambridge University Press).

Chalmers, D. (1996), *The Conscious Mind* (New York: Oxford University Press).

Chalmers, D. (2003), 'The content and epistemology of phenomenal belief', in *Consciousness: New Philosophical Perspectives*, ed. Q. Smith and A. Jokic (New York: Oxford University Press).

Chalmers, D. (2006), 'Phenomenal concepts and the explanatory gap', in *Phenomenal Concepts and Phenomenal Knowledge: New Essays on Consciousness and Physicalism*, ed. T. Alter and S. Walter (New York: Oxford University Press).

Fodor, J. (1990), *A Theory of Content and Other Essays* (Cambridge, MA: MIT Press).

Hill, C. (1997), 'Imaginability, conceivability, possibility, and the mind-body problem', *Philosophical Studies*, **87**, pp. 61–85.

Jackson, F. (1986), 'What Mary didn't know', *Journal of Philosophy*, **83**, pp. 291–5.

Kripke, S. (1972), 'Naming and necessity', in *Semantics and Natural Language*, ed. G. Harman and D. Davidson (Reidel).

Levine, J. (1983), 'Materialism and qualia: The explanatory gap', *Pacific Philosophical Quarterly*, **64**, pp. 354–61.

Levine, J. (2001), *Purple Haze: The Puzzle of Consciousness* (New York: Oxford University Press).

Loar, B. (1990), 'Phenomenal states', *Philosophical Perspectives*, **4**, pp. 81–108.

Nagel, T. (1974), 'What is it like to be a bat?', *The Philosophical Review*, **82**, pp. 435–50.

O'Dea, J. (2002), 'The indexical nature of sensory concepts', *Philosophical Papers*, **31** (2), pp. 169–81.

Papineau, D. (2002), *Thinking About Consciousness* (New York: Oxford University Press).

Perry, J. (1979), 'The problem of the essential indexical', *Noûs*, **13**, pp. 3–21.

---

[10] One of the issues outstanding will concern the selection of the *best* third-person description of the nature and role of phenomenal concepts. About this matter we have said nothing.

Perry, J. (2001), *Knowledge, Possibility, and Consciousness* (Cambridge, MA: MIT Press).

Putnam, H. (1975), 'The Meaning of "Meaning" ', in *Mind, Language and Reality*, (Philosophical Papers, Vol. II), H. Putnam (Cambridge University Press).

Rey, G. (1998), 'A narrow representationalist account of qualitative experience', *Philosophical Perspectives*, **12**, pp. 435–58.

Stoljar, D. (2005), 'Physicalism and phenomenal concepts', *Mind and Language*, **20**, pp. 469–94.

Sturgeon, S. (1994), 'The epistemic basis of subjectivity', *Journal of Philosophy*, **91**, pp. 221–35.

Tye, M. (2000), *Color, Consciousness and Content* (Cambridge, MA: MIT Press).

Tye, M. (2003), 'A theory of phenomenal concepts', in *Minds and Persons*, ed. A. O'Hear (Cambridge, MA: Cambridge University Press).

Simon Baron-Cohen, Daniel Bor,
Jac Billington, Julian Asher,
Sally Wheelwright and Chris Ashwin

Savant Memory in a Man with Colour Form-Number Synaesthesia and Asperger Syndrome

Abstract: *Extreme conditions like savantism, autism or synaesthesia, which have a neurological basis, challenge the idea that other minds are similar to our own. In this paper we report a single case study of a man in whom all three of these conditions co-occur. We suggest, on the basis of this single case, that when savantism and synaesthesia co-occur, it is worthwhile testing for an undiagnosed Autism Spectrum Condition (ASC). This is because savantism has an established association with ASC, and the combination of ASC with synaesthesia may increase the likelihood of savantism. The implications of these conditions for philosophy of mind are introduced.*

The Assumption that all Human Minds are Wired the Same

The problem of other minds has been of interest to researchers in fields as diverse as philosophy of mind (Goldman, 2006; Nagel, 1974; Wittgenstein, 1958), developmental and clinical psychology (Baron-Cohen & Cross, 1992; Baron-Cohen, Golan *et al.*, 2004; Baron-Cohen, Wheelwright & Jolliffe, 1997; Perner, 1991) and neuroimaging (Baron-

Cohen & Ring, 1994; Baron-Cohen, Ring *et al.*, 2000; Frith & Frith, 1999; Iacoboni *et al.*, 2005).

This article focuses on two clinical conditions, autism and synaesthesia, that challenge the assumption that all human minds are wired the same. Even though only one percent of the population at most may have each of these conditions (Baird *et al.*, 2006; Baron-Cohen, Burt *et al.*, 1996), this illustrates a basic problem that there may be other minds that are wired differently at a neuronal level. Neurodevelopmental conditions like autism and synaesthesia invalidate the assumption that all humans share similar conscious experiences because they share similar neural architecture.

In the next section, we summarize previous studies of these two neurodevelopmental conditions, before reporting a single case study of a young man who has both. One reason for reporting this case is that currently it is not known how rare or common it is to have both conditions. We wish to encourage other clinicians or researchers to document such cases in order for us to understand if they are related in any way. If each condition separately has a prevalence of 1%, and if these were truly independent, then the probability (p) of them co-occurring would be calculated using the multiplication law: p (synaesthesia) x p (autism) = 0.01 x 0.01 = 1 in 10,000 (i.e. quite rare). However, if they share some common causal mechanism, such as neural over-connectivity (Baron-Cohen, Harrison *et al.*, 1993; Belmonte *et al.*, 2004; Rouw and Scholte, 2007), then they may co-occur more often than chance. Their possible independence or association remains to be tested and epidemiological methods are required to find out if they are related.

The single case study we report below in whom both conditions co-occur is all the more interesting because he has a third 'condition': savantism. We not only wish to document his unusual profile but also wish to speculate on the relationship between these three conditions. In particular, we put forward the proposal that whenever autism and synaesthesia co-occur, the likelihood of savantism is increased. Such a proposal requires empirical validation through the documentation of further cases.

Synaesthesia

Synaesthesia is defined as occurring when stimulation of one sensory modality automatically triggers a perception in a second modality, in the absence of any direct stimulation to this second modality (Cytowic, 1989, 1993; Marks, 1975; Motluk, 1994; Vernon, 1930). For example, a sound automatically and instantly triggers the perception of vivid colour: a person describes the sound of the word MOSCOW as

'Darkish grey, with spinach green and pale blue' (Baron-Cohen, Wyke & Binnie, 1987). Many combinations of synaesthesia are reported to occur naturally, including sound giving rise to visual percepts ('coloured-hearing') and smell giving rise to tactile sensation (Cytowic, 1993).

The standard test for the presence of synaesthesia involves assessing a subject's *consistency* in reporting sensory descriptions for words across two or more occasions, when the subject has no prior warning of the retest, and irrespective of the length of interval between testing sessions (Baron-Cohen, Harrison *et al.*, 1993; Baron-Cohen, Wyke & Binnie, 1987). Using this method, consistency is typically as high as 90%, even when retested over years and even when stringent criteria are set for retest descriptions. Recently the 'Test of Genuineness' (TOG) has been revised for precise quantitative scoring (Asher *et al.*, 2006), and psychophysical studies of synaesthesia (Ramachandran & Hubbard, 2001) also confirm that synaesthesia is highly consistent within an individual.

'Developmental synaesthesia' is distinguished from acquired or drug-induced synaesthesia and has several characteristics:

1. childhood onset before 4 years of age;
2. differentially diagnosed to hallucination, delusion or other psychotic phenomena;
3. distinct from imagery arising from imagination;
4. not induced by drug use;
5. vivid;
6. automatic/involuntary; and
7. unlearnt.

Regarding the latter claim, that synaesthesia is unlearnt, the key arguments against a learning account are as follows:

1. The sex ratio in synaesthesia is 6:1 (f:m);
2. consecutive letters may be closely related colours (e.g. 'M' = olive green, 'N' = emerald green, 'O' = washed out pale green). Coloured alphabet books logically go to great lengths to ensure that consecutive letters are printed in very different colours;
3. the coloured alphabets of family members often show substantial variation, ruling out imitation;
4. typically subjects lack of recollection of any learning.

Two biological theories of synaesthesia have been put forward. The *neural connectivity* theory is based on the evidence of connective pathways between auditory and visual areas of the brain in other species (Dehay *et al.*, 1984; Kennedy *et al.*, 1996; Kennedy *et al.*, 1989). These projections are transient, typically disappearing approximately 3 months *post partum*. These transitory pathways may get 'pruned' as part of the biological maturation of the brain. Synaesthesia might be due to the persistence of neural information passing from auditory to visual brain areas, beyond the neonatal stage. At the cognitive level, the neural connectivity theory would be compatible with the *modularity breakdown* theory. This states that whereas in non-synaesthetes audition and vision are functionally discrete, in individuals with synaesthesia a breakdown in this modularity has occurred, such that there is cross-talk (Baron-Cohen, Harrison *et al.*, 1993).

Secondly, the *genetic* theory argues that synaesthesia is heritable (Galton, 1883). This has some support from a family study in which the pedigrees of seven families of probands suggested that the condition is transmitted as an autosomal dominant X chromosome linked condition (Baron-Cohen, Burt *et al.*, 1996). This is currently being tested (Asher *et al.*, submitted). Candidate mechanisms include genes that regulate the migration and maturation of neurons within the developing brain, or those that regulate 'neuronal pruning' (apoptosis). The first total genome linkage study of synaesthesia has recently been completed (Asher *et al.*, submitted).

As mentioned above, a neuroimaging study of synaesthesia using PET (Paulesu *et al.*, 1995) compared brain activity in synaesthetes and control whilst listening to either words or pure tones. Activity was seen in the synaesthetic group alone during auditory stimulation by words, in the posterior infer-temporal cortex and the parietal-occipital junction, both of which have known involvement in colour perception. An fMRI study (Nunn *et al.*, 2002) also found activity in the colour-selective regions V4/V8, as would be predicted. Both of these neuroimaging studies confirm atypical brain function in synaesthesia, though do not allow us to test the modularity breakdown theory directly. It may be that diffusion tensor imaging (DTI) would enable such a test (cf. Rouw and Scholte, 2007). But from the functional neuroimaging studies it has been argued that this condition is a good illustration of how atypical neural wiring can produce radically different conscious experience (Gray *et al.*, 2002).

The case of synaesthesia we report below is a man who came to our attention because of his savant memory: he is the European champion for memorizing the number Pi. His name is Daniel Tammet (DT). His identity can be disclosed because he has written an autobiography (Tammet, 2006) and he agreed to take part in a television documentary investigating the nature of his savantism (*The Boy with the Incredible Brain*, May 2005, Channel 5). In 2004 he recited Pi to 22,514 decimal places from memory. His synaesthesia takes the form of numbers being experienced as colours with texture and shape. In many ways, DT is the modern-day Shereshevsky (S), otherwise known as Luria's 'Mnemonist' (Luria, 1988). Like DT, S could recall long lists of words or letters in order, could recall the list in reverse, his memory was described as 'seemingly limitless', and recall was possible decades later. Like DT, for S each letter had a shape and a colour, and he described his memory as going along 'the mental walk', where he could 'see' each item to be remembered as landmarks in a mental landscape. Today, like DT, S would be regarded as a 'savant'.

Such cases raise 4 possible theories:

1. *Savant memory is caused by synaesthesia*. It is easy to rule this theory out as there are many documented cases of savant memory in whom there is no apparent synaesthesia. (The names of winners of international memory championships — so-called mnemonists — are available on the internet). Whilst it might be objected that people who have trained their memories are not really savants, even in cases of savants (e.g. Kim Peek), it could be argued that synaesthesia may not have been formally tested and there would have been no reason to ask about synaesthesia prior to the present case study. It remains the case that even one case of a memory savant without synaesthesia would disprove the theory that savant memory is the result of synaesthesia.

2. *Synaesthesia is caused by savant memory.* Like the previous theory, this is also easy to rule out because there are many synaesthetes who have average (but not superior) memory (Baron-Cohen, Wyke & Binnie, 1987).

3. *Synaesthesia has a facilitation effect on memory*: This theory has some plausibility. Since each item to be recalled has a visual (colour, shape, texture) dimension, this might enable a superior mnemonic strategy to be used. For example when S listened to a pure 250 Hz tone with 64 decibels, he saw 'a velvet cord with fibres jutting out on all sides. The cord was tinged with a delicate pink-orange hue'. This was quite distinct from what he saw when he heard a 250 Hz tone that was 86 decibels. DT also reported vivid 3D descriptions for numbers, with many facets to them, including colour, shape, height, size and texture. One might therefore imagine that their unusually rich form of synaesthesia facilitated the development of their prodigious memory abilities.

To test this theory would require a comparison of two groups: those with synaesthesia and those without (matched for age, education and

IQ) and assessed using standardized memory tests. As far as we know, such a relatively straight-forward experiment has not yet been conducted. Note that if the null hypothesis was supported (no difference in memory between the two groups) this would disprove the theory. If the synaesthetic group was found to have memory abilities superior to controls, this would be consistent with this third theory, though it would not be water-tight proof for it, since correlation does not prove cause.[1]

4. *In cases of savantism, there is also an autism spectrum condition (ASC).* In this article we can begin to test this fourth theory. This theory is at least plausible because savant skills are most often found in ASC (Hermelin, 2002). That is, it is already established that ASC increases the likelihood of savantism, so at a minimum it is important to test cases of savants for whether they have an ASC. Even well-documented cases of savants who have apparently intact social skills cannot be taken as clear counter-evidence for this theory, if they have never been formally tested for an ASC. ASC exist on a spectrum and a reliable way to measure this spectrum within high functioning individuals is to use the Autism-Spectrum Quotient (AQ) (Baron-Cohen, Wheelwright *et al.*, 2001). So a way of testing this fourth theory is to ask if savants have an elevated AQ. Whilst DT had no prior ASC diagnosis (and no prior measure of his AQ), in the study reported below, we conducted a full diagnostic assessment for Asperger Syndrome (AS) (a sub-group on the autistic spectrum), to test the hypothesis that in DTs case the AS might be present but undiagnosed. Before we describe our study, we first summarize what is meant by ASC.

Autism Spectrum Conditions

Autism is defined in terms of abnormalities in social and communication development, in the presence of marked repetitive behaviour and limited imagination (A.P.A, 1994). Asperger Syndrome (AS) is defined in terms of the individual meeting the same criteria for autism but with no history of cognitive or language delay, and not meeting the criteria for Pervasive Development Disorder (PDD) (I.C.D-10, 1994). Language delay itself is defined as not using single words by two years of age and/or phrase speech by three years of age. There is growing evidence that autism and AS are of genetic origin. The evidence is strongest for autism and comes from twin and behavioural genetic family studies (Bailey *et al.*, 1995). Family pedigrees of AS also implicate heritability (Gillberg, 1991).

---

[1] While this paper has been in press, a study has been published showing that synaesthesia does facilitate memory (see Yaro and Ward, 2007).

Children and adults with AS show empathizing deficits on age-appropriate tests (Baron-Cohen, Jolliffe *et al.*, 1997). This deficit in their empathizing is thought to underlie the difficulties in social and communicative development (Tager-Flusberg, 1993) and in the imagination of others' minds (Baron-Cohen, 1987). Children and adults with AS also show intact or even superior systemizing, defined as the drive to analyse systems, in order to understand and predict the behaviour of inanimate events (Baron-Cohen, 2002). Studies suggest systemizing in autism is at least in line with mental age, or superior (Baron-Cohen, Richler *et al.*, 2003). The hyper-systemizing that may be the core characteristic of ASC (Baron-Cohen, 2006) may be the key reason for the strong association between ASC and savantism. Put differently, savantism may be nothing more than the end-product of good systemizing. If one systemizes calendars, one could show the signs of 'calendrical calculation' (Hermelin & O'Connor, 1986). If one systemizes drawing, one could develop remarkable accuracy as an artist (Myers *et al.*, 2004). If one systemizes number patterns, one could develop a facility for identifying prime numbers (Baron-Cohen & Bolton, 1993). And if one systemizes syntax, one could develop a talent for acquiring languages (Hermelin, 2002).

Anatomical abnormalities have been identified in many brain areas in autism. These include the cerebellum (Courchesnen *et al.*, 1994), the brain stem (Hashimoto *et al.*, 1995), frontal lobes (Carper & Courchesne, 2000), parietal lobes (Courchesne *et al.*, 1993), hippocampus (Aylward *et al.*, 1999) and the amygdala (Aylward *et al.*, 1999). In terms of neuropathology, the number of Purkinje cells in the cerebellar cortex is abnormally low (Williams *et al.*, 1980). Abnormalities in the density of packing of neurons in the hippocampus, amygdala and other parts of the limbic system have also been reported (Bauman & Kempner, 1985). Using either MRI volumetric analysis or measures of head circumference, the autistic brain appears to involve transient postnatal macroencephaly (Courchesne, 2002). The *overgrowth* may reflect a failure of synaptic pruning or an excess of synaptogenesis. We now turn to describe DT, to confirm his synaesthesia and to test him for AS.

Daniel Tammet (DT)

Biographical information

At the time of testing DT was 26 years old (born 31 January 1979). He had epilepsy at age 3 years. He did well at school in terms of academic progress, though reports having been unhappy as a child and teenager, in feeling isolated from others. He has 3 A levels, in History, French,

German (grade Bs). He has worked as a mathematics tutor. Currently he lives with his male partner whom he met through the internet, and he runs his own website providing language-learning tutorials.

Family structure

He is the oldest of nine siblings, one of whom has AS. All nine siblings have an area of strong narrow interest, ranging from music through to literature and politics. His father has a diagnosis of schizophrenia.

His savantism

DT speaks 10 languages, including Estonian and Finnish, has invented his own language (Manti) and learnt Spanish in one weekend. He performs mathematical calculations at lightning speed, including multiplying six-digit numbers together. He commented that 31, 19, 79 and 1979 are all prime numbers, an indication of how he sees patterns in numbers very rapidly. As mentioned earlier, as part of a formal competition he recited Pi to 22,514 decimal paces, earning the title of European champion. He did not do this as part of a competition but to raise money for an epilepsy charity.

His synaesthesia

DT reports that he has always seen numbers as shapes, colours and textures. He also experiences some words as having colour. When calculating, the shape of two numbers combines to produce a new shape (the solution). This has been investigated at the neural level using fMRI, the results of which are reported elsewhere (Bor *et al.*, submitted).

Tests and Results

1. *The Test of Genuineness-Revised* (Asher *et al.*, 2006). On this test to validate synaesthesia, DT was over 90% consistent. This confirms his synaesthesia.

2. *The Autism Spectrum Quotient (AQ)* (Baron-Cohen, Wheelwright *et al.*, 2001). On the AQ he scored 39. People with AS score a mean of 35.8 (sd = 6.5), whilst controls score a mean of 16.3 (sd = 6.2). He is therefore in the clinical range on the AQ. The recommended clinical cut-off on the AQ for AS is 32 or more out of 50.

3. *The Empathy Quotient (EQ)* (Baron-Cohen & Wheelwright, 2004). On the EQ he scored 8 out of a maximum of 80. People with AS score a mean of 20.4 (sd = 11.6) and controls score a mean of 45.3 (sd = 10.5). This is clearly in the below average range. The recommended clinical cut-off for AS on the EQ is 30 or less. Whilst the AQ and EQ

are not diagnostic of AS, they are screens for clinical use to check for possible AS. DT's scores are below the cut-off on the EQ and above the cut-off on the AQ, indicating likely AS on both measures. In order to test for AS, a full diagnostic assessment was undertaken, described next.

4. *The Adult Asperger Assessment (AAA)* (Baron-Cohen, Wheelwright *et al.*, 2005). The AAA was used as part of a formal diagnostic assessment for AS. DT's mother served as informant for his developmental history. He scored 13 out of a maximum of 18 symptoms, and a diagnosis is made if the individual scores at least 10. His *social difficulties* were evident across his development. For example, he had no friends at school and instead counted leaves in the playground. He reported that numbers were his friends. He taught himself eye-contact at 13 years old. He tends to takes things literally and is reported to commit frequent *faux pas*. He avoids social situations and finds parties confusing. He is aware that he talks too much and has taught himself to stop. He has also been told that he doesn't notice if someone is upset. Examples of his *obsessions* are that he has to have strict order in his routines and he showed severe tantrums at change of routine as a child. He constructed a library in his house, alphabeticizing the books and giving out tickets. He collected hundreds of ladybirds as a child and read books about numbers for hours as a child. He was obsessed with play-doh shapes for numbers, and with Rubic cubes. He showed head-banging in his cot. As a child, he sat with fingers in his ears in primary school and with his eyes tight shut.

The combination of his social difficulties and his obsessional interests were the basis for giving him a diagnosis of AS. He fulfilled the criteria because these symptoms had interfered with his development, causing him unhappiness whilst at school when he did not understand why he couldn't fit in. The fact that he has made an excellent adjustment in his adulthood raised the question as to whether he still needed the diagnosis of AS, even though there was no question that it would have been helpful to him as a child. This was discussed with him and on balance he decided he would like the diagnosis because it helped him understand his own development.

5. *The Systemizing Quotient (SQ)* (Baron-Cohen, Richler *et al.*, 2003). On the SQ he scored 50 out of a maximum of 80. Controls score a mean of 27.2 (sd = 7.6) and people with AS score a mean of 35.9 (sd = 15.2). He is therefore above average on the SQ.

6. *Standard memory tests*. On the visual digit span test he scored 11.5 (where controls score 6.5). On the spatial span task he scored 6.5 (where controls score 5.3). His memory for faces was tested by

showing him 82 photographs of faces expressing one of the basic emotions or neutral. He was then given a surprise face memory task one hour later, with 42 of the photos taken from the face task he had just done and 42 foil face photos that were novel, and asked to say whether he had seen each face in the previous task or not. DT had an accuracy rate of 57.1% for the faces he had seen only an hour before, which is at chance level or guessing. His performance on the foil faces was somewhat better, with an accuracy score of 69%. These facial memory accuracy scores by DT are comparable to data in a current study in our lab involving 6–8 year old children. Thus, his short-term memory appears normal, his face memory appears impaired, whilst his number memory is superior.

Discussion

In this article we report a case of a savant memory. He had self-reported synaesthesia which we validated using the Test of Genuineness-Revised (Asher *et al.*, 2006). Because of the well-established association between ASC and savantism, we predicted he might also have one form of ASC, namely Asperger Syndrome (AS). This was confirmed. Whilst the existence of his AS may be sufficient to explain his savantism, we speculate that his unusual combination of conditions (synaesthesia *and* AS) may have increased the likelihood of his savant memory. This idea requires testing in a group study.

Future work needs to address the following questions. First, what percentage of people with an ASC also have synaesthesia? Currently this is unknown, perhaps because in classic autism it would be difficult to distinguish. Synaesthesia depends on verbal self-report, and in classic autism the language skills and self-reflection may not be sufficient. But in people with AS, this question should be answerable. Certainly, there are autobiographical accounts of people with AS or High Functioning Autism who have strong visual processing or sensory hyper-sensitivity (Grandin, 1996). We are currently conducting such a survey in our lab.

Second, what percentage of people with synaesthesia have an ASC? This has never been investigated as far as we are aware. If these two conditions are significantly associated, is this for genetic reasons? We mentioned earlier that neurological theories of both autism and synaesthesia refer to an excess of neural connectivity, perhaps due to a failure of pruning or apoptosis. It is interesting to speculate as to whether these two apparently very different conditions may share a common neural abnormality.

Third, does having both an ASC (which involves strong systemizing (Baron-Cohen, 2006) and synaesthesia (which arguably allows for mnemonic enhancement) increase the likelihood of savantism over and above the rate that would be expected if the person only had an ASC? To test this would require comparison of separate populations (no diagnosis, vs. ASC alone, vs. ASC with synaesthesia) in terms of their prevalence rates of savantism.

In this article we are studying DT as a savant with autism and synaesthesia. We regard the first of these (savantism) as a possible effect of the other two (autism and synaesthesia). Since savantism is the main focus of the study, we have not spent much time discussing the nature of autism. However, given the focus of this Special Issue is on consciousness, it is worth mentioning that autism has attracted considerable attention from philosophers of mind because of the idea that — hardwired into the typical brain — there is an innate module for 'mind-reading' which for genetic reasons is impaired in autism. Such 'mindblindness' would be expected to have major implications for consciousness. It would mean that whilst the person could think with ease about objects in the world, or about facts and patterns in the world, their idea of what another person might be thinking, and especially of what another person might be thinking about them, might be quite limited. A person with mindblindness might spend hours thinking about a favourite topic, becoming lost in the details and going deeply into it, all the while remaining relatively oblivious of how they appear to others or what others think of their behaviour.

Such a state was certainly true of DT when he was a child in school, since it appears he had little insight into how odd his behaviour seemed to the other children in the class. When he sat on the carpet during story-time, with his eyes tight shut and his fingers in his ears, picturing numbers in his mind and their shapes and colours, whilst the other children looked at each other or at the teacher and listened to the story, DT was in some sense in a world of his own. With age, DT has developed more of an idea of how to behave and how he seems to others, raising the possibility that mindreading skills are not completely absent but are simply delayed. It helped when, at the age of 13, his mother was able to give him some feedback and tell him to look at others' eyes and not at his own feet. This suggests that in individuals on the autistic spectrum, for whom such social insight and consciousness of others' minds does not develop naturally at the right point in development, learning to consciously attend to key parts of the environment (faces, eyes, expressions) may help. A recent study evaluating whether people on the autistic spectrum could learn to recognize facial expressions with conscious effort suggests that this is possible (Golan *et al.*, 2006). Quite what the relationship is between such atypical development of mindreading and the presence of savantism remains to be established.

In conclusion, following the validation of both synaesthesia and ASC in one case of savantism, we recommend that in future savants should be tested for both of these possible co-occuring conditions. It is of course possible that savant memory could be the result of the application of mnemonic training strategies, such as the 'loci' method, and without any effects of factors such as ASC or synaesthesia. Whether it is possible to distinguish such 'acquired' savantism from the kind shown by cases such as DT or by others with ASC will be important to establish. Finally, concerning the relevance of atypical minds for theories of consciousness, we contend that there is much to learn from the study of such rare cases. They illustrate the general principle that other minds might think or feel differently, if they are wired differently.

Acknowledgements

Simon Baron-Cohen, Jac Billington, Daniel Bor and Sally Wheelwright were supported by the MRC during the period of this work. Chris Ashwin was supported by NAAR. Julian Asher was supported by the Cambridge Overseas Trust. We are grateful to Martin Weitz for introducing us to DT, and to DT and his mother for all their help with our research. We thank Matthew Belmonte for discussions of the neurological literature of autism and Rick Griffin for discussions on the philosophical aspects. This article is dedicated to the memory of the late Professor Jeffrey Gray, who drew out the philosophical implications of synaesthesia for the philosophy of consciousness.

References

A.P.A. (1994), *DSM-IV Diagnostic and Statistical Manual of Mental Disorders, 4th Ed.* (Washington DC: American Psychiatric Association).

Asher, J., Aitken, M.R.F., Farooqi, N., Kurmani, S. & Baron-Cohen, S. (2006), 'Diagnosing and phenotyping visual synaesthesia — a preliminary evaluation of the revised test of genuineness (TOG-R)', *Cortex*, **42** (2), pp. 137–46.

Asher, J., Baron-Cohen, S., Monaco, A.P., Lamb, J., Maestrini, E., Bolton, P., Rahman, S. & Waine, H. (submitted), 'A genetic scan of the X-chromosome and implications for the genetics of synaesthesia'.

Aylward, E.H., Minshew, N.J., Goldstein, G., Honeycutt, N.A., Augustine, A.M., Yates, K.O., Barta, P.E. & Pearlson, G.D. (1999), 'MRI volumes of amygdala and hippocampus in non-mentally retarded autistic adolescents and adults', *Neurology*, **53** (9), p. 2145.

Bailey, A., Le Couteur, A., Gottesman, I., Bolton, P., Simmonoff, E., Yuzda, E. & Rutter, M. (1995), 'Autism as a strongly genetic disorder: Evidence from a British twin study', *Psychological Medicine*, **25**, pp. 63–77.

Baird, G., Simonoff, E., Pickles, A., Chandler, S., Loucas, T., Meldrum, D. & Charman, T. (2006), 'Prevalence of disorders of the autism spectrum in a population cohort of children in South Thames: The Special Needs and Autism Project (SNAP)', *Lancet*, **368** (9531), pp. 210–15.

Baron-Cohen, S. (1987), 'Autism and symbolic play', *British Journal of Developmental Psychology*, **5**, pp. 139–48.

Baron-Cohen, S. (2002), 'The extreme male brain theory of autism', *Trends in Cognitive Science*, **6**, pp. 248–54.

Baron-Cohen, S. (2006), 'Two new theories of autism: Hypersystemizing and assortative mating', *Archives of Diseases in Childhood*, **91**, pp. 2–5.

Baron-Cohen, S. & Bolton, P. (1993), *Autism: The Facts* (Oxford University Press).

Baron-Cohen, S., Burt, L., Laittan-Smith, F., Harrison, J.E. & Bolton, P. (1996), 'Synaesthesia: Prevalence and familiarity', *Perception*, **25**, pp. 1073–9.

Baron-Cohen, S. & Cross, P. (1992), 'Reading the eyes: Evidence for the role of perception in the development of a theory of mind', *Mind and Language*, **6**, pp. 173–86.

Baron-Cohen, S., Golan, O., Wheelwright, S. & Hill, J.J. (2004), *Mindreading: The Interactive Guide to Emotions* (London: Jessica Kingsley).

Baron-Cohen, S., Harrison, J., Goldstein, L. & Wyke, M. (1993), 'Coloured speech perception: Is synaesthesia what happens when modularity breaks down?', *Perception*, **22**, pp. 419–26.

Baron-Cohen, S., Jolliffe, T., Mortimore, C. & Robertson, M. (1997), 'Another advanced test of theory of mind: Evidence from very high functioning adults with autism or Asperger Syndrome', *Journal of Child Psychology and Psychiatry*, **38**, pp. 813–22.

Baron-Cohen, S., Richler, J., Bisarya, D., Gurunathan, N. & Wheelwright, S. (2003), 'The Systemising Quotient (SQ): An investigation of adults with Asperger Syndrome or High Functioning Autism and normal sex differences', *Philosophical Transactions of the Royal Society*, **358**, pp. 361–74.

Baron-Cohen, S. & Ring, H. (1994), 'A model of the mindreading system: Neuropsychological and neurobiological perspectives', in *Origins of an Understanding of Mind*, ed. P. Mitchell & C. Lewis (Hove, E. Sussex: Lawrence Erlbaum Associates).

Baron-Cohen, S., Ring, H., Bullmore, E., Wheelwright, S., Ashwin, C. & Williams, S. (2000), 'The amygdala theory of autism', *Neuroscience and Behavioural Reviews*, **24**, pp. 355–64.

Baron-Cohen, S. & Wheelwright, S. (2004). 'The Empathy Quotient (EQ): An investigation of adults with Asperger Syndrome or High Functioning Autism, and normal sex differences', *Journal of Autism and Developmental Disorders*, **34**, pp. 163–75.

Baron-Cohen, S., Wheelwright, S. & Jolliffe, T. (1997), 'Is there a "language of the eyes"? Evidence from normal adults and adults with autism or Asperger syndrome', *Visual Cognition*, **4**, pp. 311–31.

Baron-Cohen, S., Wheelwright, S., Robinson, J. & Woodbury-Smith, M. (2005), 'The Adult Asperger Assessment (AAA): A diagnostic method', *Journal of Autism and Developmental Disorders*, **35**, pp. 807–19.

Baron-Cohen, S., Wheelwright, S., Skinner, R., Martin, J. & Clubley, E. (2001), 'The Autism Spectrum Quotient (AQ): Evidence from Asperger Syndrome/

High Functioning Autism, males and females, scientists and mathematicians', *Journal of Autism and Developmental Disorders*, **31**, pp. 5–17.

Baron-Cohen, S., Wyke, M. & Binnie, C. (1987). 'Hearing words and seeing colours: An experimental investigation of a case of synaesthesia', *Perception*, **16**, pp. 761–7.

Bauman, M. & Kempner, T. (1985), 'Histoanatomic observation of the brain in early infantile autism', *Neurology*, **35**, pp. 866–74.

Belmonte, M.K., Allen, G., Beckel-Mitchener, A., Boulanger, L.M., Carper, R. & Webb, S.J. (2004), 'Autism and abnormal development of brain connnectivity', *J. Neurosci.*, **24**, pp. 9228–231.

Bor, D., Billington, J. & Baron-Cohen, S. (submitted), 'Savant memory for digits in a case of synaesthesia and Asperger Syndrome is related to hyperactivity in the lateral prefrontal cortex'.

Carper, R.A. & Courchesne, E. (2000), 'Inverse correlation between frontal lobe and cerebellum sizes in children with autism', *Brain*, **123**, pp. 836–44.

Courchesne, E. (2002), 'Abnormal early brain development in autism', *Molecular Psychiatry*, **7**, pp. 21–3.

Courchesne, E., Press, G.A. & Yeung-Courchesne, R. (1993), 'Parietal lobe abnormalities detected with MR in patients with infantile autism', *AJR*, **160**, pp. 387–93.

Courchesne, E., Townsend, J., Akshoomof, N.A., Saitoh, O., Yeung-Courchesne, R., Lincoln, A.J., James, H.E., Haas, R.H., Schreibman, L. & Lau, L. (1994), 'Impairment in shifting attention in autistic and cerebellar patients', *Behavioural Neuroscience*, **108**, pp. 848–65.

Cytowic, R.E. (1989), *Synaesthesia: A Union of the Senses* (New York: Springer-Verlag).

Cytowic, R.E. (1993), *The Man who Tasted Shapes* (New York: Putnam).

Dehay, C., Bullier, J. & Kennedy, H. (1984), 'Transient projections from the fronto-parietal and temporal cortex to areas 17, 18, and 19 in the kitten', *Experimental Brain Research*, **57**, pp. 208–12.

Frith, C. & Frith, U. (1999), 'Interacting minds — a biological basis', *Science*, **286**, pp. 1692–5.

Galton, F. (1883), *Inquiries into Human Faculty and its Development* (London: Dent & Sons).

Gillberg, C. (1991), 'Outcome in autism and autistic-like conditions', *Journal of the American Academy of Child and Adolescent Psychiatry*, **30**, pp. 375–82.

Golan, O., Baron-Cohen, S., Wheelwright, S. & Hill, J.J. (2006), 'Systemising empathy: Teaching adults with Asperger Syndrome to recognise complex emotions using interactive multi-media', *Development and Psychopathology*, **18**, pp. 589–615.

Goldman, A. (2006), 'Interpretation Psychologized', reprinted from *Mind and Language* (1989), **4**, pp. 161–85, in *Folk Psychology: The Theory of Mind Debate*, ed. M. Davies & T. Stone (Oxford: Blackwell).

Grandin, T. (1996), *Thinking in Pictures* (Vancouver, WA: Vintage Books).

Gray, J., Baron-Cohen, S., Brammer, M.J., Chopping, S., Nunn, J., Parslow, D., Gregory, L. & Williams, S. (2002), 'Implications of synaesthesia for functionalism: Theory and experiments', *Journal of Consciousness Studies*, **9** (12), pp. 5–31.

Hashimoto, T., Tayama, M., Murakawa, K., Yoshimoto, T., Miyazaki, M., Harada, M. & Kuroda, Y. (1995), 'Development of the brainstem and cerebellum in autistic patients', *Journal of Autism and Developmental Disorders*, **25**, pp. 1–17.

Hermelin, B. (2002), *Bright Splinters of the Mind: A Personal Story of Research with Autistic Savants* (London: Jessica Kingsley).

Hermelin, B. & O'Connor, N. (1986), 'Idiot savant calendrical calculators: Rules and regularities', *Journal of Child Psychology and Psychiatry*, **16**, pp. 885–93.

I.C.D-10 (1994), *International Classification of Diseases*, 10th ed. (Geneva: World Health Organisation).

Iacoboni, M., Molnar-Szakacs, I., Gallese, V., Buccino, G., Mazziotta, J.C. & Rizzolatti, G. (2005), 'Grasping the intentions of others with one's own mirror neuron system', *PLoS Biol*, **3**, p. 79.

Kennedy, H., Bartardiere, A., Dehay, C. & Barone, P. (1996), in *Synaesthesia: Classic and Contemporary Readings*, ed. S. Baron-Cohen & J. Harrison (London: Blackwells).

Kennedy, H., Bullier, J. & Dehay, C. (1989), 'Transient projection from the superior temporal sulcus to area 17 in the newborn macaque monkey', *Proceedings of the National Academy of Science*, **86**, pp. 8093–7.

Luria, A. (1988), *The Mind of a Mnemonist* (Cambridge, MA: Harvard University Press).

Marks, L. (1975), 'On coloured-hearing synaesthesia', *Psychological Bulletin*, **82** (3), pp. 303–31.

Motluk, A. (1994), 'The sweet smell of purple', *New Scientist*, **143**, pp. 32–7.

Myers, P., Baron-Cohen, S. & Wheelwright, S. (2004), *An Exact Mind* (London: Jessica Kingsley).

Nagel, T. (1974), 'What is it like to be a bat?', *Philosophical Review*, **83**, pp. 435–50.

Nunn, J., Gregory, L., Morris, R., Brammer, M., Bullmore, E., Harrison, J., Williams, S., Baron-Cohen, S. & Gray, J. (2002), 'Functional magnetic resonance imaging of synaesthesia: Activation of colour vision area V8 by spoken words', *Nature Neuroscience*, **5**, pp. 371–5.

Paulesu, E., Harrison, J., Baron-Cohen, S., Watson, J., Goldstein, L., Heather, J., Frakowiak, R. & Frith, C. (1995), 'The physiology of coloured hearing: A Positron Emission Tomography activation study of coloured-word synaesthesia', *Brain*, **118**, pp. 661–76.

Perner, J. (1991), *Understanding the Representational Mind* (Cambridge, MA: Bradford Books/MIT Press).

Ramachandran, V.S. & Hubbard, E.M. (2001), *Number-Colour Synesthesia arises from Cross Wiring in the Fusiform Gyrus* (La Jolla, CA: Centre for Brain and Cognition, University of California).

Rouw, R. and Scholte, H.S. (2007), 'Increased structural connectivity in grapheme-colour synaesthesia', *Nature Neuroscience*, **10**, pp. 792–7.

Tager-Flusberg, H. (1993), 'What language reveals about the understanding of minds in children with autism', in *Understanding Other Minds: Perspectives from Autism*, ed. S. Baron-Cohen, H. Tager-Flusberg & D. Cohen (Oxford: Oxford University Press).

Tammet, D. (2006), *Born on a Blue Day* (London: Hodder & Stoughton).

Vernon, P.E. (1930), 'Synaesthesia in music', *Psyche*, **10**, pp. 22–40.

Williams, R.S., Hauser, S.L., Purpura, D.P., Delong, G.R. & Swisher, C.N. (1980), 'Autism and mental retardation: Neuropathologic studies performed in four retarded persons with autistic behaviour', *Arch Neurol*, **37**, pp. 749–53.

Wittgenstein, L. (1958), *Philosophical Investigations*, translated by Anscombe, G.E.M. (1963) (Oxford: Blackwell).

Yaro, C. & Ward, J. (2007), 'Searching for Shereshevskii: What is superior about the memory of synaesthetes?', *Quarterly Journal of Experimental Psychology*, **60** (5), pp. 681–95.

Index